# MILLER'S

# pictures

HUGH ST. CLAIR *General Editor*

MILLER'S

# Contents

# How to use this book

It is our aim to make this book easy to use. In order to find works by a particular artist, consult the index which starts on page 237. If you are looking for the special sections consult the contents list on page 5.

## Gladys Nelson Smith
### (1888–1980)

An art critic has hailed Gladys Nelson Smith as a fine social Realist. Gladys Smith painted her portraits and figures in landscapes which did not depict the rich and the noble but the lives of ordinary people. Her inspiration was from the likes of the founding fathers of the American Realist movement, Winslow Homer (1836–1910), Thomas Eakins (1844–1916) and John Sloan (1871–1951) who in their painting sought to draw attention to the plight of the huddled masses for whom the reality of the American Dream was very different from what they had been led to believe.

A native of the State of Kansas, Gladys Nelson Smith studied at Corcoran School of Art in Washington and then settled in Washington DC. She had a weekend retreat on a farm in Frederick county, Maryland where she loved to paint. She was also an accomplished painter of still lifes.

▶ Gladys Nelson Smith
American (1888–1980)
Stoop Sitting in Georgetown
Signed, oil on canvas laid on board
17 x 19¼in (43 x 49cm)
**£2,000–2,500 / $3,000–3,600** ↗ SLN

Louisa Jordan Smith
American (1873–1928)
Eastern Mountain Landscape
Signed, oil on canvas
18 x 30¼in (45.5 x 77cm)
**£1,200–1,500 / $1,750–2,250** ↗ JAA

## Cincinnati Art Museum

■ 953 Eden Park Drive, Cincinnati, Ohio 45202, www.cincinnatimuseum.com

■ Founded in 1881, the museum is one of the country's oldest visual arts institutions.

■ Eight galleries provide for the display of Cincinnati's permanent collection of over 80,000 works of art.

Mary T. Smith
American (b1904)
Untitled
Enamel on wood, c1986
24 x 28in (61 x 71cm)
**£6,000–6,600 / $8,700–9,500** ⊞ RMG

▲ For further information
see Outsider Art (pages 144–147)

Sir Matthew Smith
British (1879–1959)
Still life with figurine
Signed, pastel
29½ x 21½in (75 x 54cm)
**£3,300–4,000 / $4,800–5,800** ↗ S(O)

Reginald Smith
British (1855–1925)
Wet sands, Fistral Bay, Cornwall
Signed, watercolour
28 x 20½in (71 x 52cm)
**£1,000–1,200 / $1,500–1,750** ↗ G(L)

**Running Head**
this refers to the first or last artist appearing alphabetically on a left or right hand page.

**Artist Profile**
provides further information on an artist's life and work together with a sample(s) of their work.

**Information Box**
covers relevant information on artists, care and restoration of pictures, important information on museums and galleries.

**Price Guide**
this is based on actual prices realized. Remember that Miller's is a price guide not a price list and prices are affected by many variables such as location, condition, desirability and so on. Don't forget that if you are selling it is quite likely you will be offered less than the price range. Price ranges for items sold at auction include the buyer's premium and VAT if applicable. Prices shown have been converted from the currency in which the picture was sold into UK£ and US$.

**Caption**
includes the artist's name, dates and country of birth, title of the work, medium, year it was produced and size.

**For Further Information Box**
directs the reader to related topics elsewhere in the book.

**Source Code**
refers to the Key to Illustrations on page 234 that lists the details of where the item was offered for sale. The ↗ icon indicates the item was sold at auction. The ⊞ icon indicates the item originated from a gallery.

# Acknowledgments

The publishers would like to acknowledge the great assistance given by all galleries, auction houses and their press offices, in particular:

Tony Haynes — Haynes Fine Art of Broadway, Picton House Galleries, 42 High Street, Broadway, Worcestershire WR12 7DT

John Maizels — Raw Vision, PO Box 44, Watford, Hertfordshire WD25 8LN

James Rawlin — Bonhams, 101 New Bond Street, London W1S 1SR

Ian Whyte — Whyte's Fine Art Auctioneers, 38 Molesworth Street, Dublin 2, Ireland

We would like to extend our thanks to the following publications and events organizers who have assisted us in the production of this book.

Art London, Ebury Events

Galleries Magazine, London

The Art on Paper Fair, London

Antiques & Fine Art Fairs, London

The Watercolours and Drawings Fair, London

The 20/21 British Art Fair, London

Maine Antique Digest, USA

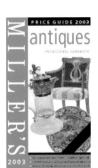

# Introduction

I feel that you can never have enough pictures in your house. Hang pictures and the four walls of a room no longer hem you in; pictures are a window on the world, they can transport you to another time and another place – maybe to a beautiful landscape or into your own mind when looking at abstract art.

Pictures are to be enjoyed not revered. I wouldn't keep that dark and dreary landscape picture just because it belonged to Granny and you think it may be valuable. Sell, and with the proceeds buy something you like. Investment potential should not be at the front of your mind. The art market, like stocks and shares, can rise and fall, however a picture makes a much nicer wall decoration than a share certificate!

The price of art is, of course, affected by the state of the economy. In the 1980s the Japanese bought Impressionist art but since their economy crashed these art prices have fallen. History tells us that the art market is always behind the financial markets, it takes longer to recover but also longer to fall. The world may have recently been in recession but prices have shown no signs of falling and they may not, spending habits have not been affected. Indeed some record prices were reached this year, including a Turner landscape which sold for over £2m ($2.8m).

Pictures should engender emotions in the viewer, they should not just be pretty and decorative – we buy wallpaper for this effect. Of course a picture can be of a beautiful place or represent an exquisite object but it must inspire the senses.

The merit of a picture can often be judged on its originality, and artists who threaten the art establishment with pictures that shock today are often tomorrow's masterpieces. The Impressionists were revolutionary in their time, but a picture painted today in the Impressionist style will never be worth as much. My tip is, if you see a picture unlike any other buy it, and have confidence in your own judgement, don't play safe.

Pictures are in one respect like Hollywood blockbusters, just because the original movie breaks box office records it does not guarantee that the sequel will be as successful.

There are many factors deciding the price of a picture – if the location of a landscape can be identified it is worth more than just a picture described as 'English Landscape'. An over-restored picture will be worth less than an un-touched, dust-covered work. Provenance is important, and if the history of a picture can be verified it will be more valuable. When personal collections of art are sold high prices are reached. The private collection of British art belonging to the reclusive American millionaire Stanley J. Seeger was sold recently in New York and record prices were fetched. These prices may well not have been achieved had the pictures appeared individually in a general sale.

Picture prices can too be affected by interior design trends. Modern tastes have changed. For example, some homes now mix ancient with modern, and European furniture with tribal artefacts. Abstract and modern art mix happily with older pictures and, therefore, prices for modern mid-20th century abstract works such as those by the St Ives masters are rising.

*Miller's Pictures Price Guide 2003* is an invaluable guide to a wide variety of 18th century to contemporary pictures by international artists. I wanted to include pictures that you might find not only at an auction, gallery or hidden in an attic, but also pictures by well-known artists that you might want to buy. Some great names in art feature in the guide but the works I have included are not huge museum-quality oils but affordable art by a master – a limited edition Picasso print, a Gainsborough watercolour or a small Turner landscape, the subject matter and style being different from his well-known works.

*Miller's Pictures Price Guide* will now be published every year so if you don't see an artist in this edition maybe they will be in the next. Enjoy this book.

Hugh Gillan

# Artists A–Z

**Pierre Abrogiani**
French (1907–85)
Champ de Blis a la Grande
Signed and inscribed, oil on canvas
23¾ x 36½in (60.5 x 93cm)
**£2,200–2,650 / $3,200–3,800** ➚ B(Ba)

**Eileen Agar**
British (1899–1991)
Confrontation
Signed, oil on canvas
20 x 24in (51 x 61cm)
**£2,500–3,000 / $3,600–4,400** ➚ P

**Craigie Aitchison, RA**
Scottish (b1926)
Star, Tree and Sheepdog
Oil on canvas
14 x 10in (35.5 x 25.5cm)
**£20,000–24,000 / $29,000–34,800** ➚ S

## Locate the source

The source of each illustration in Miller's can be found by checking the code letters below each caption with the Key to Illustrations, pages 234–236.

**James Aitken**
British (c1880–1935)
Low Tide, Firth of Forth
Signed, oil on board
10 x 13½in (25.5 x 34.5cm)
**£430–500 / $630–720** ➚ G(L)

▶ **Jean-Michel Alberola**
French (b1953)
Suzanne et les Veillards:
Peinture Occidentale
Signed and dated 1984, cloth
78¾in (200cm) square
**£2,600–3,200**
**$3,800–4,600** ➚ BUK

**Marc Aldine**
French (20thC)
La Giudecca on San Giorgio Maggiore
Signed, oil on canvas
25½ x 36in (65 x 91.5cm)
**£36,000–40,000 / $52,000–58,000** ⊞ HFA

**Frederick James Aldridge**
British (1850–1933)
Entering Harbour
Watercolour heightened with white
14 x 21in (35.5 x 53.5cm)
**£1,200–1,500 / $1,750–2,200** ⤢ Bon

◀ **Franz Althaus**
British (fl1881–1914)
Village Cottages
Watercolour
10 x 14in
(25.5 x 35.5cm)
**£3,350–3,700**
**$4,800–5,400** ⊞ HFA

**Axel Amuchastegui**
Argentinian (b1921)
White Faced Duck
Oil on canvas
30 x 20in (76 x 51cm)
**£9,250–10,200 / $13,500–14,800** ⊞ HFA

**John Anderson**
British (19thC)
An Evening Stroll
Oil on canvas
24 x 20in (61 x 51cm)
**£4,000–4,350 / $5,800–6,300** ⊞ HFA

**Sophie Anderson, RA**
British (1823–1903)
Love in a Mist
Signed and inscribed, oil on canvas
14¼ x 12in (36 x 30.5cm)
**£14,000–16,800 / $20,300–24,500** ⤢ P

> **Miller's is a price GUIDE not a price LIST**

**Torsten Andersson**
Swedish (b1926)
Untitled
Signed and dated, canvas laid on board
10¾ x 17in (27 x 43cm)
**£2,150–2,600 / $3,200–3,800** ⤢ BUK

**Richard Andsell and William Powell Frith**
British (1815–85 and 1819–1909)
Feeding Time
Oil on canvas
36 x 28in (91.5 x 71cm)
**£85,000–93,500**
**$123,250–135,550** ⊞ HFA

*Artists who can paint animals often find it
very difficult to accurately reproduce people.
Richard Andsell, Queen Victoria's favourite
animal painter, was no exception. At that
time it was perfectly respectable for two
artists to work on the same picture and
for both to sign it. Andsell decided to
collaborate with William Powell Frith, whose
pictures* Derby Day *and* The Railway Station
*gained him respect and fame as one of the
19th century's outstanding figure painters,
for a picture combining animals and people.*
  *Andsell and Frith worked together on only
a handful of pictures at a time when they
were both at the peak of their powers.
Andsell was admired by Queen Victoria
because he romanticized the Scottish
Highlands in his pictures.*

## Insuring your picture

No one likes to pay high insurance premiums. To get coverage at the best price
here are some points to consider:

■ Have your picture valued at an auction house or specialist gallery and update
the valuation every three years.

■ If your works of art have a combined value over £50,000 ($72,500) it is worth
insuring them with a company specializing in fine art. It may be cheaper than
using a general insurance company.

■ Many insurance companies allow a discount off the premium if a burglar alarm
is fitted to the premises.

■ In case of theft keep a photographic record of your pictures. If you are the victim of
theft, post photographs on the Internet website of Art Loss Register www.artloss.com

**Karel Appel**
Dutch (b1921)
Untitled
Signed, paper pasted on card panel
15¾ x 21¼in (40 x 54cm)
**£5,000–6,000 / $7,250–8,750**  ↗ BUK

◄ **Edward Jeffrey
Irving Ardizzone,
CBE, RA**
British (1900–79)
Hampstead Fun Fair
Oil on board
21½ x 25in
(54.5 x 63.5cm)
**£14,000–15,400**
**$20,000–22,300**
⊞ P&H

## Collaborations

In a label conscious age we want our paintings to be the
vision of one artist, however, the Victorians did not care.
If one artist was not good at both landscape and portrait
painting then they did not mind him calling in a colleague
to do the part he could not. Although collaborations are
now rare the exception are the artists Gilbert and George.

**Maxwell Armfield, RWS**
British (1882–1972)
Black Beauties
Signed with monogram, oil on canvas laid down on board
5¼ x 7¼in (13.5 x 18.5cm)
**£15,500–18,500 / $22,500–27,000**  ↗ S

**Mary Armour, RSA, RSW**
Scottish (1902–99)
Imachar, Arran
Signed and dated 1970,
oil on canvas
19¾ x 23¾in (50 x 60cm)
**£7,250–8,500**
**$10,500–12,500** ⚒ **Bon**

▶ **Karl Aspelin**
Swedish (1857–1932)
Portrait of a Girl
Signed and dated 1891,
oil on canvas
46¾ x 30in (119 x 76cm)
**£2,250–2,700**
**$3,250–4,000** ⚒ **DORO**

**Eddie Arning**
American (1898–1993)
Dog Training
Crayon/craypas on paper
20 x 25in (51 x 63.5cm)
**£3,500–3,850 / $5,000–5,600** ⊞ **RMG**

▲ **For further**
**information**
see Outsider Art
(pages 144–145)

**John Atkinson,**
**RA, RI, RSA**
British (1863–1924)
Haymaking
Watercolour
10½ x 14½in (26.5 x 37cm)
**£4,000–4,350 / $5,800–6,300** ⊞ **WrG**

**Frank Auerbach**
British/German (b1931)
Study for 'To the Studios'
Signed and dated 1977, coloured crayon and black felt tip
10 x 11in (25.5 x 28cm)
**£1,800–2,000 / $2,600–3,000** ⚒ **B**

**Gillian Ayres**
British (b1930)
Untitled
Signed and dated, gouache
21¾ x 29½in (55.5 x 75cm)
**£2,600–3,000 / $3,800–4,400** ⚒ **P**

► **William Baillie, CBE, PPRSA, PPRSW, RGI, HRA**
Scottish (b1923)
Banner and Paper Flowers
Oil on canvas
39½in (100.5cm) square
**£7,250–8,000**
**$10,500–11,600** ⊞ **WrG**

*Born in Edinburgh, William studied at Edinburgh College of Art 1941–51, although between 1942 and 1946 he served in the British army in the Far East. In 1955 he became resident tutor at the National Gallery of Canada in Ottawa and from 1960 to 1988 he taught at Edinburgh College of Art in Scotland. He travelled extensively in India, Nepal and Sikkim and this eastern influence is seen in much of his work. He was made an honorary RA in 1991.*

**Francis Bacon**
British (1909–92)
Man Writing Reflected in Mirror
Signed, dated 1976 and numbered 108/180, lithograph printed in colours on Arches paper
40¼ x 28in (102 x 72cm)
**£2,750–3,300 / $4,000–4,800** ➚ **BUK**

► **Thomas Baker**
British (1809–69)
Cattle Watering
Oil on canvas
13 x 19in (33 x 48.5cm)
**£12,400–13,600 / $18,000–19,700** ⊞ **HFA**

◄ **Margaret Ballantyne**
Scottish (20thC)
Autumn Woods, Ayrshire
Signed, oil on canvas
30in (76cm) square
**£3,000–3,300**
**$4,400–6,400**
⊞ **WrG**

*Margaret Ballantyne attended the Glasgow School of Art. She exhibits regularly with the Royal Glasgow Institute of Fine Arts, the Royal Scottish Academy, the Royal Scottish Society of Painters in Watercolours and the Royal Academy.*

**Brian Ballard**
Irish (b1943)
Three Jugs
Oil on canvas
15 x 19½in (38 x 49.5cm)
**£5,000–5,450 / $7,250–7,900** ⊞ **WrG**

**Hurst Balmford**
British (19thC)
Borth y Gest, North Wales
Oil
18 x 22in (45.5 x 55cm)
**£1,700–1,850 / $2,500–2,700 ⊞ Dr**

**Gustav Barbarini**
Austrian (1840–1909)
Goat Herder by Mountain Stream
Signed, oil on canvas
26 x 40½in (99 x 103cm)
**£2,600–3,200 / $3,800–4,500 ⚒ DORO**

**Alfred Banner**
British (fl1878–1914)
A Chat at the Cottage Door
Signed, oil on canvas
12 x 18in (30.5 x 45.5cm)
**£5,850–6,450 / $8,500–9,350 ⊞ HFA**

**Ranelagh Barrett**
British (d1768)
Four of Sir Robert Walpole's Hounds in a Landscape
Signed and inscribed 1744, oil on canvas
60 x 94in (152.5 x 239cm)
**£24,000–28,000 / $35,000–40,000 ⚒ S(NY)**

*This painting, after the original version of the same title by John Wootton, is representative of a number of dog portraits and hunting scenes that Wootton painted for Sir Robert Walpole (1725–42), first Earl of Orford, the first British Prime Minister. Although the original version by Wootton has remained untraced since its sale to Catherine the Great of Russia in 1779, several of the 17 Wootton paintings known to have been in Walpole's collection by 1736 survive. Wootton's primary version of the present work hung in the Hunting Hall of Walpole's Houghton Hall, Norfolk and this painting is recorded in the Breakfast Room in the 1792 inventory.*

◄ **David Bates**
British (1841–1921)
A Scotch Burn
Oil on canvas
18¼ x 14in (46.5 x 35.5cm)
**£5,800–7,000 / $8,400–10,200 ⊞ HFA**

**Edward Bawden, RA**
British (1903–89)
Rocky Mountains
Signed and dated 1949, pen and ink and watercolour
16 x 24in (40.5 x 61cm)
**£3,000–3,600 / $4,400–5,250** ⚖ Bon

◀ **Walter Emerson Baum**
American (1884–1956)
An Autumn Day
Signed, oil on canvas
36 x 30in (91.5 x 76cm)
**£24,500–30,000 / $35,000–43,500** ⚖ S(NY)

**Edward Bawden, RA**
British (1903–89)
Brighton Pier
Signed and inscribed, linocut, printed in
colours on wove, with margins, faint staining
20¾ x 56in (52.5 x 142cm)
**£2,400–2,800 / $3,500–4,000** ⚖ P

**Charles Baxter**
British (1809–79)
The Shy Maiden
Oil on canvas
24 x 18in (61 x 45.5cm)
**£7,500–8,200 / $11,000–12,000** ⊞ HFA

**Sir Cecil Beaton**
British (1904–80)
My Bolivian Aunt
Pen, ink and watercolour
18 x 13½in (45.5 x 34.5cm)
**£4,000–5,000 / $5,800–7,250** ⊞ MP
*This picture was a design for a book cover,
My Bolivian Aunt, published by Weidenfeld
& Nicholson in 1971.*

◀ **Sir William Beechey**
British (1753–1839)
Portrait of Charles Ogilby
Signed, dated 1823 and inscribed, oil on canvas
36 x 28in (91.5 x 71cm)
**£2,000–2,800 / $3,500–4,000** ⚖ P(Ba)

► **Gordon Bennett**
Australian (b1955)
Notes to Basquiat: Picture
No Artist Can Paint, 1999
Signed and dated 1999,
synthetic polymer paint on linen
39⅜in (101cm) square
**£2,300–2,700**
**$3,400–4,000** ➚ SHSY

◄ **Vanessa Bell**
British (1879–1961)
Asolo, Italy
Signed, oil on canvas
20 x 13in (51 x 33cm)
**£5,000–6,000**
**$7,250–8,750** ➚ Bon

**Alexander von Bensa**
Austrian (1820–1902)
Elegant Figures in Belvedere Castle Park
Signed, oil on panel
17¾ x 10¼in (45 x 26cm)
**£3,300–3,800 / $4,800–5,800** ➚ DORO

**Thomas Hart Benton**
American (1889–1975)
Smugglers
Signed, oil on board
10 x 8¼in (25.5 x 21cm)
**£24,000–29,000 / $35,250–42,500** ➚ S(NY)

◄ **Valentin Bernadski**
(Russian b1917)
Valentin's Garden
Signed and dated 1966, oil on board
26¾ x 18½in (68 x 47cm)
**£1,000–1,200 / $1,500–1,750** ➚ B&B

► **John Berry**
British (b1920)
Life Saving (The Scouts)
Signed, gouache
10 x 7in (25.5 x 18cm)
**£375–420 / $560–620** ⊞ Dr
*This is an original illustration for Ladybird Books.*

**John Billinghurst, RBA**
British (1880–1963)
By the Pool – Wimbledon Common
Signed, oil on canvas
12 x 16in (30.5 x 40.5cm)
**£3,250–3,600 / $4,800–5,250** ⊞ Dr

**A. W. Bryan Binns**
British (20thC)
Sheep Beneath Oak Trees
Signed and dated,
oil on board
8½ x 11½in
(21.5 x 29cm)
**£220–270**
**$320–400** ↗ G(L)

**Samuel John Lamorna Birch, RA**
British (1869–1955)
Early Summer on the Deveron
Signed, oil on panel
12¾ x 15¼in (31 x 38.5cm)
**£2,000–2,400 / $3,000–3,500** ↗ B

▶ **Peter Blake, RA**
British (b1932)
Babe Rainbow
Signed and numbered
66/500, screenprint
printed on sheet metal
26 x 17¼in (66 x 44cm)
**£450–550**
**$650–800** ↗ Bon(C)

▶ **Peter Blake, RA**
British (b1932)
Long Live the Queen
Signed, pen and black ink, coloured pencils, watercolour and gouache
9 x 11½in (23 x 29cm)
**£46,000–56,000 / $67,000–80,000** ↗ S

*This painting was executed by Blake in the year of the coronation of
Queen Elizabeth II in 1952. Blake had just been relieved from National
Service in the Royal Air Force but had not yet begun his three years at
the Royal College of Art (1953–56), where he won a first-class
diploma. As such, this rare early work marks the beginning of his
series of 'autobiographical' creations executed during the 1950s and
culminating with Self Portrait With Badges (1961), in which the seeds
of his later associations with popular imagery and the materials of
mass culture had already been sown.*

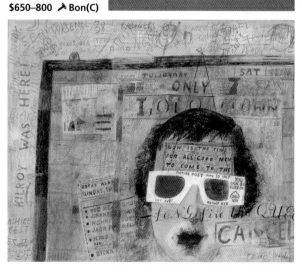

◀ **Thomas Blinks**
British (1860–1912)
Full Cry
Signed and dated 1887,
oil on canvas
35 x 26in (89 x 66cm)
**£14,800–18,000**
**$21,500–26,000** ⚒ S(NY)

**Henry John Boddington**
British (1811–65)
River Scene With Figures
Oil on canvas
29 x 41in (73.5 x 104cm)
**£45,000–50,000**
**$65,000–72,500** ⊞ HFA

**Henry John Boddington**
British (1811–65)
Fetching Water from the Stream
Oil on canvas
12 x 16in (30.5 x 40.5cm)
**£7,300–8,000**
**$11,000–11,600** ⊞ HFA

**David Bomberg**
British (1890–1957)
Composition
Signed, thinned oil on paper
16 x 12¼in (40.5 x 31cm)
**£1,300–1,500 / $1,900–2,200** ⚒ P

▶ **Elias P. van Bommel**
Dutch (1819–90)
Amsterdam
Oil on panel
10½ x 15¾in (26.5 x 40cm)
**£2,500–2,800**
**$3,600–4,000** ⚒ DORO

## Abbreviations

Letters after the artist's name denote that the
artist has been awarded the membership of an
artistic body. See page 233 for the explanation
of abbreviated letters.

**Owen Bowen**
British (1873–1967)
Roses and Delphiniums in a China Bowl
Oil on canvas
24 x 30in (61 x 76cm)
**£2,250–2,500 / $3,200–3,600** ⊞ **Dr**

**Arthur Boyd**
Australian (1920–99)
Susannah and the Elders
Signed, oil on board
9¼ x 8½in (24.5 x 22cm)
**£4,000–4,500 / $5,800–6,500** ⚲ **B**

◄ **Edward Borein**
American (1872–1945)
Two Cowboys
Oil on board
9 x 12½in (23 x 31cm)
**£15,500–18,000**
**$22,000–26,000**
⚲ **CdA**

► **Guiseppe Bortignoni**
Italian (17thC)
An Amusing Recital
Oil on panel
15 x 20in (38 x 51cm)
**£18,500–20,300**
**$26,750–29,500**
⊞ **HFA**

◄ **Hugh Boycott-Brown**
British (1909–90)
Dunwich
Signed, oil on board
6 x 8¼in (15.5 x 21cm)
**£850–1,000**
**$1,250–1,500**
⚲ **P(Nor)**

**John Boyd, RP, RGI**
Scottish (1940–2001)
Men with Boats
Oil on canvas
12 x 16in (30.5 x 40.5cm)
**£4,500–5,000 / $6,500–7,300** ⊞ **P&H**

*Boyd was recently described by fellow painter Michael Scott as 'the quiet master of contemporary Scottish painting'. John's paintings have received wide recognition and many of the country's better private collections hold at least one example of his work. He is represented in public collections worldwide and many corporate boardrooms, not least the Fleming Collection at Robert Fleming Holdings Ltd, in London. He won many awards and prizes over the years at the Royal Scottish Academy and the Royal Glasgow Institute. His work is regularly shown in London at the Royal Academy and the Royal Society of Portrait Painters where he was a member.*

# Helen Bradley (1900–79)

Helen Bradley has been compared to Laurence Stephen Lowry in that their styles were similarly naïve and that they both lived and worked in the industrial north of England at about the same time. However, experts are at pains to point out that they have little in common. Lowry's breadth of work over his long painting career was huge, Helen Bradley's style never changed and her subjects were of nostalgic childhood picnics and trips to Blackpool. She took up painting in her seventies to amuse her grandchildren and was married to Tom Bradley, a well-respected local Oldham artist, who was totally dismissive of her work. It was just luck that a gallery owner from London saw her pictures and decided to put on a show. It sold out immediately and she embarked on a frantic few years of painting and illustrating books until she died, always writing a little story on the back of her pictures, based on the memories of her childhood.

**Helen Bradley**
British (1900–79)
Our First Christmas Tree
Signed and inscribed, oil on canvas board
11¾ x 15½in (29.5 x 39.5cm)
**£26,000–32,000 / $38,000–46,000** ⚲ P
*This painting is signed and inscribed with a fly monogram, and is also signed, titled and extensively inscribed on the artist's label on the backboard: 'Because Lees and Oldham were so close to the bleak Yorkshire moors we never saw Christmas Trees, it was far too cold for them to grow, and, as there were only horses and carts in those days, it would cost so much to bring them to the towns, so great was the excitement when Father came home just before Christmas saying that there was a beautiful Christmas tree outside the church in St Annes Square in Manchester so the next day Mother, the Aunts, George and I also Miss Carter (who wore pink) travelled down to Manchester to see the lovely decorated Christmas tree and the year was 1907'.*

**Helen Bradley**
British (1900–79)
A Walk in the Park
Signed and inscribed, watercolour and bodycolour
9½ x 11in (24 x 28cm)
**£9,000–11,000 / $13,000–16,000** ⚲ B

**Helen Bradley**
British (1900–79)
The First Carol on Christmas Morning
Signed dated 1976 and inscribed, watercolour and bodycolour
9½ x 13¼in (24 x 33.5cm)
**£14,000–16,500 / $20,000–24,500** ⚲ B
*The inscription reads 'The First Carol on Christmas Morning Mother, The Aunts, Miss Carter (who wore pink) Mr Taylor (the Bank Manager) Grandma, George and I (also Gyp and Barney) walked with the Singers as far as the Hope-Ainsworth's House down Milking Green, because the First Carol on Christmas Morning was always 'Christians Awake, salute this Happy Morn', Then, as we sang, we all felt that Christmas was really here. Mother, Grandma, George and I were about to go home when some boys gave Grandma two long lengths of Ivy to decorate our Christmas Table and the year was 1907'.*

**Helen Bradley**
British (1900–79)
We Loved our Walks Through The Little Woods
Signed, dated 1975 and inscribed, watercolour and bodycolour
10¾ x 15in (27.5 x 38cm)
**£8,500–10,000 / $12,500–14,750** ⚲ B

**John Bratby, RA**
British (1928–92)
Rima with Everlasting Reflections
Oil on canvas
48 x 35¾in (122 x 91cm)
**£4,000–4,800 / $5,800–7,000** ⚒ P(Ba)

**William A. Breakspeare, RI**
British (1855–1944)
In the Garden
Oil on canvas
16 x 12in (41 x 31cm)
**£3,900–4,300**
**$5,750–6,200** ⊞ CFA

**Carlo Brioschi**
Italian (1826–95)
View of Venice from the Lido
Signed and dated 1891, oil on canvas
14¼ x 32in (36 x 81cm)
**£3,000–3,600 / $4,500–5,250** ⚒ DORO

◀ **Sophy Bristol**
British (b1973)
Breakfast in
Shepherd Market
Signed, oil on canvas
21 x 26½in
(53.5 x 67.5cm)
**£800–900**
**$1,200–1,300** ⊞ P&H

*Born in Brighton,
Sophy graduated
from the Surrey
Institute of Fine Arts
in 1995 and has
painted full time,
dividing the year
between her Brixton
studio and a family
farm in South Africa.
Her work is regularly
exhibited worldwide.*

**Allan Brooks**
Canadian (1869–1946)
Hummingbirds, Chickadees
and Wrens
Signed, gouache on paper laid on
heavy cardboard, four items
14 x 15in (35.5 x 38cm)
**£1,000–1,400**
**$1,500–2,000** ⚒ SLN

**Elizabeth Brophy**
Australian/Irish (20thC)
Chatting
Signed, oil on board
16 x 20in (41 x 51cm)
**£1,650–1,800 / $2,400–2,600 ⊞ WrG**

*Elizabeth Brophy was born in Australia and
studied art at East Sydney Technical College.
She exhibited widely in Australia before
moving to Portugal and then Ireland in 1993.
She has worked and exhibited in Ireland ever
since and is now an important contributor
to the field of Irish Impressionism. She now
lives in Co. Wicklow.*

**Sir Edward Coley Burne-Jones, ARA**
British (1833–98)
A Group of Italian Poets and their Ladies
Pen and ink on vellum
8¼ x 21½in (21 x 54.5cm)
**£35,500–42,750 / $51,000–62,000 ➹ Bon**

> **Miller's is a price GUIDE not a
> price LIST**

**William Hickling Burnett**
British (19thC)
Entrance to Canareggio from the Grand
Canal, Venice
Oil on board
10 x 14in (25.5 x 35.5cm)
**£1,400–1,700 / $2,000–2,600 ➹ G(L)**

**Chris Bushe, RSW**
Scottish (b1958)
Party Night
Oil on board
38in (96.5cm) square
**£875–970 / $1,250–1,400 ⊞ P&H**

*Born in Aberfeldy, Perthshire, Scotland,
Chris studied at the Gray's School of Art in
Aberdeen. He has had many solo exhibitions
in Scotland and his recent awards include
the Morton Fraser Milligan Award, Russell
Flint Trust, Glasgow Arts Club Fellowship
and Scottish Arts Club Award. His work
can be found in the collections of Murray
International Metals, Premier Property
Group, Aberdeen Hospitals Trust, Grampian
Regional Council, Edinburgh Hospitals Trust
and Scottish Life.*

▶ **Simon Bussy**
French (1869–1954)
Long Tailed Bird on a Branch
Signed, oil on canvas, 24 x 19¾in (61 x 50cm)
**£4,000–4,800 / $5,800–7,000 ➹ P**

**Mary E. Butler**
British (fl1867)
Spion Kop, South Africa
Signed, watercolour
7 x 9½in (18 x 24cm)
**£500–580 / $720–820 ⊞ LH**

**Hector Caffieri, RI, RBA**
British (1857–1932)
Faraway Thoughts
Watercolour
13½ x 20in (34.5 x 51cm)
**£3,500–3,900 / $5,000–5,800** ⊞ WrG

**John Callow**
British (1822–78)
Fishing Vessels off the Coast
Signed, oil on canvas
18 x 32in (45.5 x 81.5cm)
**£8,000–8,800 / $11,600–12,500** ⊞ WG

*Callow was a marine and landscape painter. He was the pupil of his elder brother William Callow who took him to Paris in 1835 where he studied for several years. In 1844 he returned to England and began to work as a landscape painter in watercolours. He was appointed Professor of Drawing at the Royal Military Academy at Addiscombe, and later became Professor of Drawing at Woolwich.*

◀ **Ercole Calvi**
Italian (1824–1900)
Fishing Family on the River Bank
Signed and dated 1887, oil on canvas
28½ x 48¾in (72.5 x 124cm)
**£23,500–28,500 / $34,000–41,000** ⚒DORO

◀ **From the studio of Miguel Canals after Edgar Degas**
Spanish (1925–95)
On the Track
Oil on canvas
19¾ x 23¾in
(50 x 60cm)
**£1,850–2,200**
**$2,680–3,200**
⚒Bon(C)

▲ **For further information**
see Forgers (page 80)

▶ **Margaret Carpenter**
British (1793–1872)
The Young Bridesmaid
Oil
40 x 30in (101.5 x 76cm)
**£7,500–8,250**
**$10,800–12,000** ⊞ FdeL

**Neil Cawthorne**
British (b1936)
End of a Day
Signed, oil on canvas
24 x 36in (61 x 91.5cm)
**£4,000–4,750 / $5,750–7,000** ⚒ **S(NY)**

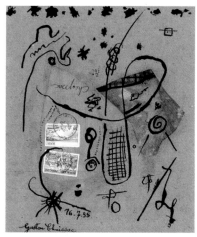

**Gaston Chaissac**
French (1910–64)
Composition
Signed and dated 1955, Indian ink and collage
10¼ x 8½in (26 x 22cm)
**£1,500–1,800 / $2,200–2,600** ⚒ **BUK**

**R. Hamilton Chapman**
British (19thC)
Woman, Geese and Bridge, near Cookham
Signed and dated 1880, watercolour
10½ x 18½in (26.5 x 47cm)
**£680–750 / $1,000–1,100** ⊞ **LH**

**Paul Charlot**
French (1906–85)
Untitled
Signed and dated, tempera on paper
15¾in (40cm) square
**£330–375 / $475–560** ⚒ **SLN**

◀ **George Chinnery**
British (1774–1852)
Villagers Washing at the River
Watercolour over pencil
6¾ x 9¼in (17 x 23.5cm)
**£7,000–7,750 / $8,700–11,000** ⚒ **P**

*George Chinnery left Britain for colonial India in 1902, arriving initially in Madras before travelling extensively. He worked in oils, painting portraits of British ex-patriot dignitaries, as well as miniatures but had a personal preference for landscape as a subject. For his own enjoyment he painted scenes of village life, generally on a modest scale, in a realistic manner and sensitive to both the local culture and nature.*

*Although recognized as an important portraitist, Chinnery is best remembered for his representations of the exotic landscape of the outposts of British Imperialism which provide a fascinating as well as beautiful record of the East in the early 19th century.*

# Oliver & Vincent Clare

Brothers Oliver and Vincent Clare fulfilled a Victorian craving for real nature, the demand for which had been created by the Industrial Revolution as people moved away from the countryside to work in towns and cities. Oliver, the more prolific of the two, painted in oil, but Vincent occasionally used watercolours. The subject matter was always fruit, flowers, bird's eggs and nests, often set against a mossy bank. Originally collected by the new industrial rich of Birmingham and London, today they are much sought after for their pleasing decorative quality and very good examples, in original frames, can fetch up to £15,000 ($21,750) per picture.

Painting was in the Clare's blood, their father George had also been a still life painter. The brothers were born in Aston, near Birmingham, and Oliver lived in the area all his life, whereas Vincent moved to Southgate, London as a young man and lived there until he died. Both men were fond of drink and Oliver often settled his bar bills with a painting. A collection of his work was recently sold by a pub in the Birmingham area.

**Oliver Clare**
British (1853–1927)
Still Life of Fruit
Oil on board
6 x 9in (15 x 23cm)
**£4,000–4,500 / $5,800–6,500** ⊞ HFA

**Oliver Clare**
British (1853–1927)
Still Life of Flowers
Oil on canvas
7 x 10in (18 x 25.5cm)
**£5,850–6,500 / $8,500–9,400** ⊞ HFA

**Oliver Clare**
British (1853–1927)
Still Life of Fruit
Oil on board
6 x 9in (15 x 23cm)
**£4,000–4,500 / $5,800–6,500** ⊞ HFA

**Vincent Clare**
British (1855–1930)
Summer's Bloom
Oil on canvas
20 x 24in (51 x 61cm)
**£13,000–13,300 / $18,800–19,600** ⊞ HFA

▶ **Vincent Clare**
British (1855–1930)
Still Life of Flowers
and Bird's Nest
Signed, oil on canvas
8 x 10in
(20.5 x 25.5cm)
**£4,350–4,800**
**$6,300–7,000** ⊞ HFA

**John Coburn**
Australian (b1925)
Gardens at Aubersson
Signed, synthetic polymer paint on paper board
20½ x 28¼in (52 x 72cm)
**£3,200–3,800 / $4,700–5,700** ⚒ P(Sy)

▶ **Bernard Cohen**
British (b1933)
Composition in
Orange
Signed and dated
1957, oil on paper
laid onto board
28¾ x 34in
(73 x 86.5cm)
**£1,600–1,800**
**$2,300–2,600** ⚒ P

**Michael Coleman**
American (b1946)
Monarch
Signed, oil on board
20 x 30in (51 x 76cm)
**£9,000–10,000 / $13,000–14,500** ⚒ CdA

▶ **Samuel David Colkett**
British (1806–63)
Woodland river landscape with figures in conversation
by a flock of sheep and a church ruin beyond.
Oil on panel
8¾ x 10¼in (22 x 26cm)
**£1,400–1,700 / $2,000–2,500** ⚒ CGC

**Maurice Cockrill, RA**
British (b1936)
Woman in Landscape
Signed, oil on canvas
24 x 30in (61 x 76cm)
**£4,750–5,250 / $7,000–7,500** ⊞ BRG

**George Cole**
British (1810–83)
Unloading the Cart
Oil on canvas
20 x 30in (51 x 76cm)
**£19,800–22,000 / $28,500–32,000** ⊞ HFA

**◄ Julia Collins**
British (19thC)
Flower Girl
Inscribed, oil on canvas
24 x 16in (61 x 40.5cm)
**£300–360 / $440–550** ⚒ RBB

**► Patrick Collins, HRHA**
British (1910–94)
The Rook
Signed, oil on board
17¾ x 23¼in (45 x 59cm)
**£15,000–18,000**
**$22,000–26,000** ⚒ JAd

*This painting is an allegory of
Collins' early years which were
spent in an orphanage. The bird
represents his mother, her head
facing away from the nest where
her offspring wait.*

**Peter Collis, RHA**
Irish (b1911)
Snowscape, Wicklow
Signed, oil on canvas
27½ x 30in (70 x 76cm)
**£2,000–2,500 / $2,900–3,600** ⚒ JAd

**Robert Colquhoun**
Scottish (1914–62)
Pig
Oil on canvas
12 x 16in (30.5 x 40.5cm)
**£4,800–5,800 / $7,000–8,500** ⚒ P

**Edward Theodore Compton**
British (1849–1921)
Windermere
Signed, inscribed and dated 1862, watercolour
17 x 31in (43 x 78.5cm)
**£1,800–2,200 / $2,600–3,000** ⚒ GAK

**► Alfred Charles
Conrade**
British (1863–1955)
Street and Tower at
Córdoba
Signed, watercolour
20½ x 14½in
(52 x 37cm)
**£1,000–1,100**
**$1,500–1,600** ⊞ LH

**John Constable, RA**
British (1776–1837)
Brighton Beach
Oil on canvas
11¾ x 16½in (30 x 42cm)
**£55,000–60,500 / $80,000–87,000** ⊞ **BRG**

*This picture is surely a bargain when his painting* The White Horse *sold at auction for nearly £10m ($14.5m). It was painted in the 1830s in Suffolk and his paintings from this period are very expensive. You can still find a Constable drawing for £2,000 ($3,000).*

**George Hamilton Constantine**
British (1875–1967)
The Ploughing Team
Watercolour
10 x 14in (25.5 x 35.5cm)
**£2,350–2,600 / $3,500–3,800** ⊞ **HFA**

◄ **George Hamilton Constantine**
British (1875–1967)
Low Tide
Signed, watercolour
6 x 8in (15 x 20.5cm)
**£1,700–2,000**
**$2,450–2,900** ⊞ **HFA**

**Gerald Cooper**
British (1898–1975)
Still Life with Flowers
Oil on canvas
30 x 25in (76 x 63.5cm)
**£19,000–21,000 / $27,500–30,500** ⊞ **HFA**

◄ **Joseph Teal Cooper**
British (1682–1743)
Peaches, pears, melons, plums and white and red grapes in a landscape with a basket of more fruit behind
Signed, oil on canvas
30¾ x 39¼in (78 x 99.5cm)
**£4,500–5,500 / $6,500–8,000** ⚒ **P**

*In 1739, Cooper is recorded by George Vertue who wrote 'Cooper who lives at Lambeth has arrived to great skill and perfection in painting fruit and flowers in the manner of Michael Angel de Caravaggio ...' His paintings of fruits and nature strongly suggest the influence of Italian still life painting.*

▶ **Thomas Sidney Cooper, RA**
British (1803–1902)
Three Cows in a Meadow
Signed and dated 1877, oil on canvas
16 x 24¼in (41.5 x 61.5cm)
**£13,000–15,500 / $18,800–22,500** 🔨 Bon

◀ **Augusto Corelli**
Italian (b1853)
Lady seated in a
botanic garden
Signed and inscribed,
watercolour
18 x 24½in
(47 x 62cm)
**£6,500–7,750**
**$9,500–11,250**
🔨 JAd

**George Cope**
American (1855–1929)
A pair, Quail (Short Bill) and Snipe (Long Bill)
Signed and dated 1911 and 1912 respectively, oil on canvas
22½ x 15in (57 x 38cm)
**£12,500–15,000 / $18,000–21,500** 🔨 S(NY)

◄ **Giovanni Costa**
Italian (1833–93)
A Friend in Need
Oil on canvas
16½ x 12in
(42 x 30.5cm)
**£11,850–13,000**
**$17,250–18,750**
⊞ **HFA**

**David Cox Snr, OWS**
British (1783–1859)
A Brigg Entering Dieppe Harbour
Signed and dated 1833, watercolour
7¼ x 10¼in (18.5 x 26cm)
**£8,000–8,800 / $11,600–12,750** ⊞ **JSp**

*This watercolour is a good example of Cox's middle period beach scenes in Northern France. He first visited Dieppe and Boulogne in 1832. The fishermen on the beach watching the ship approaching the harbour adds perspective and colour to the scene.*

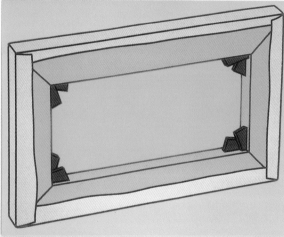

**Michael Craig-Martin**
Irish (b1941)
Painting, 1999
Screenprint, edition of 100
15 x 19in (38 x 48.5cm)
**£600–660 / $870–950** ⊞ **ACG**

**Thomas Creswick**
British (1811–69)
On the Banks of the River
Oil on panel
18 x 24in (45.5 x 61cm)
**£7,850–8,700 / $11,500–16,700** ⊞ **HFA**

◄ **Frederick Cuming, RA, NEAC**
British (b1930)
The Spinnaker
Signed, oil on panel
10 x 14in (25.5 x 35.5cm)
**£14,000–15,500 / $20,000–22,500** ⊞ **BRG**

*Born in London, Frederick trained at Sidcup School of Art from 1945 to 1949 and after National Service attended the Royal College of Art from 1951 to 1952, winning an Abbey Minor Travelling Scholarship which took him to Italy. Throughout his highly successful career he has exhibited extensively and recently his work has been well received in America, where he has shown in Pennsylvania, Texas, California and Illinois. Since 1953 he has shown at the Royal Academy and was elected RA in 1974. At the 2001 Summer Exhibition one gallery was devoted entirely to his work and 21 pieces were included. Examples of his work can be found in numerous collections including the National Museum of Wales, Lloyds of London and the Monte Carlo Museum.*

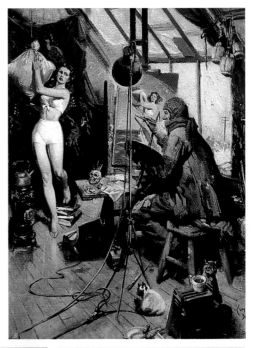

◄ **Frederick Cuming, RA, NEAC**
British (b1930)
The Crescent Moon
Signed, oil on board
50 x 39in
(127 x 99cm)
**£16,800–18,500**
**$24,500–27,000**
⊞ **P&H**

► **Terence Cuneo**
British (1907–98)
The Summer Number
Signed, oil
29 x 22in
(73.5 x 56cm)
**£5,500–6,000**
**$8,000–8,700** ⊞ **Dr**

► **Peter Curling**
Irish (b1955)
Riding Out
Signed, oil on canvas
31 x 27in (78.5 x 68.5cm)
**£8,000–9,000**
**$11,500–13,000** ⤳ **WA**
*Born in Waterford in 1955, Curling spent his early years in County Clare before moving to England. His interest in art was stimulated by his parents – his father worked in the Abbey Theatre and his mother had been involved with selling sporting paintings and prints. In England, Curling won an art scholarship to Millfield School, after which he went to Italy to study. After two years he returned briefly to England where he worked under John Skeaping RA. Curling returned to Ireland in 1975 and has since lived in County Tipperary where he and his wife Louise (who is also an artist) run a horse stud farm.*

**Roger Curtis**
British (20thC)
Summer, St Michael's Mount
Signed, acrylic
10 x 12in (25.5 x 30.5cm)
**£200–220 / $280–320** ⊞ **Stl**

◄ **Ernst Czernotzky**
Austrian (1869–1939)
Still Life
Oil on panel
10½ x 8¼in (26.5 x 21cm)
**£7,000–7,700 / $10,000–11,000** ⊞ **HFA**

► **Ernst Czernotzky**
Austrian (1869–1939)
Still Life
Oil on panel
11 x 8in (28 x 20.5cm)
**£8,000–8,800 / $11,500–12,750** ⊞ **HFA**

# Camden Town Group

Just as the Impressionists were greeted with disdain by the London based art establishment so were the paintings of a small group of artists who became known as the Camden Town Group. Having seen what the French artists were doing, they were inspired to break with the Victorian Classical tradition. Walter Richard Sickert (1860–1942) completely changed his style after meeting Edgar Degas (1834–1917). Spencer Gore (1878–1914) and Harold Gilman (1876–1919) studied Cézanne and Van Gogh's colours which had a profound effect on them. Robert Polhill Bevan (1865–1925) spent some time in Pont Aven in Brittany where Gauguin was working and learned from him how to soften form and colour.

They took their name from the area of London where they met at Walter Sickert's house from 1908 onwards. Sickert was very well respected by French Impressionists, who were not over-generous with their compliments to English painters.

Camden Town in those days was mostly a poor area and Sickert became fascinated by its inhabitants and their surroundings. His pictures are suffused with the real brown and murky light of London before electricity. Gilman, on the other hand, hated brown, preferring the stronger, brighter colours of his guru, Van Gogh, but the subject matter is unmistakably English. Spencer Gore applies the pointillist techniques of Camille Pissarro to London scenes.

**Robert Polhill Bevan, NEAC, LG**
British (1865–1925)
Goulds Farm, Luppitt
Signed, oil on canvas
20 x 30in (51 x 76cm)
**£3,500–4,500 / $5,000–6,500** ⚒ Bon

**Harold Gilman, PLG**
British (1876–1919)
Hampstead Road
Oil on canvas
10 x 12in (25.5 x 30.5cm)
**£18,500–22,000 / $26,850–32,000** ⊞ PN

**Further information**
Artists mentioned in the introduction above may have works appearing elsewhere in this Guide. Consult the index for page numbers.

◀ **Charles Ginner, ARA**
British (1878–1952)
Shepherd Market
Signed, pen, ink and watercolour
15¾ x 12in
(40 x 30.5cm)
**£4,200–5,000**
**$6,000–7,250** ⚒ B

**Spencer Gore, NEAC, LG**
British (1878–1914)
Le Cours Bourbon, Dieppe
Signed, oil on canvas
11¼ x 14in (28.5 x 35.5cm)
**£5,500–6,600 / $8,000–9,500** ⚒ Bon
*Spencer Gore first visited Dieppe in 1904 on a trip with Albert Rothenstein to see Sickert. This trip was followed by two others in 1905 and 1906 when Sickert lent Gore his house in Neuville, near Dieppe.*

**Spencer Gore, NEAC, LG**
British (1878–1914)
Somerset Landscape
Oil on canvas
25 x 30in (63.5 x 76cm)
**£40,000–48,000 / $58,000–70,000** ⊞ PN

*Gore stayed on a large farm owned by Harold Harrison at Applehayes, Clayhidon, Devonshire during the summers of 1909, 1910 and 1913. Bevan and Ginner followed in 1912 and 1913. Bevan subsequently rented various cottages for several summers and eventually bought one in the area.*

*Harrison, a retired rancher from the Argentine, studied at the Slade with Gore, Gilman and John. This is the largest of Gore's Somerset paintings.*

**Lucien Pissarro, NEAC**
French (1863–1944)
Compass Rocks, Dartmouth (September)
Signed, oil on canvas
17¾ x 22in (45 x 56cm)
**£38,500–46,000 / $55,000–65,000** ⊞ MSM

**Walter Richard Sickert, ARA**
British (1860–1942)
The Taming of the Shrew, 1937
Oil on canvas
24 x 20in (61 x 51cm)
**£13,500–16,500 / $20,000–24,000** ⚒ P

*This shows a scene from the 1937 New Theatre production of The Taming of the Shrew.*

**Walter Richard Sickert, ARA**
British (1860–1942)
La Maison Blanche, Dieppe
Signed, oil on panel
7 x 5½in (18 x 14cm)
**£19,000–23,000 / $28,000–33,000** ⚒ S

◀ **Salvador Dali**
Spanish (1904–89)
Tristan et Iseult
Book with 21 drypoint etchings printed in
colours on Arches paper, text pages,
frontispiece signed in pen, etchings signed
with initials in pen, copy number 81 (from the
French edition of 118) published by Editions
Ramos Anstalt Oeuvres Graphiques
Contemporaines, Paris 1970. Loose in paper
wrappers and white calfskin-covered boards,
in cloth-covered slipcase.
18½ x 13¾in (47 x 35cm)
**£3,000–3,500 / $4,400–5,000** ⚒ BUK

*An original picture by a famous artist is out
of reach for most people. However, as shown
here, it is possible to buy signed etchings and
prints for much less, see Limited Edition Prints
(pages 104–107).*

**Wilder M. Darling**
American (1856–1933)
The Haymaker
Signed and dated 1887, oil on canvas
24 x 19in (61 x 48.5cm)
**£5,800–7,000 / $8,500–10,000** ⚒ JAA

**Sir Robin Darwin**
British (1910–74)
The Berkshire Landscape
Signed and dated 1936,
oil on canvas
22 x 48in (56 x 122cm)
**£3,300–4,000**
**$4,700–5,700** ⚒ B

Miller's is a
price GUIDE
not a price LIST

**William Davies**
British (1826–1910)
Mountain Pastures
Oil on canvas
10 x 14in (25.5 x 35.5cm)
**£9,350–10,300 / $13,500–15,000** ⊞ HFA

▶ **Charles Frederick Dawson**
British (fl1909–33)
Getting ready for the Masked Ball
Pastel
21 x 9in (53.5 x 23cm)
**£880–1,000**
**$1,300–1,500** ⊞ WrG

*Charles Frederick Dawson studied
at Shipley School of Art and was
known to have worked in Bradford,
Manchester and Newlyn.*

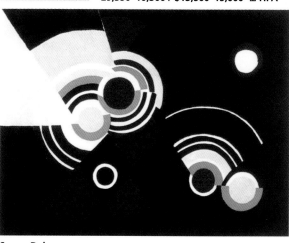

**Sonya Delaunay**
French (1885–1979)
Abstract Composition
Signed, lithograph on paper, edition 30/75
17¾ x 23in (45 x 58cm)
**£700–850 / $1,000–1,250** ⚒ P(Sy)

◄ **Eugène Delacroix**
French (1798–1863)
Figure Study, standing
Pencil
5¼ x 3in (13.5 x 7.5cm)
**£5,000–6,000 / £7,250–8,700 Bon**
*This drawing could be related to the series of preparatory studies for the* Portrait du Comte Palatiano en Costume Souliote *conserved at the Louvre.*

**Robyn Denny**
British (b1930)
Night Out
Signed and dated, oil on board
48in (122cm) square
**£4,000–4,800 / $5,800–7,000 P**
*Whilst the influence of American and European art on the St Ives painters in the late 1950s has been well documented, the effect on the slightly younger generation of artists centred around the Royal College of Art has, until relatively recently, been less thoroughly investigated. Denny was at the centre of this group and this painting demonstrates clearly the direction in which these younger artists were moving. Usually on a large scale, the use of non-art materials such as bitumen and unprimed found boards combined with collage and household paints to produce images of great freedom that were considered to be at the very edge of artistic practice by contemporaries.*

**Marie d'Epinay**
French (fl1908–10)
Picture of Elegance
Oil on canvas
21¾ x 18in (55.5 x 45.5cm)
**£18,500–20,500 / $26,850–29,750 HFA**

◄ **For further information**
see Nudes
(pages 140–141)

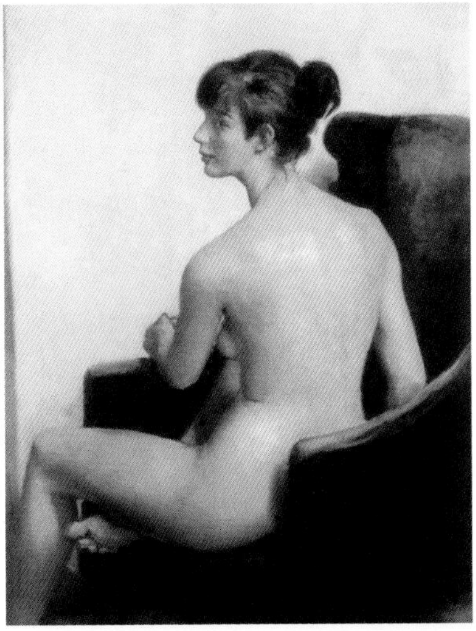

◄ **Anthony Devas**
British (1911–58)
Nude
Signed, oil on canvas
36 x 28in (91.5 x 71cm)
**£2,000–2,400**
**$3,000–3,500 P**

**Jules Ernest Devaux**
French (19thC)
A pair, The Escaped Bird and The Young Pipe Smoker
Signed, oil on panel
12½ x 9¾in (32 x 25cm)
**£4,000–4,800 / $5,800–7,000 TEN**

◄ **Wynford Dewhurst**
British (1864–1941)
Field Workers
Signed and dated 1897, oil on canvas
24 x 32in (61 x 81.5cm)
**£3,000–3,500 / $4,400–5,000 P**

◄ **Sir Frank Dicksee, PRA**
British (1853–1928)
Portrait of Maude Moore
Signed and dated 1894, oil on panel
16 x 12in (40.5 x 30.5cm)
**£25,000–28,000 / $36,000–40,000** ⊞ CW

► **Jim Dine**
American (b1935)
Oil Can
Signed in pen and numbered 38/75,
softground etching, printed in brown.
25½ x 19¾in (64.5 x 50cm)
**£950–1,100 / $1,400–1,600** ⚹ BUK

**Otto Dix**
German (1891–1969)
Recumbent Nude (Sitzende with a Cigarette)
Signed, dated 1923 and numbered 27/36,
lithograph
24 x 19¾in (61 x 50cm)
**£2,000–2,500 / $3,000–3,500** ⚹ SLN

**Charles Edward Dixon**
British (1872–1934)
North River, New York
Signed and dated 1898, watercolour
heightened with white
17½ x 33in (44.5 x 84cm)
**£15,000–18,000**
**$21,750–26,000** ⚹ P(S)
*In this watercolour, Charles Dixon has
transferred his love of painting the bustling
River Thames to the North River, New York.*

◄ **Josef Dobrowsky**
Austrian (1889–1964)
Landscape of Lower
Austria
Signed and dated
1946, gouache
on paper
19 x 25in
(48 x 63cm)
**£2,300–2,800**
**$3,400–4,000**
⚹ DORO

**W. Anstey Dollond**
British (fl1880–1911)
Distant Thoughts
Oil
20 x 16in (51 x 40.5cm)
**£2,400–2,700 / $3,500–3,900** ⊞ Dr

▶ **Mary Donnelly**
Irish (b1964)
The Mountains throw a Shadow
Signed, oil on tracing paper
11 x 15in (28 x 38cm)
**£320–350 / $450–500** ⚒ WA

**J. E. Downing**
British (fl1913)
Sailing Vessel in Harbour
Signed, watercolour
7½ x 11½in (19 x 29cm)
**£470–520 / $680–750** ⊞ LH

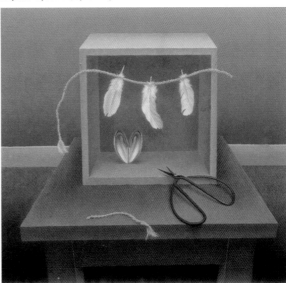

**Alfred de Dreux**
French (1810–60)
An Arabian Horse
Watercolour
9½ x 12¼in (24 x 31cm)
**£2,600–3,000 / $3,800–4,400** ⚒ P

◀ **Alexander John Drysdale**
American (1870–1934)
Oak Bayou under Yellow Skies
Signed, oil wash on board
20 x 30in (51 x 76cm)
**£2,200–2,600 / $3,200–3,800** ⚒ NOA

▶ **Alison Dunlop, RSW**
Canadian (b1958)
The First Cut
Oil on canvas
24in (61cm) square
**£2,000–2,200 / $2,900–3,200** ⊞ P&H

*Alison Dunlop began her studies in Canada before continuing in
France and Britain. In 1982, she went to Scotland to undertake
postgraduate studies at Edinburgh College of Art, and has made
Scotland her home. In 1989, Alison was elected a member of the
Royal Scottish Society of Painters in Watercolour and served as
President of Visual Arts Scotland for three years in the 1990s.*

**Sir Alfred East**
British (1849–1913)
Girl, Geese and Thatched Cottages
Signed, watercolour
9 x 13½in (23 x 34.5cm)
**£670–750 / $950–1,500** ⊞ LH

**Henry East**
British (19thC)
Fishing on a Summer's Day
Oil on canvas
18 x 24in (45.5 x 61cm)
**£2,275–2,500 / $3,300–3,600** ⊞ HFA

## Lionel Edwards (1878–1966)

Foxhunting has certainly been in the news in Britain over the last few years. Eighty years ago it was a popular pastime, with many city and country dwellers keen to participate. Lionel Edwards was one such person and he managed to combine his love of the sport with his work. His oils, paintings and books, including his autobiography, *Memoirs of a Sporting Artist*, record a way of life now fast disappearing.

As an artist he has been in the shadow of Alfred Munnings, another famous equestrian artist (see page 129). Not only was Edwards a popular artist, contributing drawings of fox and stag hunting and military subjects to Punch and other magazines, but he was also an accomplished painter in oils. His signed prints of hunts *The Cheshire*, The *Whaddon Chase* and *The Duke of Beaufort's,* are vignettes of life on the hunting field and fetch between £350 ($500) and £500 ($720). Unsigned prints published by Eyre and Spottiswoode in the 1930s and 1940s cost from £140–150 ($200–220).

Lionel Edwards was a well-loved man in rural England. With the appearance and demeanour of an old soldier, he was on the hunting field jumping gates into his eighties.

**Lionel Dalhousie Robertson Edwards, RI, RCA**
British (1878–1966)
Away from the Prince of Wales Covert, The Quorn
Signed and inscribed 'The Quorn', oil on canvas
20 x 30in (51 x 76cm)
**£11,000–13,000 / $16,000–18,500** ⚒ P

**Lionel Dalhousie Robertson Edwards, RI, RCA**
British (1878–1966)
The Hunt
Signed and dated 1932, watercolour and bodycolour
19¾ x 29½in (50 x 75cm)
**£2,600–3,200 / $3,800–4,600** ⚒ P

**Lionel Dalhousie Robertson Edwards, RI, RCA**
British (1878–1966)
A pair, Across Country and Hold Hard, Please
One signed and dated 1904, oil on board
14½ x 17in (37 x 43cm)
**£5,800–7,000 / $8,400–10,200** ⚒ JAd

**Frank Egginton, RCA**
British (1908–90)
Lough Leane, Killarney
Watercolour
10 x 14in (25.5 x 35.5cm)
**£2,900–3,200 / $4,250–4,650** ⊞ **WrG**

**Edward S. England**
British (19thC)
On the Scent
Oil on canvas
24 x 36in (61 x 91.5cm)
**£6,400–7,000 / $9,400–10,200** ⊞ **HFA**

**Sir Jacob Epstein**
British/American (1880–1959)
Epping Forest
Signed, watercolour
22 x 17in (56 x 43cm)
**£2,200–2,600**
**$3,200–3,800** ↗ **P**

**Max Ernst**
German (1891–1976)
Birds in Peril
Signed and numbered 5/100,
etching with collage on paper
11¾ x 9¾in (30 x 25cm)
**£1,000–1,200**
**$1,500–1,750** ↗ **BUK**

**Tracey Emin**
British (b1963)
Dog Brains
Signed, numbered and dated 2000 by the artist, limited edition of
300, silkscreen
30 x 40in (76 x 102cm)
**£350–400 / $500–580** ⊞ **CEL**

*Tracey Emin graduated from Maidstone College of Art in 1986 and
completed her MA at the Royal College of Art, London in 1989. She
has presented numerous solo shows, a number of other significant
projects, including The Shop in 1993, a kind of art boutique which she
ran with Sarah Lucas; Exploration of the Soul – a reading/performance
tour of the US in 1994, and the Tracey Emin Museum in Waterloo,
London from 1995 to 1998.*

*Tracey Emin's work is essentially introspective. She has risen rapidly
to a position of central prominence in the London art scene. Her
Turner Prize show of 1999, which included her now famous unmade
bed, attracted all the attention, although it did not win the prize. She
has made known her life, beliefs and feelings in the form of diaristic
drawings, films, sculptures and written stories, in a manner full of
compassion and wit as well as frustration and pain. Drawings remain
at the heart of Emin's work, and over the last ten years she has
produced a steady flow of monotype prints direct from her drawings.
Dog Brains has been selected from a collection of her most recent
drawings and has the trademark Emin line – a hesitant, slightly blurred
line suggesting a fragile immediacy of experience.*

▲ **For further information**
see Limited Edition Prints (pages 104–107)

**Bernard Walter Evans, RI, RBA**
British (1848–1922)
Knaresborough Park
Watercolour
17½ x 26½in (44.5 x 67.5cm)
**£2,600–3,000 / $3,800–4,400** ⊞ **WrG**

**Mary Fedden, OBE, RA, PPRWA**
British (b1915)
Three Eggs
Signed and dated 1989, oil on board
5½ x 8in (14 x 20.5cm)
**£4,200–4,500 / $6,000–6,500 ⊞ NZ**

**Arnaldo Ferraguti**
Italian (1862–1925)
In the Roman Campagna
Signed, oil on canvas
29 x 66in (73.5 x 167.5cm)
**£2,300–2,600 / $3,400–3,800 ⤳ Bon**

**Mary Fedden, OBE, RA, PPRWA**
British (b1915)
The Conch Shell
Signed and dated, oil on canvas
20 x 24in (51 x 61cm)
**£9,500–10,500 / $13,800–15,250 ⊞ P&H**

*Born in Bristol, Mary studied at the Slade School of Fine Art from 1932 to 1936. She became the first woman tutor at the Royal College of Art where she taught between 1958 and 1964. She has had numerous major exhibitions in London and the provinces and her work is held in many private collections, including that of HM The Queen. She was President of the Royal West of England Academy and was elected RA in 1992. She was married to the artist Julian Trevelyan, who died in 1988.*

**Anthony Vandyke Copley Fielding, POWS**
British (1787–1855)
Bolton Abbey from the river with cattle
Signed and dated 1849, watercolour over traces of pencil with touches of gum arabic
20¼ x 34in (51.5 x 86.5cm)
**£2,000–2,400 / $3,000–3,500 ⤳ Bri**

◄ **Anthony Vandyke Copley Fielding, POWS**
British (1787–1855)
A View near Hythe, Kent
Signed and dated 1825, watercolour heightened with scratching out
9¾ x 14in (25 x 35.5cm)
**£8,000–8,800 / $11,600–12,600 ⊞ JSp**

*Copley Fielding was a pupil of John Varley and a member of the Dr Munro circle of artists. This expansive view of the Kent countryside near Hythe is a fine example of his middle period. He was living only a few miles away at Sandgate when he painted this picture. He moved to Brighton in 1829, and finally to Worthing in 1847.*

**James Fitton, RA**
British (1899–1982)
London Landscape
Signed, oil, pen and ink and gouache on card
20 x 24in (51 x 61cm)
**£8,800–9,500 / $12,500–13,800** 🔨 P

**Vaughan Flannery**
American (1898–1955)
Mrs Whitney and Cherry Pie
Signed, oil on panel
14 x 20in (35.5 x 51cm)
**£14,000–16,500 / $20,500–24,000** 🔨 S(NY)
*A bay gelding, Cherry Pie by Chicle out of Cherry Malotte won the Jerome Handicap, the Nursery Handicap and the Keene Memorial during his successful racing career.*

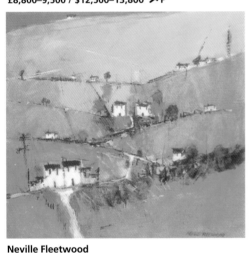

**Neville Fleetwood**
British (b1932)
Yellow Fields
Signed, acrylic on board
30 x 32in (76 x 81.5cm)
**£2,000–2,200 / $3,000–3,200** ⊞ P&H

**Francis Russell Flint**
British (1915–77)
Star Shell in E-Boat Alley – M.L's in Trouble
Signed, watercolour
10 x 14in (25.5 x 35.5cm)
**£220–260 / $320–380** 🔨 G(L)

◀ **William Gilbert Foster, RBA**
British (1855–1906)
Cottage Near Staithes
Signed, oil on canvas
72 x 112in (183 x 284.5cm)
**£2,000–2,200 / $3,000–3,200** ⊞ TBJ
*Foster taught art at Leeds Grammar School before being appointed Under-Master at Leeds School of Art. He taught private pupils too, including Owen Bowen, (see page 19). In 1890, he bought a cottage at Runswick Bay and spent his summers painting in the area, encouraging his students to do likewise. His works are in the collections of many public galleries including Bradford, Leeds, Huddersfield, Hull, Manchester, Redcar and Whitby. It was around this time that his work began to lose its traditional Victorian tightness and take on the atmospheric plein-air characteristics for which he is most admired.*

**Robert Fowler**
British (1853–1926)
Young Ballerina
Signed, watercolour
12½ x 9in (32 x 23cm)
**£650–720 / $950–1,000** ⊞ **LH**

**E. M. Fox**
British (19thC)
Study of a Shorthorn
Signed and dated 1869, oil on board
10¼ x 14in (26 x 35.5cm)
**£620–750 / $900–1,100** ⚒ **WL**

▶ **William Arnee Frank**
British (1808–97)
Cattle Watering
Signed, watercolour
12 x 18½in (30.5 x 47cm)
**£950–1,150 / $1,400–1,600** ⊞ **LH**

**Henry Branston Freer**
British (fl1870–1900)
A Busy River
Signed, watercolour
8½ x 12½in (21.5 x 32cm)
**£500–600 / $700–850** ⚒ **Bon**

**William Percy French**
British (1854–1920)
Meandering stream in a hilly landscape
Signed and dated 1907, watercolour
11 x 17½in (28 x 44.5cm)
**£2,700–3,200 / $4,000–4,600** ⚒ **WA**

◄ **Arthur Friedenson**
British (c1872–1955)
View across Staithes
Signed and dated, oil on wood
13 x 16in (33 x 40.5cm)
**£1,500–1,800 / $2,200–2,600** ⚒ G(L)

**Dame Elizabeth Frink, DBE, CH, RA**
British (1930–92)
Horse, 1982
Signed and dated, pencil on paper
22 x 30in (56 x 76cm)
**£8,000–8,800 / $11,660–12,750** ⊞ P&H

◄ **Katherine Mary Fryer, RBSA**
British (b1910)
Sheep Judging – Bingley Hall
Oil
24 x 30in (61 x 76cm)
**£1,750–2,000 / $2,500–3,000** ⊞ Dr

# Henry Fuseli (1741–1825)

Fuseli was born in Switzerland to Swiss and German parents and trained as a priest. He had no formal art training. He loved Shakespeare and the German legends, such as *Niebelungenlied* and came to England on the suggestion of the English Ambassador who had seen his drawings of scenes from Shakespeare's plays. While in London he met Joshua Reynolds who encouraged him to take up painting full time. Fuseli then went to Rome to study Michelangelo. He finally settled in England, setting up a studio in Fulham, London.

Fuseli is considered to be one of the most outstanding artists working in Britain during the late 18th century. His muscular and heroic men and his images of women, often in reckless sexual abandon, were a huge influence on the Expressionist and Surrealist artists who were fascinated by his interpretation of sex and power. His drawings have a fluidity that has been an inspiration for modern artists.

◄ **Henry Fuseli, RA**
Swiss (1741–1825)
A naked warrior attacking with raised sword – a scene from *The Niebelungenlied*
Inscribed and dated 20 May P.C., pen and brown ink over pencil on the back of a cover sheet of a letter
6¾ x 4¼in (17 x 11cm)
**£7,200–8,000 / $10,500–11,500** ⚒ S

*This drawing, dated to c1805, depicts a helmeted warrior with a large upraised sword. He appears to be involved in one of the numerous combats described in the bloody Germanic epic, The Niebelungenlied. This seems likely as Fuseli drew another subject from this text on the same day entitled Kriemhild and Brunhild Dispute whether Siegfried or Gunther is the Better Man (Schiff 1973, no.1383).*

*This drawing was made at Purser's Cross (hence the initials P.C.), the Fulham retreat of Fuseli's friend and publisher, Joseph Johnson.*

**Thomas Gainsborough**
British (1727–88)
A landscape
c1747, drawing
11¾ x 15¾in (30 x 40cm)
**£35,000–40,000 / $50,000–60,000** ✏ P

*East Anglian-born Thomas Gainsborough is well-known for his portraits of the British aristocracy and the Royal Family but he started his career as a landscape artist. This finished pencil drawing of the Suffolk countryside is very rare. It comes from a group of studies much admired because it shows the artist revelling in the different textures of the pencil to describe the landscape in considerable detail. Unfortunately, since two hundred years have elapsed since he drew this picture there has been little success in identifying the individual views. The drawing came from a group of studies, one of which is in the house he grew up in, now the Gainsborough House Museum, Sudbury, Suffolk.*

*Gainsborough served his apprenticeship in London under the landscape painter Francis Hayman and was regarded by his urban contemporaries as something of a landscape specialist, providing backgrounds to other painter's portraits. William Hogarth rated him highly and asked him to submit a little circular oil on canvas landscape to hang in the Court Room in the Foundling Hospital, London, as part of the decorative scheme he was organizing.*

*The price of this Gainsborough is more affordable due to the small size of the picture, the fact that it was a drawing as opposed to an oil and that it was completed very early in the artist's career.*

**Henry G. Gastineau**
British (1791–1876)
River Trent and Nottingham Castle
Signed, watercolour
7 x 9½in (18 x 24cm)
**£900–1,100 / $1,300–1,600** ⊞ LH

**Simon Gales**
British (b1964)
The Mantel of a Wanderer
Oil on linen mounted on panel
27¼in (69cm) square
**£5,200–5,800 / $7,500–8,500** ⊞ BrS

*Simon Gales is much more than a latter-day surrealist. A superficial glance at his work might suggest a Magritte-like eye for composition or a Dali-esque penchant for the deliberate juxtaposition of commonplace objects with grand vistas. However, closer inspection of Gales' intriguing paintings will reward the observer with the realization that he transcends mere stylistic references and delivers instead a determinedly cerebral aesthetic. His thought-provoking works are deeply concerned with the communication and exploration of fundamental concepts or eternal paradigms through a wholly visual medium. In particular, Gales is fascinated by the human condition, the central questions of faith and possibility of the existence of God. These are the philosophical questions that constantly obsess him, and his canvasses are the forum in which he strives for the answers. Gales himself says, 'I have tried to perfect a visual parlance concerning faith. I seem to cling to the forever floating straw of possibility – the eternal balance that although the existence of God cannot be proved it has yet to be disproved. Still life can seduce the mind and focus it upon the spiritual and temporal basis for our existence. I am probing for the immortal; I thirst to comprehend its being.'*

*Gales' quest has proved to be a popular one. Inspired by the visual power of these sincere artworks, collectors ensured that Gales' previous one-man exhibition at the Bruton Street Gallery was a complete sell-out.*

## Tate galleries

■ Admission to the Tate Galleries is free. www.tate.org.uk

■ Tate Britain, Millbank, London SW1P 4RG
(020 7887 8000)

■ Tate Modern, Bankside, London SE1 9TG (020 7887 8000)

■ Tate Liverpool, Albert Dock, Liverpool L3 4BB
(0151 702 7400)

■ Tate St Ives, Porthmeor Beach, St Ives, Cornwall,
TR26 1TG (01736 796226)

**Henri Gaudier-Brzeska**
French (1891–1915)
Study of a Male Nude
Black chalk, watercolour and gouache
21 x 16in (53.5 x 40.5cm)
**£10,000–12,000 / $14,500–17,500** ⚒ S

*Gaudier-Brzeska was a brightly burning star. Strikingly handsome in the mould of the poet Lord Byron, he was a sculptor who produced a small collection of drawings that were largely unappreciated at the time. Soon after his death, he became a cult figure and has been the subject of many books and films. Today his spontaneous pen and ink drawings are highly collected, as are his rarer pastel portraits influenced by the Fauvist movement. He is now regarded as one of the most important sculptors of his generation.*

*Henri Gaudier-Brzeska was born in St Jean de Braye in France and became a sculptor in Paris through obsession and determination. He had no formal training.*

**Paul Gaugin**
French (1848–1903)
Noa Noa
Woodcut printed in black, yellow, ochre and red on heavy cream japan paper
14 x 8in (35.5 x 20.5cm)
**£16,500–19,000 / $24,000–28,000** ⚒ BUK

◀ **Oscar Ghiglia**
Italian (1876–1945)
L'Enfant Dormi
Signed, oil on board
13¼ x 18½in
(33.5 x 47cm)
**£6,000–7,000**
**$8,500–10,000** ⚒ P

▶ **Madge Gill**
British (1882–1961)
Untitled
c1940, pen and ink
on card
9 x 7½in (23 x 19cm)
**£850–950**
**$1,250–1,350** ⊞ BOX

# George Gillespie (1924–96)

George did not begin painting until the age of 50. He had his first one-man show at the Oriel Gallery, Dublin in 1979 and went on to exhibit regularly in Dublin. His work was shown at both the Royal Hibernian and Ulster Academies. He was greatly influenced by the Ulster School of Painting, particularly the great artists McKelvey, Craig and Wilks and his work is highly regarded in the UK.

**George Gillespie, RUA**
British (1924–96)
On the road to Achill Sound, County Mayo
Signed, oil on canvas
15 x 30in (38 x 76cm)
**£4,000–4,500 / $5,800–6,500** ↗ **WA**

◀ **George Gillespie, RUA**
British (1924–96)
Low Tide, Ards Point, County Donegal
Signed, oil on board
12 x 15½in (30.5 x 39.5cm)
**£4,500–5,000 / $6,500–7,250** ⊞ **WrG**

> **For further information**
> see Irish Art
> (pages 72–75)

◀ **Sir William George Gillies**
British (1898–1973)
Gladhouse
Signed and dated 1962, watercolour
22½ x 30¼in (57 x 77cm)
**£3,600–4,200 / $5,200–6,000** ↗ **TRL**

A VOLUPTUARY under the horrors of Digestion.

▶ **James Gillray**
British (1757–1815)
A Voluptuary under the horrors of Digestion and Temperance enjoying a Frugal Meal
A pair, published 1792, etchings with stipple engraving, contemporary hand colour, finished with touches of gum arabic
14¾ x 11½in (37.5 x 29cm)
**£4,600–5,400 / $6,800–8,000** ↗ **P**

*At the time of Gillray's satire, the Prince was estranged from his parents by his politics, his choice of friends and lifestyle. He would be frustrated in efforts to follow his younger brothers into the military. Self-centred, self-indulgent, vain, his princely aptitude for enjoyment had boosted the royal physique to an estimated 17 stones. The caricaturist surrounds his subject with trappings of excess. Contrasted with the Prince's life is the somewhat more severe regimen observed by his royal parents at Windsor. The other half of the royal generation gap shows George III and Queen Charlotte in an orgy of self-denial and restraint.*

**Charles Ginner, CBE, ARA**
British (1878–1952)
The Hunted Stag
Signed, 1930, oil on canvas
24 x 20in (61 x 51cm)
**£38,000–45,000 / $55,000–65,000** 🔨 PN

*Born in Cannes, the son of an English doctor, Ginner studied art at the Académie Vitti and Ecole des Beaux-Arts in Paris after initially training as an engineer and architect. He exhibited at the Allied Artists' Association in London in 1908 where his work was first noticed by Gore. Friendship with Gilman and Gore, of the Camden Town Group, followed as a result of their meeting at the 1910 exhibition. His earliest work, influenced by the Spanish artist Hermen Anglada y Camarasa, was thickly painted with large strokes of impasto, but he quickly absorbed the influence of Impressionism and Post-Impressionism, particularly that of Van Gogh whom he studied on a visit to Paris in 1911. From 1939 to 1945 he was an Official War Artist and made a CBE in 1950.*

▲ **For further information**
see Camden Town Group (pages 32–33)

## Auction or gallery?

All the pictures in our price guide originate from auction houses or galleries. When buying at auction, prices can be lower than those of a gallery, but a buyer's premium and VAT will be added to the hammer price. Equally, when selling at auction, commission, tax and photography charges must be taken into account.

Both galleries and auctioneers can provide professional advice, so it is worth researching both sources before buying or selling your pictures.

**Wilfred Gabriel de Glehn**
British (1870–1951)
Dornford, Wiltshire
Signed, oil on canvas
20 x 30in (51 x 76cm)
**£3,000–3,500 / $4,500–5,000** 🔨 P(S)

**Alfred Glendening**
British (1861–1907)
A Day at the Seaside
Signed with monogram and dated 1886, oil on canvas
20 x 30in (51 x 76cm)
**£24,000–28,800 / $34,800–42,000** 🔨 P

*The son of a successful landscape painter, Glendening spent his life painting in the countryside to the east of London. Among a wide variety of genre and landscape subjects, riverside scenes feature regularly and, occasionally, seaside scenes such as this. Like his contemporaries, Marcus Stone and Edmund Blair Leighton, Glendening often chose a late 18th-century setting for his genre scenes. He worked in both oil and watercolour and exhibited at the Royal Academy, the Royal Society British Artists, the British Institution and elsewhere. His painting entitled* Haymaking *(1898) was bought for the nation by the Chantrey Bequest and is now in the Tate Gallery.*

**Frederick E. J. Goff**
British (1855–1931)
St Paul's from Blackfriars
Signed and inscribed, watercolour
heightened with white
6¼ x 4½in (16 x 11.5cm)
**£2,000–2,400 / $3,000–3,500** ↗ B

**George Bouverie Goddard**
British (1832–86)
First Meet of the Cotswold Hounds on the London Road, 1858
Oil on canvas
28 x 36in (71 x 91.5cm)
**£58,000–65,000 / $85,000–95,000** ⊞ HFA

▶ **Philip R. Goodwin**
American (1882–1935)
Into New Country
Signed, oil on canvas
24 x 33in (61 x 84cm)
**£38,000–45,000 / $55,000–65,000** ↗ CdA

**Richard Labarre Goodwin**
American (1840–1910)
Snagging the Catch
Inscribed, oil on canvas
25½ x 17in (65 x 43cm)
**£850–1,000 / $1,250–1,500** ↗ SLN

▶ **Sidney Goodwin**
British, (1867–1944)
Fishing Vessels In
Strong Breeze
Signed and dated
1914, watercolour
14½ x 21in
(37 x 53.5cm)
**£1,200–1,400
$1,750–2,000** ⊞ LH

**Robert Gordy**
American (1933–86)
Night Garden
Signed and dated 1980, magic
marker and ink
24½ x 30½in (62 x 77.5cm)
**£2,000–2,400**
**$3,000–3,500** ⚒ NOA

▶ **Thomas Cooper Gotch**
British (1854–1931)
Dalphane
Signed, watercolour
9 x 7½in (23 x 19cm)
**£4,000–4,500**
**$5,800–6,500** ⚒ P

**Frederick Gore, CBE, RA**
British (b1913)
Portrait of Lily
Oil on canvas
20 x 16in (51 x 40.5cm)
**£7,500–8,500 / $11,000–12,500** ⊞ P&H

*One of the Royal Academy's most senior members,
Frederick Gore studied at the Ruskin School while at
Oxford in the 1930s, and later at Westminster School
of Art and the Slade. While at Westminster, his
effective influences were Mark Gertler and Bernard
Meninsky and, while at the Slade, he roomed above
Cedric Morris whose artistic circle he gravitated towards.
His paintings adorn the walls of most public art galleries
up and down the UK and his popular views of France
have been widely reproduced. An important artist,
Gore's paintings from the 1940s and 1950s are
considered his strongest, and consequently are hardest
to find.*

**Alfred Fitzwalter Grace, RBA**
British (1844–1903)
The South Downs, near Hastings
Watercolour
9½ x 14in (24 x 35.5cm)
**£1,200–1,350 / $1,750–2,000** ⊞ WrG

**Brian Graham**
British (b1945)
Shelter, Culverwell
Signed and dated 2000, acrylic on Fabriano paper
9½ x 13in (24 x 33cm)
**£400–450 / $580–650** ⊞ HG

**Carleton Grant**
British (fl1885–99)
The Marius Lake with Boats on a Grey Day
Signed and dated 1895, watercolour
13 x 24in (33 x 61cm)
**£750–900 / $1,100–1,300** ✗ TAY

▶ **Duncan Grant**
British (1885–1975)
Woman Arranging Flowers
Oil on panel
19¾ x 13in (50 x 33cm)
**£5,800–6,500 / $8,500–9,500** ✗ TRL

**James Ardern Grant**
British (1885–1973)
The Red Shawl
Signed and inscribed, oil on canvas
50 x 32in (127 x 81.5cm)
**£1,200–1,400 / $1,750–2,000** ✗ S(O)

**James Green**
British (fl1882–1901)
The Tranquility of a Winter Landscape
Signed, watercolour
19¾ x 27¾in (50 x 70.5cm)
**£1,650–1,800 / $2,300–2,600** ⊞ JC

◀ **J. Greenhalgh**
British (fl1882–97)
Punting on the River
Signed and dated 1881, watercolour
14 x 20in (35.5 x 51cm)
**£300–350 / $450–500** ✗ G(L)

**Ninel Grigoreva**
Russian
Untitled
1917, mixed media
22¾ x 16¼in (58 x 41.5cm)
**£1,000–1,200 / $1,500–1,750** ⚒ **B&B**

## Arthur E. Grimshaw

Arthur Grimshaw didn't paint many pictures but when he did it was in the style of his father John Atkinson Grimshaw (1836–93) who commands around £100,000 ($145,000) a picture. Arthur's brother Louis (1870–1943) was also a painter, and his work sells for around £25,000 ($36,000) a picture.

▶ **Ken Grimes**
American (b1947)
We Must Collect, Examine and Evaluate as Much Evidence as Possible
Dated 1993, acrylic on canvas
48 x 66in (122 x 167.5cm)
**£3,700–4,200**
**$5,500–6,000** ⊞ **RMG**

▶ **For further information**
see Outsider Art
(pages 144–147)

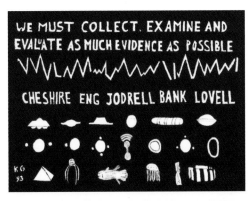

**Arthur E. Grimshaw**
British (1868–1913)
Evening, Whitby Harbour
Signed and dated 1893, oil on board
8 x 12in (20.5 x 30.5cm)
**£7,500–9,000 / $11,000–13,000** ⚒ **P**

**Daniel Charles Grose**
American (1865–90)
Fisherman on a Riverbank
Signed, oil on canvas
15 x 26in (38 x 66cm)
**£800–1,000 / $1,200–1,500** ⚒ **SLN**

**George Grosz**
German (1893–1959)
God with Us
Signed, 1920, photo-lithograph, No. 19 of 20 numbered copies of Edition A without typographic satirical captions
25¾ x 19in (65.5 x 48.5cm)
**£10,500–12,000 / $15,000–17,500** ⚒ **DORO**

◀ **Isaac Grünewald**
Swedish (1889–1946)
Skogslandskap med Slingrande Stig
Signed, pastel
39½ x 26¾in (100 x 61cm)
**£3,000–3,300**
**$4,400–4,800** ⚒ **BUK**

**Emile Albert Gruppe**
American (1896–1978)
Bass Rocks
Signed, oil on canvas
25 x 30in (63.5 x 76cm)
**£1,900–2,200**
**$2,750–3,200** ⚒ **SK**

◀ **Emile Albert Gruppe**
American (1896–1978)
Cloudy Day
Signed, oil on canvas
12 x 16in (30.5 x 40.5cm)
**£4,400–5,200 / $6,300–7,500** ⚒ **SK**

**Robin Craig Guthrie, RP, NEAC**
Scottish (1902–71)
Resting Model
Signed, oil on canvas
20 x 24in (51 x 61cm)
**£3,200–3,500 / $4,650–5,000** ⊞ **P&H**

*Guthrie studied at the Slade School of Art from
1918 to 1922 under Wilson Steer and Henry Tonks.
In the early 1930s he was joint director of painting
and drawing at the School of the Museum of Fine Arts
in Boston, USA and later taught at St Martin's School
of Art and the Royal College of Art in London. Guthrie
exhibited widely and his work can be found in the
collections of the Tate, the British Museum, the Victoria
and Albert Museum and the National Portrait Gallery.*

◀ **Constantin Guys**
French (1802–92)
Scene from the
Crimean War
Watercolour
10 x 13½in
(25.5 x 34.5cm)
**£4,000–4,800**
**$5,800–7,000** ⚒ **S(O)**

**Louis Haghe, PRI**
Belgian (1806–85)
St Bavon, Ghent
Signed and dated 1867, watercolour over pencil
heightened with white
23½ x 19½in (59.5 x 49.5cm)
**£1,000–1,200 / $1,500–1,750** ⚹ Bon

**Fred Hall**
British (1860–1948)
In the Craven Country
Signed and inscribed, oil on panel
13¾ x 16¼in (33.5 x 41.5cm)
**£3,000–3,500 / $4,500–5,000** ⚹ AG

◄ **Maggi Hambling**
British (b1945)
Redhead in Bedroom
Signed and dated 1983, oil on canvas
51¼ x 38¼in (130 x 97cm)
**£3,800–4,500 / $5,500–6,500** ⚹ P

*Maggi Hambling is one of Britain's most respected living artists. She was the first
artist in residence at the National Gallery. This painting is reminiscent of Grünewald
(see page 52) in the flamboyant hair, awkwardly angular body and gnarled toes
tipped with wickedly sexy scarlet. The redhead is poised between two points of utter
stillness: on the left, Hambling's quizzical black cat, Parole, who often crept into her
paintings of Max Wall, and on the right a beautiful still life featuring an orchid on a
mock-Oriental lacquer corner cupboard. One of her last and most fully resolved full-
length figures, Redhead in Bedroom is an important transitional work between the
portrait likeness, and her purely imaginative interpretations of the human spirit.*

▶ **Arthur Henry Knighton Hammond, RI, RSW**
British (1875–1970)
Summer Breakfast on the Lawn (the Artist's Family)
Watercolour
21½ x 29in (54.5 x 73.5cm)
**£4,250–4,700 / $6,250–6,750** ⊞ WrG

**James Hardy Jnr**
British (1832–1889)
Reading to Grandma
Oil on panel
6 x 8in (15 x 20.5cm)
**£6,500–7,000 / $9,400–10,200** ⊞ HFA

**Dudley Hardy RI, ROI, RBA**
British (1865–1922)
Mending the Nets
Signed, watercolour
10¼ x 14in (26 x 35.5cm)
**£1,000–1,200 / $1,500–1,750** ↗ Bon

**Miller's is a price GUIDE not a price LIST**

# Thomas Bush Hardy (1842–97)

Hardy is one of the most popular maritime watercolourists with collectors today. Born in Sheffield, he is best known for his watercolours but he also painted in oils. Hardy travelled extensively in Europe, especially in France, Holland and Italy. He exhibited at the Royal Academy from 1872–97 as well as the New Watercolour Society.

**Thomas Bush Hardy**
British (1842–97)
Clearing the wreck near Boulogne
Signed, dated 1882 and inscribed, watercolour heightened with white
13 x 9¾in (33 x 25cm)
**£3,200–3,800 / $4,650–5,500** ↗ P

**Thomas Bush Hardy**
British (1842–97)
On the Lagoon, Venice
Signed and dated 1888, watercolour heightened with white
9 x 12in (23 x 30.5cm)
**£6,000–7,000 / $8,700–10,200** ↗ P(S)

| **For further information** see Marine Art (pages 130–133) | ▶ **Thomas Bush Hardy** British (1842–97) On the Quayside, Venice Signed, watercolour 5 x 6¾in (12.5 x 17cm) **£2,000–2,400 / $3,000–3,500** ↗ Bon |

**Edward Steele Harper**
British (1878–1951)
Isle of Eigg
Oil on canvas
20 x 30in (51 x 76cm)
**£1,500–1,600 / $2,200–2,300** ⊞ Dr

▶ **Edwin Harris**
British (1855–1906)
A Pinch of Snuff
Signed, oil on canvas
5 x 12in (12.5 x 30.5cm)
**£17,250–19,000 / $25,000–27,500** ⊞ HFA

**James R. Harrington**
American (20thC)
Pinnacle
Signed, oil on canvas
16 x 14in (40.5 x 35.5cm)
**£350–400 / $500–580** ⚒ TREA

▶ **John Cyril Harrison**
British (1898–1985)
Pink-footed geese at Holkham, Norfolk
Signed, watercolour
13 x 18½in (33 x 47cm)
**£900–1,000 / $1,300–1,500** ⚒ Bon

**Henri Joseph Harpignies**
French (1819–1916)
A woodland pool
Signed, indistinctly inscribed and dated 1878, watercolour
11½ x 19¾in (29 x 50cm)
**£500–600 / $725–875** ⚒ Bon

▶ **Heine Hartwig**
American (b1937)
Below Mt Moran
Signed, oil on board
30 x 24in (76 x 61cm)
**£2,300–2,800**
**$3,500–4,000** 🔨 JAA

**Hans Hartung**
French/German (1904–89)
Abstract Composition
Signed, dated 1966 and inscribed, acrylic on canvas
9¼ x 7½in (23.5 x 19cm)
**£3,600–4,200 / $5,250–6,000** 🔨 B(Ba)

**Childe Hassam**
American (1859–1935)
Dryads
Signed and dated 1906, oil on canvas
13½ x 16¾in (34.5 x 42.5cm)
**£63,000–70,000 / $92,000–100,000** 🔨 S(NY)

*Childe Hassam was born in Dorchester, Massachusetts, the son of a*
*hardware merchant. His ancestors included a number of sea captains*
*and revolutionary war patriots. He also had family ties with the*
*Boston painter, William Morris Hunt.*
  *Hassam was apprenticed to a Boston wood engraver in 1876 and was*
*soon employed locally as a freelance illustrator. After attending evening*
*classes at the Boston Art Club during 1877 and 1878 and studying*
*privately, his first non-commercial work was in watercolour, a medium*
*that he would continue to favour for the rest of his career. Hassam visited*
*Europe in 1883 and exhibited 67 watercolours to much critical acclaim.*
*After 1915, he developed an interest in printmaking, etching in particular.*
*He died at his summer residence at East Hampton, Long Island in 1935.*

**John Rabone Harvey**
British (1866–1933)
Wayside Gossips
Signed, oil on canvas
20 x 24in (50.5 x 61cm)
**£2,000–2,200 / $3,000–3,200** 🔨 DN

**Alfred Charles Havell**
British (1855–1928)
Richard Marsh leading his string at Newmarket
Signed, oil on canvas
12 x 22in (30.5 x 56cm)
**£6,000–7,000 / $8,700–10,200** ⚒ S

**William Havell, OWS**
British (1782–1857)
Covent Garden Market
Initialled, dated and inscribed, watercolour
11¼ x 16in (28 x 41cm)
**£5,000–5,500 / $7,250–8,000** ⊞ BG

◄ **Charles W. Hawthorne**
American (1872–1930)
The Lovers
Signed, tempera on panel
40in (101.5cm) square
**£8,200–9,800 / $13,500–14,250** ⚒ S(NY)

**Peter Alexander Hay**
Scottish (1866–1952)
Silk and Straw
Oil on canvas
24 x 20in (61 x 51cm)
**£6,500–7,100 / $9,500–10,250** ⊞ Dr

◄ **Claude Hayes, RI**
Irish (1852–1922)
Anglers beside stream with red brick bridge
Signed, watercolour
9½ x 13½in (24 x 43.5cm)
**£850–1,000 / $1,250–1,500** ⊞ LH

**Claude Hayes, RI**
Irish (1852–1922)
The Drinking Place
Watercolour
13½ x 20in (34.5 x 51cm)
**£1,750–2,000 / $2,500–3,000 ⊞ WrG**

**Claude Hayes, RI**
Irish (1852–1922)
The Wheatfield
Signed, watercolour heightened with white
13 x 20in (33 x 51cm)
**£1,200–1,500 / $1,750–2,200 ⚒ WA**

**Edwin Hayes, RHA, RI**
British (1820–1904)
Sailing boat at sunset with lookout tower in distance.
Signed, inscribed 'Langham' and dated 1873, oil on panel
7 x 11in (18 x 28cm)
**£2,000–2,400 / $3,000–3,500 ⚒ WA**

**Edwin Hayes, RHA, RI**
British (1820–1904)
St Malo Harbour
Signed, oil on board
7¾ x 12½in (19.5 x 32cm)
**£4,000–4,800 / $5,800–7,000 ⚒ JAd**

**Colette Pope Heldner**
American (1902–90)
The Little Theatre Courtyard, French Quarter
Signed, oil on canvas panel
16 x 20in (40.5 x 51cm)
**£1,750–2,000 / $2,500–3,000 ⚒ NOA**

► **Eileen Hemsoll, RBSA**
British (b1924)
Stripes – Swanage
Pastel
12 x 16in (30.5 x 40.5cm)
**£375–420 / $560–620 ⊞ Dr**

Ludwig Hermann
German (1812–81)
On the Rhine
Signed and dated 1878, oil on canvas
12 x 19in (30.5 x 48.5cm)
£5,500–6,000 / $8,000–8,700 ⊞ Ben

## Hanging your picture

■ Never let the hanging wire show above the picture. Some interior designers cover the hanging wire above nondescript prints with coloured ribbon, to give a decorative effect.

■ If you only have a few pictures on one wall do not hang them too high – about 60in (152.5cm) from the floor should be about right. Pictures hung too high look lonely and lost.

■ With groups of pictures, create interest by putting different shapes and sizes together. Lay out the arrangement on the floor first, before hanging, playing with shapes and patterns until you are happy with your design.

■ The key to a harmonious arrangement of pictures is frame compatability. Do not be afraid to mix prints, watercolours and drawings together. The frames can be any colour but they should be the same width and depth. A heavy decorated frame close to a simple wooden one will overpower it and thus also the picture.

◀ Glen Cooper Henshaw
American (1885–1946)
New York
Signed and dated 1916, pastel on paper
8½ x 11in (21.5 x 28cm)
£450–550 / $650–800 ⚲ TREA
*Born in Windfall, Indiana, Henshaw studied at the Ecole des Beaux-Arts Academy in Paris. He exhibited at the Art Institute of Chicago, the Addison Gallery and the Herron Art Institute.*

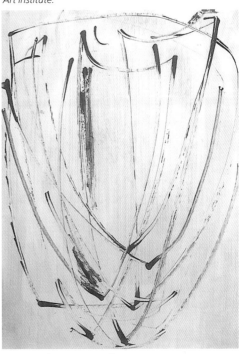

Dame Barbara Hepworth
British (1903–75)
Dance (Greek) 1958
Signed and inscribed, oil on board
17¼ x 13¼in (44 x 33.5cm)
£14,500–17,500 / $21,000–25,500 ⚲ P

Ludwig Hermann
German (1812–81)
Traders along the Rhine
Oil on board
27 x 38in (68.5 x 96.5cm)
£19,800–21,800 / $28,700–30,700 ⊞ HFA
*Ludwig Hermann was a painter of marine and architectural scenes. He was born in Greifswald in 1812. He made his debut in Berlin in 1850 and exhibited in Leipzig and London 1862–73.*

# John Frederick Herring, Snr and Jnr

Painting was the Herring family business. John Frederick Snr, born in 1795 and his brother Benjamin, both painted sporting scenes. John Frederick Snr, who was far more talented than his brother, started his career driving coaches from London to Halifax and painted in his spare time. Perhaps it was his first-hand observation of horses and the countryside that made him a consummate illustrator of horses and other animals. He took up painting full time in 1820, having exhibited at the Royal Academy in 1818.

John Frederick Snr lived in Newmarket, Suffolk, later moving to London where he fell into debt. He was rescued by W. T. Copeland who set him up in a cottage on his country estate and employed him as a designer of hunting patterns for Copeland Spode porcelain. Herring eventually became rich as a result of royal and aristocratic patronage.

John Frederick's three sons, John Frederick Jnr, Charles and Benjamin were all painters and often contributed to their father's pictures. Charles died young. Benjamin was very competent but lazy, preferring to spend his father's money but many engravings exist of his paintings. John Frederick Jnr worked hard but is not considered to be as talented as his father. Their work is very similar and accusations of plagiarism on both sides caused a rift in their relationship.

**John Frederick Herring, Jnr**
British (1815–1907)
Feeding Time
Signed, oil on canvas
14 x 20in (35.5 x 51cm)
**£5,250–6,250 / $7,500–9,000**  ➹ S(O)

**John Frederick Herring, Jnr**
British (1815–1907)
A pair, Two Farmyard Scenes
Signed, watercolours
8½ x 12in (21 x 31cm)
**£2,000–2,200 / $2,900–3,200**  ⊞ LH

**John Frederick Herring, Jnr and George A. Williams**
British (1815–1907 and 1814–1901)
Off to Market
Signed, oil on canvas
10 x 19in (25.5 x 48cm)
**£8,000–8,800 / $11,600–12,500**  ⊞ CFA

**John Frederick Herring, Jnr**
British (1815–1907)
Beeswing, Queen of Trumps, and Alice Hawthorn with foals and a grey stallion in a river landscape
Signed, dated 1847 and inscribed, oil on canvas
25½ x 41½in (65 x 105.5cm)
**£11,500–14,000 / $16,750–19,000**  ➹ S(NY)

**John Frederick Herring, Snr**
British (1795–1865)
The Barnyard in Winter
Signed and dated 1858, oil on canvas
20 x 24in (51 x 61cm)
**£46,000–55,000 / $67,000–80,000**  ➹ S(NY)

**Beatrice Pauline Hewitt, RBA, ROI**
British (b1907)
Mousehole harbour
Oil on canvas
15 x 18in (38 x 45.5cm)
**£1,800–2,200 / $2,600–3,200** ✂ Bon

**Aldro Thompson Hibbard**
American (1886–1972)
Coastal view
Signed, oil on canvas
18 x 25¾in (45.5 x 65.5cm)
**£1,500–1,800 / $2,200–2,600** ✂ SK

## Abbreviations

Letters after the artist's name denote that the
artist has been awarded the membership of an
artistic body. See page 233 for the explanation
of abbreviated letters.

▶ **Nicola Hicks**
British (b1960)
Standing Hare
Signed and dated
1986, charcoal
43¾ x 32in
(111 x 81.5cm)
**£1,800–2,200**
**$2,600–3,200** ✂ P

**Dale Hickey**
Australian (b1937)
Five on Yellow, 1992
Signed and dated 1992, oil and enamel
on canvas
72in (183cm) square
**£16,000–18,000 / $23,000–26,000** ✂ P(Sy)

▶ **Douglas Hill**
British (b1953)
Porthgwidden Beach, St Ives
Signed and dated, oil
22 x 25in (56 x 63.5cm)
**£850–950 / $1,250–1,400** ⊞ Stl

**Rowland Hill, ARUA**
Irish (1915–79)
Summer haze, Port Brandon, County Antrim
Signed, oil on canvas
20 x 30in (51 x 76cm)
**£2,400–2,800 / $3,500–4,000** ⚒ WA

**Rowland Henry Hill, ARUA**
British (1873–1952)
Ellerby village with the artist's house
Signed, watercolour
9½ x 13½in (24 x 34.5cm)
**£1,600–1,750 / $2,300–2,500** ⊞ TBJ

*Originally from Halifax, Yorkshire, Hill was attracted to
art from an early age. Holiday encounters with Ralph Hedley
at Runswick Bay persuaded his father to send him to the
Herkomer School at Bushey, Hertfordshire. He subsequently
settled at Ellerby near Staithes in Yorkshire and became an
active member of the Staithes Group of Artists.*

◀ **Rowland Henry Hill, ARUA**
British (1873–1952)
Sheephaven Bay, County Donegal
Signed, oil on canvas
24 x 36in (61 x 91.5cm)
**£3,100–3,700 / $4,500–5,500** ⚒ WA

**Lawrence Hilliard**
British (fl1876–87)
A November dawn
Signed, inscribed, watercolour over traces of pencil
heightened with bodycolour
6½ x 9½in (16.5 x 24cm)
**£1,800–2,200 / $2,600–3,200** ⚒ S

◀ **Laura Coombs Hills**
American (1859–1952)
A Breezy Summer Garden
Signed, pastel on paper/board
18 x 21in (45.5 x 53.5cm)
**£12,000–14,000 / $17,500–20,000** ⚒ SK

◄ **Laura Coombs Hills**
American (1859–1952)
Tulips and chintz
Signed, pastel on board
21½ x 17in (54.5 x 43cm)
**£18,000–22,000 / $26,000–32,000** ⚒ S(NY)

*Known for miniatures and flowers paintings, Laura Coombs Hills had a long-time career in Massachusetts where she had a studio in Boston and spent the summers in Newburyport, her birthplace. She briefly studied at the Cowles Art School in Boston with Helen Knowlton but was described as 'comparatively self-taught'. She became noted for miniature portraiture, a style she learned in England. She was an illustrator for Louis Prang and Company and designed valentines and other cards. She also painted flowers in pastel and watercolour. The latter works she began in the early 1920s when her eyesight began failing and the market for the miniature work had decreased.*

**Robert Hills**
British (1769–1844)
Cattle resting
Signed and dated 1820, watercolour
16 x 11½in (41 x 29.5cm)
**£600–700 / $870–1,000** ⚒ S(O)

◄ **Harry T. Hine, RI, ROI, NWS**
British (1845–1941)
The Market Hall, Amersham, Buckinghamshire
Watercolour, exhibition label on reverse
12 x 18in (30.5 x 45.5cm)
**£500–600 / $725–875** ⚒ Bon

▶ **Ivon Hitchens**
British (1893–1979)
Cottage Interior
Signed, oil on canvas
20 x 18in (51 x 45.5cm)
**£40,000–48,000 / $58,000–70,000** ⚒ S

*Early in 1925, Ivon Hitchens went to stay with Ben and Winifred Nicholson at Banks Head, their farmhouse in Cumberland. Hitchens had seen Nicholson's first one-man exhibition the previous year, had felt in sympathy and invited him to join the group of young artists who exhibited together under the name of the Seven and Five Society. Like Winifred Nicholson, Hitchens was a natural colourist, but he was also concerned with the abstract principles of rhythm and formal structure: like Ben, he was still coming to terms with Cézanne. All three were united in their rejection of the outworn teaching of the art schools and in their realization of the need to go back to first principles. Between them there was an exchange of ideas and a sharing of enthusiasms as they worked together in close rapport.*

*Most of the paintings Hitchens made from Banks Head were of the interior of the house or of views from its windows. His outstanding watercolour, The Bridge at Lanercost, now at the Abbot Hall Gallery, Kendal, is an exception. Cottage Interior shows a new freedom in his use of colour to suggest space and a move towards abstract interpretation of interiors and landscapes. These were the particular qualities that Hitchens was to develop throughout the rest of his career, so that the Banks Head paintings can be seen as the first in which a personal style emerges. It was on the strength of such works that he was offered his first one-man exhibition in 1925. Many of his works have been offered at auction recently.*

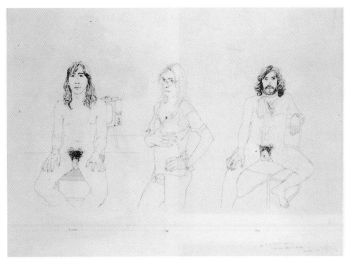

**David Hockney, RA**
British (b1937)
Portrait of Richard, Jim and Felix
Signed, inscribed and numbered 13/30, etching
28 x 37½in (71 x 95cm)
**£1,100–1,300 / $1,600–2,000** ↗ **Bon(C)**
*The inscription reads 'For the Oz obscenity bunch love from David Hockney Feb–March 1971'.*

**Howard Hodgkin**
British (b1932)
Norwich, 1999
Hand-coloured etching with carborundum, edition of 80
16½ x 18½in (42 x 47cm)
**£5,000–5,500 / $7,250–8,000** ⊞ **ACG**

▲ **For further information**
see Limited Edition Prints (pages 104–107)

**Abel Hold**
British (1815–91)
A Springer Spaniel in a landscape
Signed, dated 1847 and inscribed, oil on panel
10¾ x 18½in (27 x 47cm)
**£600–700 / $870–1,000** ↗ **TEN**

**William J. Hodgson**
British (fl1891–93)
Horse and riders leaping fences
Watercolour
9 x 13in (23 x 33cm)
**£500–600 / $725–875** ⊞ **LH**

▶ **James Holland**
British (1800–70)
Study of a Bee Orchid
Watercolour
7 x 6in (18 x 15cm)
**£130–150 / $190–220** ⊞ **LH**

## Auction or gallery?

All the pictures in our price guide originate from auction houses or galleries. The source of each picture can be found by checking the code letters after each caption with the Key to Illustrations on pages 234–236. When buying at auction prices can be lower than those of a gallery, but a buyer's premium and VAT will be added to the hammer price. Equally when selling at auction, commission, tax and photography charges must be taken into account. Galleries will often restore and authenticate pictures before putting them back on the market.

# Dora Holzhandler (b1928)

Dora Holzhandler's naïve art has many fans, Irish writer Edna O'Brien and television art historian Sister Wendy Beckett amongst others – she even painted a portrait of Charlie Chaplin. She illuminates human life with compassion, loving humour and awe. Her faces are childlike in execution but are surrounded by motifs reminiscent of Polish art, Persian miniatures and Byzantine mosaics, which give them a medieval, mystical feel. Her figures are often set into landcapes of verdant Eden-like gardens.

Born in Paris in 1928 into a family of Polish refugees who were too poor to look after her, Dora Holzhandler was sent to live with a Catholic foster family on a farm in Normandy, France. She returned to her large Jewish family and an urban life when she was five years old. In 1934 the family moved to the East End of London, where, in 1948, she attended the Anglo-French Art School in St John's Wood. Here her innate yet non-insular naïveté was recognized and she was allowed to paint in her own style. A key supporter in the early 1960s was the Manchester Guardian art critic, Eric Newton, who described her as a 'temperamental primitive'. She herself said 'there are definitely rules in art but I discover them myself and these are the answers: here in my paintings are the rules I've found'.

Dora's Jewish origins are a very important influence on her art and inspired her scenes of 19th-century Penzance in Cornwall with its Jewish community.

◄ **Dora Holzhandler**
French (b1928)
Garnett Hill Synagogue, Glasgow
Signed, oil on canvas
36 x20in (91.5 x 51cm)
**£3,800–4,200**
**$5,500–6,000** ⊞ PN

**Dora Holzhandler**
French (b1928)
Flowers for Mothers Day
Signed, oil on canvas
20 x 26in (51 x 66cm)
**£3,500–3,800 / $5,000–5,500** ⊞ PN

**Miller's is a price GUIDE not a price LIST**

**Dora Holzhandler**
French (b1928)
Girl with Roses
Signed, oil on canvas
20 x 18in (51 x 45.5cm)
**£1,200–1,350 / $1,750–2,000** ⊞ BOX

◄ **Dora Holzhandler**
French (b1928)
Sabbath Lovers
Signed, oil on canvas
20 x 24in (51 x 61cm)
**£6,500–7,200 / $9,500–10,500** ⊞ BOX

**Dora Holzhandler**
French (b1928)
Spring Lovers
Oil on canvas
50 x 35in (127 x 76cm)
**£6,500–7,100 / $9,500–13,800** ⊞ BOX

**Sidney F. Homer**
British (1912–93)
Harbour at Staithes
Signed, oil
16 x 12in (40.5 x 30.5cm)
**£450–500 / $650–720 ⊞ Dr**

**Evie Hone**
Irish (1894–1955)
Our Lady of the Hill
Signed, gouache and pastel
18in (46cm) square
**£1,400–1,600 / $2,000–2,300 ↗ WA**

▲ **For further information**
see Irish Art (pages 72–75)

**Gottfried Honegger**
Swiss (b1917)
Z 580
Signed, mixed media
40½in (103cm) square
**£2,000–2,400 / $3,000–3,500 ↗ BUK**

**Bernard de Hoog**
Dutch (1867–1943)
A Dutch interior
Signed, oil on canvas
16 x 12in (40.5 x 30.5cm)
**£6,200–7,000 / $9,000–10,500 ↗ Bon**

**Francis Powell Hopkins**
British (1830–1913)
On the Green
A pair, signed, watercolour
8 x 12in (20.5 x 30.5cm)
**£20,000–25,000 / $30,000–36,000** ⊞ **BuP**

**William H. Hopkins and Henry Jamyn Brooks**
British (d1892) British (fl 1884–1904)
George Friday Neame (1825–1913) of South Norwood, Surrey
Signed by both artists, oil on canvas
30 x 38in (76 x 96.5cm)
**£8,000–9,000 / $11,600–13,000** ⊞ **Ben**

*William Hopkins was a landscape, animal and portrait painter from
Keynsham, Bath. He exhibited at the Royal Academy from 1858. He
became a popular painter of horses, hounds and hunting scenes.
Henry Brooks was a portrait painter who exhibited from 1884–1900.
His works include portraits of the King Edward VII and Queen
Alexandra and Gladstone.*

**John Hoppner**
British (1758–1810)
Portrait of William, 2nd Lord Bagot
Signed and inscribed, oil on canvas
50 x 40in (127 x 101.5cm)
**£4,000–4,800 / $5,800–7,000** ⚒ **Bon**

▶ **Henry Silkstone Hopwood, RWS, RBC**
British (1860–1914)
Glimpsing Daybreak
Signed and dated 1906, watercolour over pencil
22¾ x 16½in (58 x 42cm)
**£4,500–5,000 / $6,500–7,250** ⚒ **B(L)**

**Jan Josef Horemans the Younger**
Dutch (c1714–1790)
A doctor bleeding a patient
Oil on canvas
19¼ x 23in (49 / 58.5cm)
**£2,600–3,000 / $3,800–4,500** ⚒ Bon

**William Hough**
British (fl1857–94)
A still life of plums, strawberries, currants and a pear on a mossy bank
Signed, watercolour and bodycolour
9¼ x 13½in (23.5 x 34.5cm)
**£1,800–2,000 / $2,600–3,000** ⚒ Bon

## Artist contact service

The National Portrait Gallery, St Martin's Place, London WC2H 0HE (020 7306 0055) and the Royal Society of British Portrait Painters at the Mall Galleries (020 7930 6844) both hold files of portraits by contemporary painters and offer a contact service between artist and sitter.

▶ **John Houston**
British (b1930)
Maid, Tawaraya Inn, Kyoto
Signed, dated 1994 and inscribed, oil on board
8 x 5¾in (20.5 x 14.5cm)
**£850–1,000 / $1,250–1,500** ⚒ AG

**Elmyr de Hory**
French (1905–78)
The 1937 Coronation
Oil on panel
10 x 14in (25.5 x 35.5cm)
**£4,500–5,000 / $6,500–7,250** ⊞ BRG

| ▲ **For further information** |
| see Forgers (page 80) |

*Elmyr de Hory, considered to be one of the master art forgers of the 20th century, was born in Hungary in 1905. He successfully deceived museums across the world into buying his pictures as authentic Impressionist and post-Impressionist paintings and claimed to have sold over 1,000 forged pictures purporting to be Modigliani, Matisse, Dufy and other contemporary masters to galleries and museums.*

*Upon his release from prison in Spain, de Hory decided to tell all. Clifford Irving wrote a book about him called F is for Fake, and in 1974 Orson Welles made a film of the book, commenting 'If the lawyers will let us we can name you one highly respected museum with an important collection of Impressionists, every single one of which is painted by Elmyr'. The irony however is that de Hory himself is now becoming valuable in his own right, his works fetching £5,000–15,000 ($7,250–21,750).*

**George Howard**
British (1843–1911)
Wooded landscape
Oil on panel
8 x 14in (20.5 x 36cm)
**£450–500 / $650–720** 🔨 S(O)

**Ken Howard, RA, NEAC, RWA**
British (b1932)
High Summer
Signed, oil on canvas
12 x 24in (30.5 x 61cm)
**£3,000–3,500 / $4,500–5,000** 🔨 Bon

**John Hoyland, RA**
British (b1934)
Composition
Signed, dated 1976
and inscribed, acrylic on canvas
35½ x 24in (90 x 61cm)
**£2,200–2,600 / $3,200–3,800** 🔨 P

**Peter Howson**
British (b1956)
Glasgow Night Club
Oil on canvas
60 x 48in (152.5 x 122cm)
**£7,000–8,000 / $10,000–11,500** ⊞ CON

▶ **Arthur Hughes**
British (1832–1915)
The Fisherman's Cottage
Signed, oil on board
10¾ x 17¾in (27 x 45cm)
**£2,000–2,400**
**$3,000–3,500** 🔨 P(S)

**Edward Hughes**
British (1832–1908)
The Secret Letter
Signed and dated 1867, oil on canvas
21 x 25in (53.5 x 63.5cm)
**£6,000–7,200 / $8,700–10,500** ⚒ Bon

**Abraham Hulk, Jnr**
British (1851–1922)
River scene with cattle watering, church beyond
Oil on canvas
23½ x 15in (59.5 x 38cm)
**£380–400 / $560–580** ⚒ AH

**Louis Bosworth Hurt**
British (1856–1929)
Highland Mist
Oil on canvas
20 x 30in (51 x 76cm)
**£27,000–30,000 / $40,000–45,000** ⊞ HFA

*Louis Bosworth Hurt was a landscape painter from Derbyshire who exhibited at the Royal Academy between 1881 and 1901. Hurt's subjects were mainly highland scenes with cattle – a popular subject in many Victorian pictures.*

▶ **Frank Townsend Hutchens**
American (1869–1937)
The Sheep Herder
Signed, oil on canvas mounted on board
24 x 20in (61 x 51cm)
**£1,200–1,400 / $1,750–2,000** ⚒ JAA

*Hutchens was born in New York and studied both in the US and at the Acadamie Julien in Paris. He was a member of many art organizations including the Society of Independent Artists. He exhibited widely including at the Paris Salon. His works can be found in the High Museum of Atlanta, at West Point, New York and the Syracuse Museum of Fine Art, New York.*

### Oil paintings

When dusting oil paintings be careful not to use a dirty duster or an abrasive cloth. Use cotton wool. Frames can be damaged by frequent vigorous cleaning. Apply a soft brush to the corner of the frame and don't clean too often.

## Royal Academy of Arts

■ Royal Academy of Arts, Burlington House, Piccadilly, London WIJ OBD Telephone 020 7300 8000 Recorded information line 020 7300 5760/1 www.royalacademy.org.uk

■ The Royal Academy is an independent fine arts institution which supports contemporary artists and promotes interest in the work of past masters through a comprehensive and ambitious exhibition programme.

■ The famous Summer Exhibition is a hugely popular show and sale of contemporary art held every year since 1769.

**John William Inchbold**
British (1830–88)
Lake Leman
Signed and inscribed 'Clarens', watercolour over pencil heightened with bodycolour
9½ x 13½in (24 x 34.5cm)
**£7,800–8,500 / $11,300–12,300** ⚒ S
*Inchbold's watercolour shows the north shore of the Lake of Geneva looking towards the west. Inchbold was born in Leeds, the son of a Yorkshire newspaper owner, and trained as a lithographer. He then studied painting at Royal Academy schools and in 1854 met Ruskin with whom he travelled to Switzerland.*

**David Inshaw**
British (b1943)
Tree and Moon
Oil on canvas
40 x 58in (101.5 x 147.5cm)
**£6,600–8,000 / $9,500–11,500** ⚒ S

**James Isherwood**
British (1917–88)
Horse Guards Parade
Signed, oil on panel
18 x 24in (45.5 x 61cm)
**£580–620 / $850–925** ⊞ BRG

# Irish Art

In the early 20th century the arts in Ireland were vibrant and exciting. It was not just the writers who were attracting worldwide fame, but artists such as Jack Butler Yeats and Charles Lamb who took up the cause of Irish nationalism. Many other Irish-born artists including Sir John Lavery and Sir William Orpen saw no future in painting local subjects. Orpen was reluctant to get involved in Irish politics preferring to seek an international reputation. He supported the British WWI effort by selling pictures for the Red Cross and travelled to France to paint trench scenes.

Jack Butler Yeats was born in London but brought up by his grandparents in Sligo. He studied in London and worked there as an illustrator but fired up with a romantic vision of Ireland he returned and started to paint in oil. His pictures don't show momentous events in the struggle for independence but depict ordinary everyday life in Ireland – travelling on a train, going to a funeral, street scenes. Yeats' style is impressionistic but he uses the colours of Ireland. The result is very powerful and the pictures are very sought after.

Sean Keating was born in Limerick and was strongly committed to the Irish Nationalistic Movement initiated by Yeats. His early work depicted political subjects – Men of the South showed a group of Republicans awaiting an ambush. From the late 1920s his subject matter was less controversial and he travelled round the country painting scenes from rural life.

Charles Lamb, who was born in Armagh, was profoundly affected by the Irish Nationalistic Movement and his work owes much to Sean Keating. He discovered in the west of Ireland what he called 'the national essence'. His subjects were scenes from rural life that he observed on his many tours of Ireland.

May Guinness fervently believed in establishing a modern Irish art movement. She exhibited in Paris and collected the works of Picasso, Matisse, Bonner and Dufy.

In the 1920s, artists such as Ulster-born Frank McKelvey celebrated Irishness through the island's beautiful landscapes. His soft and clear Irish views were acclaimed in exhibitions of Irish art worldwide. McKelvey in turn was an important influence on Ulster artist Norman McCaig.

In 1905 Mary Swanzy brought back influences from Europe that were reflected in her paintings. Working into her nineties, she flirted with many styles. Landscapes were constructed in a Cubist manner, and influenced by Futurists she depicted machines. Some of her work from the 1940s, often illustrating estranged figures, have a feeling of German Expressionism.

Louis le Brocquy is one of the most important artists of the generation after Yeats and Keating. He studied in London and Paris. The naturalistic style of his early work seems to be influenced by James McNeil Whistler. He returned briefly to Ireland in 1940 but six years later settled in London where his work became more abstract. In 1956 he won first prize at the Venice Biennale but later suffered a creative crisis and destroyed his entire 1963 output. After that his work took on an obvious Irish feel when he painted a series of head studies of Irish heroes such as James Joyce. Markey Robinson promoted a feeling of Irishness in her folk-style works (see page 161).

The partition of Ireland in 1922 saw the new capital Belfast and its industries generate money and artist patrons. Artists such as William Conor, Charles Lamb and Daniel O'Neill, who spent a lot of time in London painting the Irish abroad, were given status when their work was bought by the well funded Ulster Museum.

◄ **Louis le Brocquy, HRHA**
Irish (b1916)
Entrance to the Dark Wind (Khyber Pass, Dalkey)
Signed, oil on board
23 x 14in (58.5 x 35.5cm)
**£52,000–62,000 / $75,000–90,000** ↗ WA

**William Conor, RHA, RUA**
Irish (1881–1968)
Barges on The Lagan
Signed, watercolour drawing
10 x 15in (25.5 x 38cm)
**£5,200–6,000 / $7,500–8,700** ↗ ROSS

**William Conor, RHA, RUA**
Irish (1881–1968)
The Bellows Minder
Signed, crayon
19 x 14½in (48.5 x 36cm)
**£20,000–24,000**
**$30,000–35,000** ↗ JAd

◄ **May Guinness**
Irish (1863–1955)
Still life with apples and a
white cloth
Oil on canvas
17½ x 33½in (44.5 x 85cm)
**£3,800–4,500**
**$5,500–6,500** ↗ WA

► **Evie Hone**
Irish (1894–1955)
Single element composition
Signed, gouache and crayon
on paper
6½ x 4in (16.5 x 10cm)
**£775–950**
**$1,150–1,400** ↗ WA

◄ **Nathaniel Hone**
Irish (1831–1917)
Children by the seaside at Malahide
Signed, oil on canvas laid on board
19 x 29½in (48.5 x 75cm)
**£8,000–9,500 / $11,500–14,000** ↗ WA

*Nathaniel Hone spent much of his working
life in France where artists such as Corot
influenced him. When he returned to Ireland
in the 1870s his more fluid style was very
different from the typical Victorian Irish
artists such as Francis William Topham. Many
of Hone's seascapes were set on the flat
north Dublin coastline near Portmarnock, or
Malahide, where he lived. He often included
small figures of people in his pictures.*

◄ **Sean Keating**
Irish (1889–1978)
The Turf Man of Aran
Oil on board
30 x 36in (76 x 91.5cm)
**£32,000–35,000 / $46,000–50,000** ↗ WA

**Charles Lamb, RHA, RUA**
Irish (1893–1965)
Sailing boats in harbour
Signed, oil on board
10 x 14½in (25.5 x 36cm)
**£3,800–4,600 / $5,500–6,500** ↗ JAd

**Sir John Lavery, RA, RHA, RSA**
Irish (1856–1941)
Tangier (1920)
Oil on canvas board
10 x 14in (25.5 x 35.5cm)
**£11,000–13,000 / $16,000–18,500** ⬈ **JAd**

*Lavery preferred to paint in France and north Africa (as well as painting society portraits). This study was executed on Lavery's final tour of Morocco in 1920. He made many productive trips to Tangier, the earliest recorded being in 1893.*

**Frank McKelvey, RHA, RUA**
Irish (1895–1974)
Fishing Boat, Donegal
Signed, oil on board
12 x 16in (30.5 x 40.5cm)
**£3,000–3,500 / $4,400–5,000** ⬈ **ROSS**

◀ **Sir William Orpen, RHA, RA**
Irish (1878–1931)
Behind the Scenes
Pen and ink with watercolour and bodycolour
6in (15cm) square
**£1,150–1,400**
**$1,750–2,000** ⬈ **WA**

**Norman J. McCaig**
Irish (1929–2001)
Signed, oil on canvas board
18 x 24in (45.5 x 61cm)
**£2,200–2,600 / $3,200–3,800** ⬈ **WA**

**Daniel O'Neill**
Irish (1920–74)
Summer Night
Signed, oil on canvas
18¼ x 24in (46.5 x 61cm)
**£23,000–27,500 / $33,300–39,750** ⬈ **JAd**

**Markey Robinson**
Irish (1918–99)
Seated Figures
Oil on board
12 x 19in (30.5 x 48.5cm)
**£6,300–7,000 / $9,000–10,000** ⊞ **WrG**

**Markey Robinson**
Irish (1918–99)
Still life with apples and flowers
Signed, oil on board
16 x 20in (40.5 x 51cm)
**£1,300–1,600 / $1,900–2,300** ⚒ WA

**Mary Swanzy, HRHA**
Irish (1882–1978)
Figure in a wood
Signed, oil on canvas
21¼ x 18¼in (54 x 46.5cm)
**£18,000–22,000 / $26,000–32,000** ⚒ JAd

**Maurice Canning Wilks**
Irish (1911–80)
Redbay, County Antrim
Signed, watercolour
10 x 14in (25.5 x 35.5cm)
**£1,400–1,700 / $2,000–2,500** ⚒ ROSS

**Jack Butler Yeats, RHA**
Irish (1871–1957)
Untitled
Watercolour
8½ x 12½in (21.5 x 32cm)
**£3,000–3,500 / $4,400–5,000** ⚒ B

## Hints & tips

Irish Art is very collectable and sought after, in particular by American collectors. The most popular pictures are those depicting the romance of the Irish landscape, thanks to the recent economic boom in Ireland.

▶ **Jack Butler Yeats, RHA**
Irish (1871–1957)
On the Skibbereen Light Railway, 1924
Signed, oil on board
9 x 14in (23 x 35.5cm)
**£135,000–150,000 / $180,000–220,000** ⚒ JAd

◀ **Richard Jack, RA**
British (1866–1952)
Portrait of Jonathan Simpson Esq
Signed, oil on canvas
44 x 34in (112 x 86.5cm)
**£2,400–2,800**
**$3,500–4,000** ⚒ S

▶ **Bill Jacklin**
British (b1943)
The Couple
Signed, oil on paper on canvas
44 x 30in (112 x 76cm)
**£9,800–10,800**
**$14,000–15,500** ⊞ BRG

**David James**
British (fl1881–98)
The Flow of the Tide, Tenby
Signed and dated, oil on canvas
25 x 50in (63.5 x 127cm)
**£1,800–2,200 / $2,600–3,200** ⚒ P(S)

**Bill Jacklin**
British (b1943)
The Park II – Sheep
Meadow
Signed and dated,
oil on linen
39¼ x 48in
(99.5 x 122cm)
**£17,500–19,000**
**$25,500–27,500**
⚒ S(O)

**Lena Jameson**
British (fl1911–12)
St Mary's Le Strand
Signed, watercolour
10 x 6in (25.5 x 15cm)
**£280–330 / $400–475** ⊞ LH

▶ **Charles Jamieson**
Scottish (b1952)
Side Street,
Valldemossa
Oil on canvas
12 x 10in
(31 x 25.5cm)
**£900–1,000**
**$1,300–1,500** ⊞ P&H

**Ange-Louis Janet**
French (1815–72)
A Portrait of Queen Victoria with Prince Albert and their Family
Inscribed, pencil, brown, grey and white wash on brown paper
13¼ x 20¼in (33.5 x 51.5cm)
**£7,500–8,250 / $10,875–12,000** ⊞ CW

**W. Howard Jarvis**
British (fl1946–64)
Running up the Needles Channel
Signed indistinctly, inscribed on label on reverse, oil on canvas
25 x 30in (63.5 x 76cm)
**£750–850 / $1,100–1,250** ↗ Bon

*Jarvis exhibited two pictures at the inaugural exhibition of the Royal Society of Marine Artists and was a regular exhibitor there until his posthumous exhibition in 1964.*

**Wilfrid Jenkins**
British (fl1875–88)
Promenade at Dusk
Signed, oil on canvas
15¾ x 24½in (40 x 65cm)
**£1,800–2,200 / $2,600–3,200** ↗ S(O)

**George Henry Jenkins**
British (c1843–1914)
Fish Boats in Harbour
Signed, watercolour
16 x 11½in (40.5 x 28cm)
**£380–450 / $560–650** ↗ G(L)

▶ **Isaac Walter Jenner**
Australian (1836–1901)
Bamborough Castle, Blowing a Gale
Signed and dated 1883, oil on canvas
12 x 24in (30.5 x 61cm)
**£900–1,100 / $1,300–1,600** ↗ Bon

**Thomas Martin
Jensen**
American
(1831–1916)
Sunset on the
Wetlands
Signed, watercolour
on paper
14 x 18in
(35.5 x 45.5cm)
**£700–850**
**$1,000–1,250**
⚖ JAA

▶ **Augustus John,
OM, RA**
British (1878–1961)
Study of a Young Boy
Pencil, pen and ink
14 x 7¾in
(35.5 x 20cm)
**£2,400–3,000**
**$3,500–4,500** ⚖ P
*This drawing is
thought to depict
one of the artist's
sons, either Pyramus
or Romilly, and is
dated c1912.*

◀ **Vivien John**
British (1915–94)
Two girls with garlands of flowers
Signed, watercolour heightened
with white, pencil
13¼ x 11½in (33.5 x 29cm)
**£580–700**
**$850–1,000** ⚖ WA
*Vivien John was a daughter of
Augustus John.*

**Hilda K. Jillard**
British (1899–1975)
Gossip
Signed, oil on canvas
47¾ x 64in (121.5 x 162.5cm)
**£2,200–2,600 / $3,200–3,800** ⚖ RTo
*Born near Godalming in Surrey, Hilda Jillard trained at numerous art
schools, most notably at the Slade under Henry Tonks, at La Grande
Chaumière in Paris and at Guildford Art School under Hinchcliffe.
While working from a makeshift studio at her family home in Surrey
she painted an expression of impending war entitled 1939 What
Harvest?, now in the Imperial War Museum.*

*In 1942, Jillard moved to Cornwall and joined the already established
art colonies of St Ives and Newlyn. Her work was represented from
1944 at the influential St Ives Society of Artists Arts Club exhibitions.
In September 1947 she held exhibitions at the Castle Inn, St Ives, with
the sculptor Denis Mitchell. There were increasing tensions between
the traditional and modern arists within the St Ives Society of Artists,
which led to the latter being offered a separate space below a church;
they consequently became known as The Crypt Group.*

*In the autumn of 1948, Jillard held a solo exhibition of her paintings
and drawings and was described by the artist David Cox as being a bold
painter, 'almost an experimentalist'. In February 1949 the Penwith
Society of Arts in Cornwall was formed by a breakaway group of
progressive artists from several disciplines, including David Cox, Barbara
Hepworth, Bernard Leach, Denis Mitchell and Ben Nicholson, with the
writer and artist Herbert Read as president. Shortly after the society's
formation Jillard herself was elected to membership. After 12 years
working within the artists' community in St Ives, Hilda Jillard left and
eventually settled near Petworth in West Sussex, where she continued
to paint, exhibiting locally and in London until her death in 1975.*

**William Earl Johns**
British (1893–1968)
Three bi-planes performing acrobatics
Signed, watercolour
10¼ x 14½in (26 x 37cm)
**£1,100–1,400 / $1,600–2,000** ⚖ N

**James Johnson**
British (1803–34)
Montacute House, Somerset
Signed and dated 1825, watercolour heightened with white
9 x 16½in (22.5 x 42cm)
**£3,800–4,200 / $5,500–6,000** 🔨 **Bon**

◀ **Joseph Johnson**
American (19thC)
Young Girl with
her Dog
Signed and dated
February 8, 1840,
inscribed on reverse,
oil on ivory
6¼ x 5in
(16 x 12.5cm)
**£1,300–1,600**
**$1,900–2,300**
🔨 **SHN**

**Robert Edmond Lee Jones**
American (b1913)
Free
Oil on board
21 x 18in (53.5 x 45.5cm)
**£2,600–3,000 / $3,800–4,400** 🔨 **TREA**

*Jones was born in Lynchburg, Virginia. He moved to Chicago and studied at Hull House and the Art Institute of Chicago. He was a founding member of the National Confederation of Artists and his work is in the collections of the Negro History Hall of Fame and the Chicago Museum.*

## The Art Institute of Chicago

■ 111 South Michigan Avenue, Chicago, Illinois 60603, www.artic.edu/aic

■ Houses more than 300,000 works of art within its 10 curatorial departments.

**William Joy**
British (1803–67)
Merchant Vessels off Norfolk Coast
Watercolour
10 x 15in (25.5 x 38cm)
**£6,750–7,500 / $9,800–10,800** ⊞ **LH**

▶ **Henry Jutsum**
British (1816–69)
Sheep Grazing in Heathlands
Oil on canvas
9½ x 12in (24 x 31cm)
**£3,500–4,000 / $5,000–5,800** ⊞ **HFA**

**Christian Cornelis Kannemans**
Dutch (1812–84)
Sailing Ships off the Dutch Coast
Oil on panel
8½ x 12in (21.5 x 30.5cm)
**£2,200–2,600 / $3,200–3,800** ⚒ SWO

> **Miller's is a price GUIDE not a price LIST**

 **Tony Karpinski**
British (b1965)
Elephant
Signed, oil on board
10 x 8in (25.5 x 20.5cm)
**£5,300–5,800 / $7,600–8,400** ⊞ HFA

*Born in Westminster, London in 1965, Tony Karpinski began painting and drawing from the age of four and a half years old. He went on to study the techniques of great masters such as Rembrandt and Reubens and was privately commissioned to execute several pastiches of Dutch Masters paintings for private clients. From 1985 to 1995 he worked as a commercial illustrator. Inspired by the African wildlife paintings of Wilhelm Kuhnert, Karpinski took his first trip to Africa in 1995 and his first step towards a career as a wildlife artist.*

*After many trips to South Africa he became friends with the head ranger of the Kapama Game Reserve whose local knowledge and experience with animals helped Karpinski get the references he had been looking for.*

**Adolf Kaufmann**
Austrian (1843–1916)
Autumnal Landscape
Signed with pseudonym J. Rollin, oil on canvas
33 x 51in (83 x 130.5cm)
**£3,200–3,600 / $4,600–5,200** ⚒ DORO

◀ **Angelica Kaufmann**
Swiss (1741–1807)
Theseus raises his Father's Sword
Oil on wood
16½ x 11¾in (42 x 30cm)
**£900–1,000
$1,300–1,500**
⚒ DORO

**Tom Keating**
British (1917–84)
Still Life
Signed, oil on canvas
20 x 30in (51 x 76cm)
**£2,750–3,000 / $4,000–4,400** ⊞ BRG

*Tom Keating was a famous artist and restorer who first came to public notice in 1976 when it was revealed he had painted thirteen drawings attributed to Samuel Palmer. In his subsequent trial at The Old Bailey, it transpired that he had painted over two thousand pictures in the style of one hundred and fifty artists.*

## Forgers

Some art forgers have become collected artists in their own right. The best known are Elmyr de Hory and Tom Keating. Auction houses and dealers now sell their renditions of Claude Monet, Samuel Palmer etc, and because the fakes can be attributed to these artists they fetch from £2,000–5,000 / $2,900–7,250. Forgeries of well-known pictures such as Monet and Van Gogh's landscapes fetch the highest prices because the images are so well known.

De Hory and Keating intended to deceive whereas Miguel Canals and his studio reproduced works by artists out of copyright from 16th to early 20th century. Everyone knew these pictures were by Canals.

The studio closed last year and an auction of the remaining works took place. Prices were from £500–800 ($720–1,150) although in the 1980s when real Impressionist prices went through the roof Canal's homages fetched up to £5,000 ($7,250).

◀ **Albert von Keller**
Swiss (1844–1920)
An Afternoon Stroll
Signed, oil on panel
23 x 17½in
(58.5 x 44.5cm)
**£9,300–10,300**
**$13,500–15,000**
⊞ **HFA**

**Ellsworth Kelly**
American (b1923)
Untitled (Orange State I)
Signed, inscribed, lithograph printed in orange on Arches 88 paper
47 x 45½in (119.5 x 114.5cm)
**£2,000–2,500 / $3,000–3,600** ⚒ **S(NY)**

**Sir Gerald Festus Kelly, RHA, PRA**
Irish (1879–1972)
Portofino across the Golfo Tigullio, September 13, 1933
Inscribed on reverse, oil on canvas board,
13 x 16½in (33 x 42cm)
**£1,300–1,600 / $1,900–2,300** ⚒ **WA**

**Paul Kelly**
Irish (b1968)
Still life with Spanish jug
Signed and dated 1991, oil on board
16 x 20½in (41 x 52cm)
**£1,000–1,200 / $1,500–1,750** ⚒ **WA**

◀ **Norman Kenyon**
American (20thC)
Fishing Trip in the Chrysler
Signed, watercolour and gouache
14¾ x 19¾in (37.5 x 50cm)
**£1,800–2,000 / $2,600–3,000** ⚒ **SHN**

► **Harry Kernoff, RHA**
Irish (1900–74)
Abstract compositions
A pair, one signed, gouache
6 x 8in (15 x 20cm)
**£2,200–2,600**
**$3,200–3,800** ⚒ JAd

▼ **Harry Kernoff, RHA**
Irish (1900–74)
Kerry bull after Sunset, Killarney
Signed, watercolour
10½ x 14in (27 x 36cm)
**£3,000–3,500**
**$4,500–5,000** ⚒ JAd

**Norman Kenyon**
American (20thC)
Testing the Water
Signed, watercolour and gouache
16 x 9in (41 x 23cm)
**£480–580 / $700–850** ⚒ SHN

◄ **John Ross Key**
American (1832–1920)
Electric Building, Pan American Exposition
1901, Buffalo, N.Y.
Signed, oil on board
19 x 12½in (48.5 x 32cm)
**£2,200–2,600 / $3,200–3,800** ⚒ SHN

*John Ross Key was the grandson of Francis Scott Key, author of* The Star Spangled Banner. *John was born in Maryland and studied art in Munich and Paris. He served with the Federal Corp of Engineers in South Carolina and recorded the siege of the Confederate city Charleston in 1863. After the US Civil War he lived in San Francisco and painted many landscapes including popular subjects in the Sierra Nevadas as well as the Golden Gate Bridge.*

► **M. Khavalov**
Russian (20thC)
Portrait
Signed and dated 1959, pencil
20 x 13in (51 x 33cm)
**£850–950 / $1,250–1,400** ⊞ B&B

◄ **Frederik Kiaerskou**
Dutch (1805–91)
View of a Valley with a Castle on a Crag
Signed and dated 1849, oil on canvas
20 x 28in (51 x 71cm)
**£2,000–2,200 / $3,000–3,200** ⚒ **Bon**

**George Goodwin Kilburne**
British (1839–1924)
Dressing for a Walk
Signed, watercolour
7 x 10in (18 x 25.5cm)
**£5,000–5,500 / $7,250–8,000** ⊞ **HFA**

**George Goodwin Kilburne**
British (1839–1924)
The Courtship
Signed, watercolour
8 x 12in (20.5 x 30.5cm)
**£5,950–6,550 / $8,700–9,500** ⊞ **HFA**

◄ **Gordon King**
British (b1939)
In the Orchard
Signed, watercolour
15 x 10in
(38 x 25.5cm)
**£2,250–2,500**
**$3,300–3,600** ⊞ **Dr**

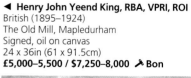

◀ **Henry John Yeend King, RBA, VPRI, ROI**
British (1895–1924)
The Old Mill, Mapledurham
Signed, oil on canvas
24 x 36in (61 x 91.5cm)
**£5,000–5,500 / $7,250–8,000** ⚘ Bon

◀ **Jessie Marion King**
British (1875–1949)
Illustration of Idleness from *The Romaunt of the Rose* by Chaucer
Signed, pen and ink on vellum with gilt highlights
10¾ x 5½in (27.5 x 14cm)
**£6,500–7,500**
**$9,500–11,000** ⚘ CGC

**Paul King**
American (1867–1947)
Afternoon Sun
Signed, oil on masonite
15 x 12in (38 x 30.5cm)
**£1,200–1,400 / $1,750–2,000** ⚘ SHN

▶ **John Kingsley, PAI**
British (b1957)
Winding Path, Montfrin, Provence
Signed, oil on canvas
26in (66cm) square
**£3,000–3,500 / $4,000–5,000** ⊞ CON

◄ **Henry John Kinnaird**
British (1861–1929)
An Old Mill in Suffolk
Signed, watercolour
11½ x 22½in (29 x 57cm)
**£2,200–2,500 / $3,200–3,600** ⊞ **WrG**

**Ethel Kirkpatrick**
British (fl from 1890)
Girl Amongst Sweet Peas
Signed, oil
20 x 28in (51 x 71cm)
**£1,200–1,400 / $1,750–2,000** ⊞ **LH**

**Joseph Kirkpatrick**
British (1898–1928)
By the Mill stream
Signed, watercolour
13½ x 9½in (34.5 x 24cm)
**£2,800–3,400 / $4,000–4,800** ⊞ **Ben**

## Do signatures matter?

Many 20th-century artists signed work executed by other artists in their studio – Salvador Dali used his signature very liberally in this manner.

It is provenance that matters. If a picture's history can be traced with receipts of purchase or details of where the picture was exhibited, a signature might not be as important as you might think.

However, signatures can be faked – if in doubt ask a reputable gallery or auction house to verify it.

◄ **Nadia Kisseleva, ARBSA**
Anglo-Russian (b1956)
Red Reef – Indian Ocean
Oil
32 x 39in (81.5 x 99cm)
**£1,250–1,400 / $1,800–2,000** ⊞ **Dr**

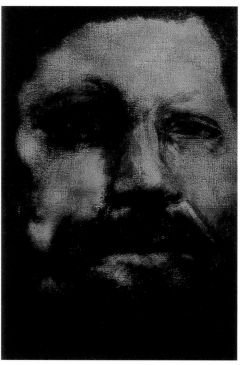

◄ **R. B. Kitaj, RA**
American (b1932)
Fenil Hague
Charcoal and oil on
canvas laid onto
canvas
18½ x 11¾in
(47 x 30cm)
**£10,000–12,000**
**$14,500–17,500** ⚒ P

► **Ernest S.
Klempner**
American/Austrian
(early 20thC)
Portrait of a Girl
Reading
Signed, watercolour
20 x 15in
(51 x 38cm)
**£500–600**
**$720–870** ⚒ TREA
*Klempner studied at
the Vienna Academy.
He exhibited at the
Art institute of
Chicago 1920–30.*

**Franz Knebel Jnr**
Swiss (1809–77)
Travellers and cattle beside a stone bridge and castle
Signed and dated 1868, oil on wooden panel
10 x 14¾in (25.5 x 37.5cm)
**£2,700–3,200 / $4,000–4,600** ⚒ G(L)

◄ **John Buxton
Knight**
British (1843–1908)
The Country Bridge
Signed, oil on canvas
23 x 35¾in
(58.5 x 91cm)
**£950–1,100**
**$1,400–1,600**
⚒ AH

**Adolphus Knell**
British (fl1860–90)
Shipping under Moonlight
Signed, oil on canvas
11 x 9¼in (28 x 23cm)
**£950–1,100 / $1,400–1,600** ⚒ Bon
*Adolphus Knell was a member of the Knell family of
painters who specialized in maritime scenes. He started
life decorating furniture in Bath before moving to Bristol
where he was influenced by the busy port scenes and
shipping plying the Bristol Channel. He started painting
small maritime pictures in oils, depicting the scenes around
him and it is for these he has become well known.*

# Dame Laura & Harold Knight

Harold Knight, the son of an architect, studied in Paris with Benjamin Constant and John Paul Laurens, and at the Academie Julian. As a young man he won numerous awards for his art. He met his wife Laura, who was later to be made a Dame of the British Empire, in 1889 when he was 17 and studying at Nottingham School of Art, and Laura was just 13 years old. Harold, a sensitive sympathetic person, was a comfort to Laura during a succession of personal tragedies. *The Letter* is a portrait of the young Laura, and is influenced by Vermeer, whose work they saw during a trip to Holland in 1904.

Harold specialized in thoughtful portraits and simple interiors, whereas Laura's work reflects her more ebullient personality. She loved colour in landscapes, and in her studies of people she was fascinated by old fashioned show-business, drawing many characters from the circus, music hall and ballet. She worked as a war artist during WWII and drew scenes from the War Crimes Tribunal at Nuremberg.

The couple first set up home in the small artistic colony of Staithes in North Yorkshire and were married in 1903. They moved to Newlyn, Cornwall in 1908 and finally settled in London in 1918.

**Harold Knight, RA, ROI, RP, RWA**
British (1874–1961)
A Lady mending Fishing Nets in a sunlit yard
Signed, pencil and watercolour
13¾ x 11¾in (34.5 x 29.5cm)
**£3,800–4,500 / $5,500–6,500** 🔨 B(L)

**Harold Knight, RA, ROI, RP, RWA**
British (1874–1961)
The Letter
Signed, oil on canvas
18in (45.5cm) square
**£38,000–45,000 / $55,000–65,000** 🔨 S

**Dame Laura Knight, RA, RWS, RE, RWA, PSWA**
British (1877–1970)
Nude study
Signed, pencil
13¾ x 9¾in (35 x 25cm)
**£2,200–2,500 / $3,200–3,600** 🔨 B

**Dame Laura Knight, RA, RWS, RE, RWA, PSWA**
British (1877–1970)
The Water's Edge
Signed, gouache over charcoal and pencil
22 x 30¼in (56 x 77cm)
**£15,000–18,000 / $22,000–26,000** 🔨 P

**Dame Laura Knight, RA, RWS, RE, RWA, PSWA**
British (1877–1970)
Off to Sleep
Signed Laura Johnson, watercolour
17½ x 13¾in (44.5 x 35cm)
**£8,600–9,200 / $12,500–13,500** 🔨 AH

**Dame Laura Knight, RA, RWS, RE, RWA, PSWA**
British (1877–1970)
Nude and Sea
Signed and inscribed, oil on canvas
25 x 20in (63.5 x 51cm)
**£7,000–8,500**
**$10,500–12,250** 🔨 P

**Dame Laura Knight, RA, RWS, RE, RWA, PSWA**
British (1877–1970)
Spring Blossom
Signed and dated, oil on panel
13 x 18in (33 x 45.5cm)
**£3,000–3,500 / $4,400–5,000** 🔨 Bon

## Oil paintings

When dusting oil paintings be careful not to use a dirty duster or an abrasive cloth. Use cotton wool. Frames can be damaged by frequent vigorous cleaning. Apply a soft brush to the corner of the frame and don't clean too often.

▶ **Henry Koehler**
American (b1927)
To the Start, Chantilly
Signed, oil on canvas
15 x 23in (38 x 58.5cm)
**£10,000–12,000 / $14,500–17,500** ⚘ S(NY)

◀ **Henry Koehler**
American (b1927)
Brandywine Action
Signed and dated 1977, charcoal, pencil and oil on paper
18 x 24in (45.5 x 61cm)
**£2,500–3,000 / $3,600–4,400** ⚘ S(NY)

**Ida Kohlmeyer**
American (1912–97)
Striae
Signed and dated 1989, mixed media on paper
24 x 30in (61 x 76cm)
**£1,600–1,800 / $2,300–2,600** ⚘ NOA

## The Metropolitan Museum of Art

■ 1000 Fifth Avenue at 82nd Street, New York 10028–0198, www.metmuseum.org

■ Houses more than three million works of art from all points of the compass, from ancient to modern times.

◀ **Andrei Andreevich Kotzka**
Ukranian (1911–80)
Young Woman
Signed, oil on canvas
26¾ x 22in (67 x 57cm)
**£2,000–2,500 / $3,000–3,600** ⊞ ARL
*Kotzka studied at the Uzhgorod School of Painting, Rome Academy of Arts and also at the Academy of Arts in Budapest.*

KUROVSKA, LENA • 89

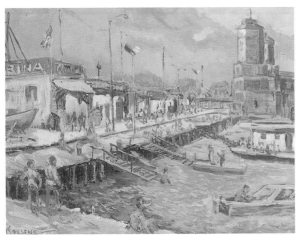

**Lou Kousens**
American (1899–1997)
Navy Pier
Signed, oil on canvas
14 x 18in (35.5 x 45.5cm)
**£600–700 / $870–1,000** ⚖ **TREA**
*Kousens studied at the Art Institute of Chicago and the Chicago
Academy of Art. He worked with Milford Zornes in Mexico and at the
University of Oklahoma.*

**Vincent
Krasnowski**
American (20thC)
Central City,
Colorado
Signed, oil on canvas
16 x 20in
(40.5 x 51cm)
**£550–650
$800–950** ⚖ **TREA**

**George Melchior Kraus**
German (1737–1806)
Family in Interior
Signed and dated, oil on canvas
15 x 19¼in (38 x 49cm)
**£2,500–2,800 / $3,600–4,000** ⚖ **SLN**

▶ **Bob Kuhn**
American (b1920)
In the High Forest –
Leopard
Acrylic on board
26 x 24in
(91.5 x 61cm)
**£30,000–35,000
£44,000–52,000**
⚖ **CdA**

▶ **Lena Kurovska**
Ukranian (b1969)
Lilacs and Apples
Signed, oil on canvas
25 x 30in (65 x 76cm)
**£1,250–1,450 / $1,800–2,200** ⊞ **ARL**

**Edward Ladell**
British (1821–86)
Still Life
Signed, oil on canvas
10 x 12in
(25.5 x 30.5cm)
**£40,000–45,000**
**$58,000–65,000**
⊞ BuP

► **Vincent Lambe**
Irish (20thC)
Stroller at Dooega
Signed, oil on
canvas board
12 x 16in (30 x 41cm)
**£250–280**
**$360–420** ⚒ WA

**James Garden Laing**
British (1852–1915)
Interior of Cathedral, Haarlem
Signed, watercolour
13½ x 9½in (34 x 24cm)
**£380–420 / $570–620** ⊞ LH

**Clement Lambert**
British (1855–1925)
Shepherd and cattle drover in landscape
Signed, oil on wooden panel
11½ x 15½in (29 x 39.5cm)
**£280–340 / $400–500** ⚒ G(L)

**Georges Lambert**
French (b1919)
Bal, 14 Juillet, Paris
Signed and dated 1962, oil on canvas
57½ x 38¼in (146 x 97cm)
**£700–800 / $1,000–1,200** ⚒ P

◀ **Percy Lancaster**
British (1878–1951)
Elegant Lady reading
a Letter
Signed, oil
24 x 19in (61 x 48.5cm)
**£1,000–1,100**
**$1,500–1,600** ⊞ LH

▶ **Sir Edwin Henry
Landseer, RA and
Henry Bright**
British (1802–73 and
1814–73)
The Sentinel
Oil on paper laid
down on canvas
24 x 18in (61 x 45.5cm)
**£11,500–13,000**
**$16,500–19,000**
🔨 Bon

**Walter Langley**
British (1852–1922)
Mending the Nets
Signed, watercolour
9¾ x 13¾in (25 x 35cm)
**£7,000–8,000 / $10,000–11,500** 🔨 B
*This watercolour is thought to date to 1887 when the same model*
*appears in another watercolour of his of the same year,* The Answer.

**William Langley**
British (fl1880–1920)
Still life of fruit and mallard
Signed, oil on canvas
20 x 30in (51 x 76cm)
**£600–700 / $870–1,000** 🔨 P(Ba)

**Mark William Langlois**
British (fl1862–73)
The New Arrival
Signed, oil on canvas
21 x 17in (53.5 x 43cm)
**£2,000–2,500 / $3,000–3,500** ⊞ Ben

**Peter Lanyon**
British (1918–64)
Study for St Just
Signed and dated 1952, charcoal and pencil on paper
9¾ x 14¼in (25 x 36cm)
**£5,000–6,000 / $7,250–8,750** 🔨 JLx

**Peter Lanyon**
British (1918–64)
Godolphin
Signed, dated 1948 and inscribed, oil on board
10¼ x 14¼in (26 x 36cm)
**£14,500–17,500 / $21,000–25,500** 🔨 P

▲ **For further information**
see St Ives School (pages 190–191)

**Giovanni G. Lanza**
Italian (1827–89)
Extensive landscape overlooking Naples with Vesuvius beyond
Signed, watercolour
17 x 29½in (43 x 75cm)
**£2,600–3,200 / $3,800–4,800** 🔨 G(L)

**Mikhail Fedorovich Larionov**
Russian (1881–1964)
Reclining Nude
Signed, oil on board
5½ x 7¼in (14 x 18.5cm)
**£4,500–5,000 / $6,500–7,250** 🔨 S

## State Hermitage Museum

■ 34 Dvortsovaya Naberezhnaya (Palace Embankment), St Petersburg 190000, www.hermitagemuseum.org

■ The Hermitage collection of works of art contain over 3,000,000 items from the Stone Age to the 20th century.

▶ **Karolina Larusdottir, NEAC, RWS**
Icelandic (b1944)
The Yellow Coat
Signed, oil on canvas
32 x 38in (81.5 x 96.5cm)
**£2,850–3,200 / $4,000–4,500** ⊞ BRG
*Karolina Larusdottir moved to England when she was sixteen. Her pictures have been used to advertise the Royal Academy Summer Show.*

**Achile Lauge**
French (1861–1944)
Still life of roses
Signed, oil on board
24 x 29¾in (61 x 75.5cm)
**£2,000–2,400 / $3,000–3,500** ⚒ P(Ba)

▶ **Sydney Laurence**
American (1865–1940)
At the Campfire
Signed, oil on canvas
24 x 20in (61 x 51cm)
**£16,500–20,000 / $23,500–30,000** ⚒ S(NY)

**Nasse Laurens**
French (20thC)
French Courtyard
Signed, watercolour
16 x 20in (40.5 x 51cm)
**£110–130 / $160–200** ⚒ TREA

**Simon Laurie, RSW, RGI**
Scottish (b1964)
Still Life with Jug
Signed, acrylic on board
22 x 24in (56 x 61cm)
**£1,200–1,350 / $1,750–2,000** ⊞ P&H
*Laurie's highly individual abstract style has won him most of the
principal awards at the Scottish societies over the last decade.*

◀ **Harold Lawes**
British (fl1890)
Bucklesham Heath
A pair, signed, watercolour
9½ x 21in (24 x 53.5cm)
**£400–460 / $580–700** ⚒ G(L)

**Michael Lawes**
British (b1948)
The Champs Elysées
Signed, pastel
18 x 24in (45.5 x 61cm)
**£700–770 / $1,000–1,200** ⊞ **Dr**

**Michael Lawes**
British (b1948)
Corporation Street, Birmingham
Pastel, 18 x 24in (45.5 x 61cm)
**£700–770 / $1,000–1,200** ⊞ **Dr**

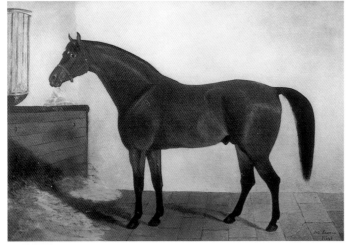

## Equestrian subjects

Pictures of equestrian events and equine subjects
have a faithful following. Most collectors will buy
specific sport themes such as hunting or racing.
With a large number of artists supplying the
market, prices and quality of work can vary
enormously. If one shops carefully you can find
what you are after at a price you can afford.

◀ **Joseph Lawrence**
British (19thC)
Chestnut hunter, 'Yaggon'
Signed, oil
15½ x 21½in (39.5 x 54.5cm)
**£3,000–3,300 / $4,400–4,800** ⊞ **LH**

**Cecil Lawson**
British (19thC)
In the Apple Orchard
Signed, oil on canvas
8 x 10in (20.5 x 25.5cm)
**£2,850–3,200 / $4,000–4,500** ⊞ **HFA**

**Frederick (Fred) Lawson**
British (1888–1968)
Lincoln
Signed, inscribed Lincoln and dated 1930, pencil, pen, ink and
watercolour on tinted paper
12½ x 15in (32 x 38.5cm)
**£900–1,000 / $1,300–1,500** ⚒ **B(L)**

# Benjamin Williams Leader (1831–1923)

Born as Benjamin Williams, the artist added the surname Leader (his father's middle name) to distinguish himself from the Williams family of painters who were unrelated. Abandoning a profession in engineering for art he became a pupil at The Royal Academy in 1853. The following year he showed his first picture there and continued to exhibit prolifically up until 1923. Leader achieved notable success with his painting *February Fill Dyke*, exhibited in 1881, which remains a very famous Victorian painting. The Royal Academy elected Leader as an Associate in 1883, and an Academician in 1898. He won the gold medal and the Legion d'Honneur in Paris in 1889.

**Benjamin Williams Leader, RA**
British (1831–1923)
Sheep at Pasture
Signed and dated 1899, oil on board
8 x 12in (20.5 x 30.5cm)
**£8,000–8,800 / $11,500–13,000** ⊞ CFA

**Benjamin Williams Leader, RA**
British (1831–1923)
Resting on the River Bank, North Wales
Signed and date 1887, oil on canvas
16 x 24in (40.5 x 61cm)
**£14,500–16,000 / $21,000–23,000** ⊞ HFA

**Benjamin Williams Leader, RA**
British (1831–1923)
The Hayfield
Signed, oil on panel
16 x 24in (40.5 x 61cm)
**£8,500–9,500 / $12,500–14,000** ⊞ SGL

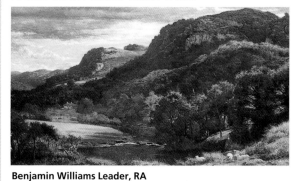

**Benjamin Williams Leader, RA**
British (1831–1923)
Betws-y-Coed, North Wales
Oil on canvas
19 x 35in (48.5 x 89cm)
**£18,500–20,500 / $27,000–29,000** ⊞ HFA

▶ **Benjamin Williams Leader, RA**
British (1831–1923)
A River in North Wales
Signed, oil on board
13 x 17in (33 x 43cm)
**£12,500–14,000 / $18,000–20,000** ⊞ CW

◄ **Noel Harry Leaver ARCA**
British (1889–1951)
Chichester Cross
Watercolour
13½ x 9½in (34.5 x 24cm)
**£3,500–3,800 / $5,000–5,500** ⊞ **HFA**

*Noel Harry Leaver was born at the School House in Austwick, near Settle in March 1889, and was educated at St. James's School, Burnley where his father, Peter Leaver, was the headmaster. Aged thirteen he attended the Burnley School of Art. He became a general craftsman and Art Master at the Halifax School of Art and was awarded RCA in 1911 and RIBA in 1912.*

**William Lee-Hankey**
British (1869–1952)
Old Woman
Signed, watercolour
10 x 7in (25.5 x 17.5cm)
**£1,500–1,800 / $2,200–2,600** ↗ **B**

## Watercolours

When framing your watercolours insist on mounting the picture on acid free boards. Poor mounting and the wrong adhesives can cause works on paper to deteriorate.

◄ **William J. Leenders**
Dutch (19th/20thC)
Dutch Harbour
Signed, watercolour
24 x 18in (61 x 45.5cm)
**£350–400 / $500–580** ↗ **TREA**

**Fernand Leger**
French (1881–1955)
Nature Morte aux Fruits
Signed and numbered 24/75, lithograph printed in colours
13¾ x 17¾in (35 x 45cm)
**£900–1,000 / $1,300–1,500** ⚒ BUK

**Rene Le Grand**
British (b1953)
Looking out ot Sea
Signed, oil
24 x 20in (61 x 51cm)
**£3,250–3,600 / $4,700–5,200** ⊞ Dr

## Abbreviations

Letters after the artist's name denote that the artist has been awarded the membership of an artistic body. See page 233 for the explanation of abbreviated letters.

**John Leigh-Pemberton**
British (b1911)
Bus – Alexander in Plain Black Double Harness
Signed and dated 1954, oil on canvas
21 x 35in (53.5 x 89cm)
**£3,250–3,750 / $4,700–5,500** ⊞ AAJ

*John Leigh-Pemberton painted in oils, tempera and gouache, specializing in natural history subjects. Born in London, he was educated at Eton and then studied art in London between 1928 and 1931. He has exhibited at the Royal Academy, the Royal Institute of Oil Painters, provincial galleries and abroad.*

▶ **Frederic Lord Leighton, PRA**
British (1830–96)
Study for two figures in *Captive Andromache*
Oil on panel
13¼ x 9in (33.5 x 23cm)
**£8,000–9,500 / $11,500–13,000** ⚒ Bon

*The Captive Andromache is arguably one of the greatest of Leighton's ambitious panoramas. Completed in 1888, it was bought from the artist for the City of Manchester Art Gallery in the following year.*

**William Leighton-Leitch, RI**
British (1804–83)
Santa Maria della Salute
Oil
14 x 18in (35.5 x 45.5cm)
**£2,400–2,700 / $3,500–4,000** ⊞ Dr

**August Leroux**
French (1871–1954)
By the Sea
Signed, oil on panel
7½ x 9½in (19 x 24cm)
**£9,000–10,500 / $13,000–15,500** ⚹ S(O)

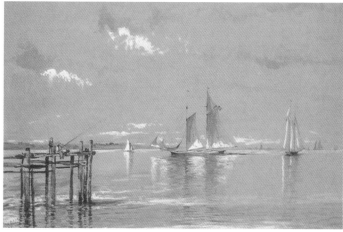

**Edmund Darch Lewis**
American (1835–1910)
Fishing in the Harbour
Signed and dated 1882, watercolour and gouache
16 x 27¼in (40.5 x 69cm)
**£1,800–2,200 / $2,600–3,200** ⚹ SHN

**Charles James Lewis, RI**
British (1830–92)
A Sunny Peep, Oxford
Signed and dated 1859, oil on paper laid on board
13¼ x 9½in (33.5 x 24cm)
**£3,500–4,000 / $5,000–5,800** ⚹ S

▶ **Edmund Darch Lewis**
American (1835–1910)
Lake View
Signed, oil on canvas
11½ x 19in (29 x 48.5cm)
**£2,600–3,000 / $3,800–4,400** ⚹ SHN

**Leonard Lewis**
British (19thC)
On the Wye
Signed watercolour
10 x 14in (25.5 x 35.5cm)
**£190–230 / $275–330** ⚒ **GAK**

**Ludolfs Liberts**
Russian/American (1895–1959)
City of Lights
Signed, oil on canvas
30 x 42in (76 x 106.5cm)
**£2,700–3,200 / $4,000–4,600** ⚒ **NOA**

**Bengt Lindstrom**
Swedish (b1925)
Face
Signed, oil on canvas
32 x 39¼in (81 x 99.5cm)
**£2,700–3,200 / $4,000–4,600** ⚒ **P(Ba)**

▶ **John Lines**
British (b1938)
Sunny Acre
Signed, oil
24in (61cm) square
**£650–720**
**$950–1,000** ⊞ **Dr**

**John Lines**
British (b1938)
*Red Lady* off Tilbury
Oil on canvas
20 x 30in (51 x 76cm)
**£1,100–1,300 / $1,600–1,900** ⊞ **Dr**

**John Linnell**
British (1792–1882)
Sunset and River
Signed and dated 1860, oil on board
8½ x 10½in (21.5 x 26.5cm)
**£10,800–13,000 / $15,750–18,750** ⚒ **S**

**Maria Liszt**
American (20thC)
The Old Elm
Signed, oil on canvas
24 x 20in (61 x 51cm)
**£250–280 / $360–420** 🔨 **TREA**

*Maria Liszt studied at the Scott Carbee School of Art in Boston. She exhibited at the North Shore Arts Association and the National Association of Women Painters and was awarded the Elizabeth T. Greenshield Memorial Award. Liszt was sought after for portrait work as well as mural work in hotels, dining rooms and ballrooms in Boston, New York and Florida.*

**Horace Mann Livens**
British (1862–1936)
Still Life
Signed and dated 1912, oil on canvas
20 x 16½in (51 x 42cm)
**£1,200–1,400 / $1,750–2,000** 🔨 **G(L)**

**Walter Stuart Lloyd**
British (fl1875–1929)
Lincoln
Signed, oil
on canvas
72 x 40in
(183 x 101.5cm)
**£15,000–17,000**
**$21,750–24,750** ⊞ **Ben**

## Abbreviations

Letters after the artist's name denote that the artist has been awarded the membership of an artistic body. See page 233 for the explanation of abbreviated letters.

**Konstantin Lomykin**
Russian (1924–93)
Evening Still Life
Signed, oil on canvas
41 x 32in (106 x 83cm)
**£7,000–7,500 / $10,200–10,800** ⊞ **ARL**

**Leonard Long**
Australian (b1911)
Shoalhaven River, Nowra, New South Wales
Signed and dated 1957, oil on board
5½ x 7½in (14 x 19cm)
**£85–100 / $125–145** ⚖ G(L)

**Charles Oglesby Longabough**
American (1885–1944)
Pirate's Alley, French Quarter
Signed and dated, watercolour
6 x 7in (15 x 18cm)
**£500–600 / $720–870** ⚖ NOA

◄ **Antonio Lonza**
Italian (1846–1918)
The Three Gypsies
Signed, oil on canvas
24½ x 19in
(62 x 48.5cm)
**£3,800–4,500**
**$5,500–6,500** ⚖ S(O)

► **Robert Lougheed**
American (1910–82)
Ontario Winter
Signed, oil on canvas
12 x 16in
(30.5 x 40.5cm)
**£3,500–3,800**
**$5,000–5,500**
⚖ CdA

# Tom Lovell (1909–97)

Lovell studied at Syracuse University, New York, and was a member of the Society of Illustrators, Westport Artists, National Association of Western Artists and the Cowboy Art Association. He exhibited at the National Academy of Western Art. His work is in the National Cowboy Hall of Fame.

◄ **Tom Lovell**
American (1909–97)
Harbour in Winter
Signed, gouache
19 x 29in
(48.5 x 73.5cm)
**£1,600–1,800**
**$2,300–2,600**
⚖ TREA

**Tom Lovell**
American (1909–97)
Study for The Pipeholder
Signed, pastel, 10 x 8in (25.5 x 20.5cm)
**£4,000–4,500 / $5,800–6,500** ⚖ CdA

**Alan Lowndes**
British (1921–78)
Stuart Street, Tiger Bay, Cardiff
Signed and dated 1972, oil on canvas
19¾ x 30in (50.5 x 76.5cm)
**£1,500–1,800 / $2,200–2,600** ⚒ S(O)

**Laurence Stephen Lowry, RA, RBA, LG, NS**
British (1887–1976)
House on the Corner of Hanover Street, Shudehill
Signed, pencil
7 x 8½in (18 x 21.5cm)
**£19,500–21,500 / $28,500–30,500** ⊞ P&H

**Henry Frederick Lucas Lucas**
British (c1848–1943)
Bellagio
Signed, oil on canvas
14 x 18in (36 x 46cm)
**£1,400–1,600 / $2,000–2,300** ⚒ B(C)

**Albert Durer Lucas**
British (1828–1918)
Still Life
A pair, both signed, one dated 1889 the other 1899,
oil on canvas
8 x 6in (20.5 x 15cm)
**£2,600–3,000 / $3,800–4,400** ⚒ Bon

▶ **William Luker**
British (1828–1905)
Summer Pastures
Signed, oil on canvas
16 x 24in (40.5 x 61cm)
**£9,800–10,800 / $14,000–15,500** ⊞ HFA

**◀ Soren Lund**
Danish (1852–1933)
Farmyard with Ducks
Signed, oil on canvas
22 x 26in (56 x 66cm)
**£1,200–1,400 / $1,750–2,000** 🔨 **TREA**

**◀ John Abernethy Lynas-Gray**
British (b1869)
Tantallon Castle, Lothian and Beach
Signed, watercolour
6 x 10½in (15 x 25.5cm)
**£320–360 / $470–550** ⊞ **LH**

**Leon Lundmark**
American (b1875)
Rock Bound
Signed, oil on canvas
29 x 36in (73.5 x 91.5cm)
**£1,200–1,400**
**$1,750–2,000** 🔨 **TREA**

**Michael Lyne**
British (1912–89)
Lady Cure's Hounds near the River Servern
Signed, watercolour
16¼ x 23in (41.5 x 58.5cm)
**£7,250–7,750 / $10,500–11,200** ⊞ **AAJ**

*Michael Lyne was born in Herefordshire, the fourth child of a country parson. He studied at Cheltenham College of Art where his love of animals and the English countryside were quickly evident in the subjects of his paintings and drawings. His first public exhibition was held in 1934 and he went on to exhibit in London in 1938. At the same time he pursued his keen interest in hunting in USA, Ireland and England. His early work was mostly in watercolour, but by the late 1950s he used mainly oils and his large dramatic canvases captured the mood and excitement of a moment in the Grand National or on the hunting field. He painted numerous commissions on both sides of the Atlantic and had many one-man shows in the 1960s and '70s. Lyne retired from active painting in the late 1970s. He illustrated a number of books, including* Horse Hounds and Country *and* From Litter to Later On.

# Limited Edition Prints

You would have to be extremely rich to buy a Matisse or a Picasso oil today, but prints by 'blue chip' artists, as they are known in the trade, are much more affordable. By prints I mean limited edition print runs, signed, originated and worked on by the artists themselves, and therefore of a value that will increase. These differ from offset lithographs, which are copies of paintings printed by a publishing house, with no involvement by the artist. Van Gogh and Gaugin never made prints.

Blue chip artists are deemed to be all French Impressionists: Toulouse Lautrec, Matisse, Renoir; and Expressionists such as Kandinsky, Picasso and Americans, Chagall and Warhol. A signed print by Toulouse Lautrec is worth £20,000 ($29,000). A small black-and-white signed lithograph by Picasso can be picked up for £7,000–8,000 ($10,200–11,600), although a large coloured linocut is worth £250,000 ($362,000).

The price of prints rises and falls in line with original works of art. If a Picasso reaches a record, then a print by him would increase in value accordingly. In the late 1980s, the Japanese were paying record prices for European 20th-century paintings; prints by these masters also rose in value. The Japanese recession of the 1990s saw picture prices fall, although they recovered in the late 1990s economic upturn and have continued to hold their value through the downturn in the world economy.

Other 20th-century prints are subject to the vagaries of fashion, and they do not necessarily rise in price. Work by young British artists are extremely desirable at the moment, although their long-term reputation is as yet unproven. London gallery, Counter Editions are working in close co-operation with artists such as Gary Hume, Matt Collishaw and Rachel Whiteread to produce limited editions of 400 signed silkscreen prints. Such a large print run enables them to charge a starting price of £400 ($580), which increases as the print run nears its end.

Currently under aesthetic reassessment are the prints of 1960s American pop artists. Extremely sought after in the late 1980s, their value plummeted by as much as 70% a decade later. Prices are regaining ground, and at a Sotheby's sale in New York earlier this year, a Robert Motherwell fetched over £14,000 ($20,300).

Mid-20th century British prints are now very collectable, with the increased interest in Graham Sutherland, John Piper and Elizabeth Frink. According to gallery owners, a print by the abstract artist William Scott or the sculptor Elizabeth Frink would have fetched little more than £75 ($110) ten years ago; now work by them could cost up to £4,000 ($5,800) and £1,000 ($1,500) respectively. John Piper prints fetch more at auction (£1,800 / $2,600) than retail at a gallery (£1,200 / $1,750). Conversely, prints by Graham Sutherland, who began his career as a printmaker, made £2,000 ($2,900) fifteen years ago, but today reach only £300–400 ($440–580) at auction.

◀ **Gillian Ayres**
British (20thC)
Greenwell's Glory, 1999
Signed, hand-coloured carborundum etching, edition of 30
25¼ x 29¼in (65 x 74.5cm)
**£1,500–1,800**
**$2,200–2,600** ⊞ ACG

### Further information
Artists mentioned in the introduction above may have works appearing elsewhere in this Guide. Consult the index for page numbers.

◀ **Jeff Burton**
American (20thC)
Untitled (Swim Trunks) (2000)
Signed, numbered and dated 2000, cibachrome print, edition of 300
12 x 17in (30.5 x 43cm)
**£350–420**
**$500–600** ⊞ CEL

**Marc Chagall**
French/Russian (1887–1985)
Soleil Rouge, Soleil Jaune (Cramer 45)
Signed, monotype printed in colours on chine
14½ x 12½in (37 x 32cm)
**£12,500–15,000 / $18,000–22,000** ↗ S(NY)

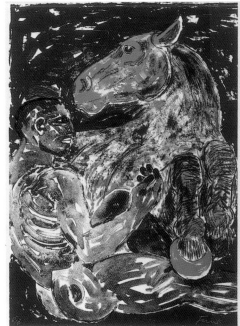

◀ **Willem de Kooning**
American/Dutch (1904–97)
Untitled
Four, signed and numbered,
lithographs printed in colours on
Arches paper, edition of 180
28¼ x 24¾in (72 x 63cm)
**£11,500–14,000**
**$16,700–20,000** 🔨 S(NY)

▶ **Elisabeth Frink**
British (1930–93)
Man and Horse
Signed, original screenprint,
edition of 70
39½ x 27¼in (100.5 x 69cm)
**£3,000–3,500**
**$4,400–5,000** ⊞ WO

**Patrick Heron**
British (1920–99)
The Brushwork Series, 1999
Etching on Velin Arches paper,
edition of 38
31½ x 26½in (80 x 67.5cm)
**£1,200–1,400**
**$1,750–2,000** ⊞ WO

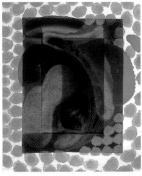

**David Hockney**
British (b1937)
Artist and Model, 1973–74
Original etching in black from a copper plate
worked in hardground, softground and sugar
aquatint, edition of 100
22½ x 17½in (57 x 44.5cm)
**£8,000–8,800 / $11,500–12,500** ⊞ WO

**Howard Hodgkin**
British (b1932)
David's Pool
Signed, original etching with
hand colouring, edition of 100
24½ x 31½in (62 x 80cm)
**£8,000–8,800**
**$11,500–12,500** ⊞ WO

**Gary Hume**
British (b1962)
The Cleric
Signed, numbered and dated, silkscreen in six colours on
Somerset tub sized paper, edition of 300
27 x 37in (69 x 94cm)
**£650–720 / $950–1,000** ⊞ CEL

*Gary Hume is one of the most acclaimed painters of his
generation and his work has met with widespread critical
approval. He had a major solo show at the Whitechapel
Gallery, London in 1999, represented Great Britain in the
1999 Venice Biennale and the 1996 Sao Paulo Biennale.
Hume has also participated in many of the significant group
shows of the last ten years, including 'Freeze', the 1990 and
1995 British Art Shows, 'Brilliant' (1995) and 'Sensation'
(1997). He was nominated for the Turner Prize in 1996.*

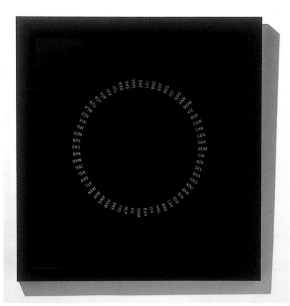

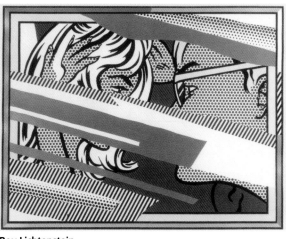

**Ben Langlands and Nikki Bell**
British (b1955 and 1959)
Frozen Sky (Night), 1999
Screenprint, edition of 45
27½ x 26in (70 x 66cm)
**£900–1,000 / $1,300–1,500** ⊞ **ACG**

**Roy Lichtenstein**
American (1923–97)
Reflections on Conversation
Signed, dated and numbered, lithograph, screenprint and woodcut
printed in colours, with metallized PVC collage and embossing,
edtion of 68
47 x 60¾in (119.5 x 154.5cm)
**£10,800–13,000 / $16,000–19,000** ↗ **S(NY)**

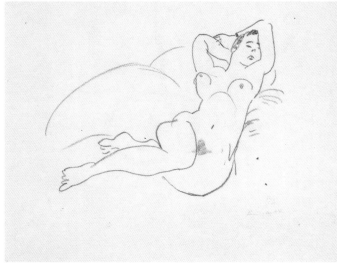

**Henri Matisse**
French (1869–1954)
Figure Endormie
Signed and numbered, lithograph, edition of 50
15½ x 22½in (39.5 x 57cm)
**£4,800–5,800 / $7,000–8,500** ↗ **BUK**

**Joan Miró**
Spanish (1893–1983)
Le Vent Parmi les Roseaux
Signed and numbered, aquatint printed in colours on
japan, edition of 150
13¼ x 10in (33 x 25.5cm)
**£3,500–4,200 / $5,000–6,000** ⊞ **WO**

◄ **Robert Motherwell**
American (1915–91)
Mediterranean Light
Numbered, lithograph printed in colours on TGL
handmade, hand-coloured paper, edition of 40
22½ x 65¾in (57 x 167cm)
**£13,500–16,000 / $20,000–23,000** ↗ **S(NY)**

**Chris Ofili**
British (b1968)
Regal (2000)
Signed, dated and numbered, lithographic print in four colours on a silkscreened glow-in-the-dark background on Colorplan 270gsm paper, edition of 300
11 x 16in (28 x 40.5cm)
**£350–420 / $500–600** ⊞ CEL

**Elizabeth Peyton**
American (b1965)
Thursday (Tony) (2000)
Signed, dated and numbered, two-colour lithographic print on silkscreened pearlescent ground, on Somerset Velvet 300gsm paper, edition of 300
24 x 19in (61 x 48.5cm)
**£350–385 / $500–580** ⊞ CEL

 **Frank Stella**
American (b1936)
Signed, dated and numbered, relief and screenprint in colours on TGL hand-made paper, edition of 30
66 x 52in (167.5 x 132cm)
**£8,500–10,000**
**$12,500–14,500** ⚒ S(NY)

**Julian Opie**
British (b1958)
Radio Wind Tyres
One of a series of eight lambda prints laminated to acrylic, edition of 40
29¼ x 43¼in (74.5 x 110cm)
**£2,000–2,400**
**$3,000–3,500** ⊞ ACG

**Pablo Picasso**
Spanish (1881–1973)
Le Vieux Roi
Signed and numbered, lithograph
25¼ x 19½in (64 x 49.5cm)
**£2,500–3,000**
**$3,600–4,400** ⚒ BUK

**John Piper**
British (1903–92)
Winter, 1981
Signed, original etching on Velin Arches 300gsm paper, edition of 100
16 x 13in (40.5 x 33cm)
**£950–1,150 / $1,400–1,750** ⊞ WO

**Andy Warhol**
American (1930–87)
Mao
Signed and numbered, silkscreen printed in colours, edition of 250
36in (91.5cm) square
**£3,500–4,200 / $5,000–6,000** ⚒ BUK

◀ **Gladys MacCabe, ROI, RUA**
British (b1918)
Castlewellan Horse Fair
Signed, oil on board
16 x 20in (40.5 x 51cm)
**£3,200–3,600 / $4,600–5,200** ⊞ **WrG**

*Born in Randelstown in Northern Ireland,
Gladys attended Belfast College of Art
between 1934 and 1938. An art critic,
lecturer and broadcaster as well as an artist,
she has also been a past president of the
Ulster Society of Women Artists and is a
member of the Watercolour Society of Ireland
as well as fellow of the Royal Society of Arts.
Her paintings observe people at leisure and at
work, often in a humorous way. She has
exhibited widely and her work can be found
in private collections in Ireland, Britain and
the USA.*

▶ **Maurice MacGonigal, PRHA**
Irish (1900–79)
Spring Waters on the Tolka
Signed, oil on canvas
14 x 18in (36 x 46cm)
**£3,500–4,200 / $5,000–6,000** ⚲ **WA**

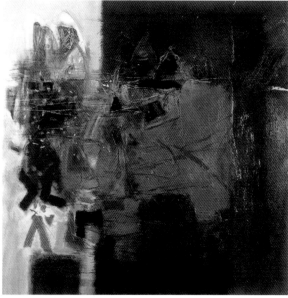

**Charles MacQueen, RSW, RSI**
Scottish (b1940)
Tunisian Saddlebags
Mixed media
19in (48.5cm) square
**£1,400–1,600 / $2,000–2,300** ⊞ **P&H**

*Charles is among the first rank of Scottish painters. His vibrant
abstracts have won him numerous awards since his days at Glasgow
School of Art. He has exhibited continually at the Royal Scottish
Academy and the Royal Glasgow Institute and was elected Vice
President of the Royal Scottish Society of Painters in Watercolour.*

◀ **Thomas
MacQuoid**
British (1820–1912)
Vannes, Brittany
Signed, watercolour
13½ x 10¼in
(34.5 x 26cm)
**£420–440**
**$600–700** ⚲ **Bea(E)**

**John MacWhirter**
British (1839–1911)
In the Italian Lakes
Signed, watercolour and bodycolour
7 x 10in (17.5 x 25.5cm)
£1,000–1,200 / $1,500–1,750 ⚒ DN

**Arthur K. Maderson**
British (b1942)
Evening Study, Clonea Strand, County Waterford
Signed and inscribed, mixed media
25 x 37in (63.5 x 94cm)
£2,700–3,200 / $4,000–4,700 ⚒ WA

**Arthur K. Maderson**
British (b1942)
Lismore River Pool, 2pm
Signed, oil on board
46in (117cm) square
£4,000–4,500 / $5,800–6,500 ⚒ WA

*Arthur Maderson studied at the Camberwell School of Art from 1959 to 1963, when he won the Anna Berry Award in open competition as a first year student. He is a series painter, the most notable being the Lismore River series and the Tallow Horse Fair series. He exhibits regularly at the Royal Academy and the Royal Hibernian Academy in Dublin.*

**Cecil Maguire, RUA**
Irish (b1930)
Ervallagh, Roundstone
Signed, oil on board
16 x 20in (40.5 x 51cm)
£5,200–5,800 / $7,500–8,500 ⊞ WrG

*Born in Lurgan, Cecil Maguire graduated from Queen's University, Belfast in 1951. He exhibited at the Royal Hibernian Academy and Royal Ulster Academy from 1967 and was elected member of the RUA in 1974. He has exhibited in many group and one-man shows, most recently at the Oriel and Leinster Galleries, Dublin and his work is held in many corporate and private collections. He now lives and works in the West of Ireland, an area which has always been the inspiration for much of his work with its ever changing landscape and tranquillity.*

**Jennie Magafan**
American (1916–52)
Autumn Wind
Signed, oil on board
24½ x 18½in
(62 x 47cm)
£3,000–3,500
$4,500–5,500
⚒ JAA

*Jennie Magafan was born in Chicago, Illinois, in 1916 and studied in Colorado, where she exhibited and won many awards. Some of her work is located in the White House as well as many private collections.*

◄ **Helena Maguire**
British (1860–1909)
Watching the Kittens
Signed, watercolour
10 x 8½in
(25.5 x 21.5cm)
**£4,750–5,250**
**$7,000–7,500**
⊞ **WrG**

► **J. L. Mallony**
British (b1920)
Figures on Seaside
Promenade
Signed, oil on canvas
17½ x 21in
(44.5 x 53.5cm)
**£1,000–1,200**
**$1,500–1,750**
⚒ **RBB**

**William Henry Mander**
British (fl1880–1922)
Welsh river scene with boys fishing
Signed, oil on canvas
15 x 23½in (38 x 60cm)
**£1,850–2,000 / $2,700–3,000** ⚒ **AH**

**Cathleen Mann**
British (1896–1959)
Tulips and Lilies
Signed, oil on canvas
18 x 24in (45.5 x 61cm)
**£8,500–9,500 / $12,300–13,800** ⊞ **NZ**

◄ **Gerard Marjoram**
Irish (b1936)
Near Maam, Co Galway
Signed, oil on canvas
14 x 18in (35.5 x 45.5cm)
**£1,400–1,600 / $2,000–2,300** ⊞ **WrG**

*Gerard was born in Dublin and studied at the National College of Art under Maurice MacGonigal and Seán Keating. Since 1970 he has exhibited frequently in Dublin and Galway and his work is held in many private and public collections worldwide including the Irish Embassy in Prague. He makes frequent trips to Connemara and the west coast of Ireland.*

**Albert Ernest Markes**
British (1865–1901)
A Second Rater in the Thames Estuary
Signed, watercolour
8¼ x 6½in (21 x 16.5cm)
**£800–900 / $1,150–1,300** ⚒ S(O)

▶ **George Marks**
British (fl1876–1922)
On Shere Heath,
Surrey
Signed, watercolour
9¾ x 14in
(25 x 35.5cm)
**£1,500–1,800**
**$2,200–2,600** ⚒ B

**Paul Marny**
French (1829–1914)
Townsfolk at the Harbour, Rouen
Signed, watercolour heightened with scratching out and white
21½ x 38½in (54.5 x 98cm)
**£1,000–1,500 / $1,500–2,500** ⚒ Bon

**Ignacio Marmol**
Spanish (1934–94)
(Untitled), No7, 1965
Signed, enamel on board
34¾ x 25¼in (88.5 x 64cm)
**£300–350 / $450–500** ⚒ P(Sy)

▶ **Reginald Marsh**
American (1898–1954)
Belles on the Broadwalk
Signed and dated 1950, brush, black ink and
watercolour on paper
21 x 28½in (53.5 x 72.5cm)
**£16,000–19,000 / $23,000–27,500** ⚒ P(NY)

◄ **Richard Marshall**
British (b1943)
Staithes Beach
Signed, oil on board
9½ x 13in (24 x 33cm)
**£675–750 / $1,000–1,200** ⊞ **TBJ**

**Roberto Angelo Kittermaster Marshall**
British (1849–1902)
Near Vall Cricis, Llangollen, West Wales
Signed, watercolour
20 x 15in (51 x 38cm)
**£3,000–3,300 / $4,500–4,800** ⊞ **HFA**

◄ **Elliott H. Marten**
British (fl1886–1910)
Wiston Pond and Chanctonbury Ring
Signed, watercolour
14 x 20½in (35.5 x 51cm)
**£700–840 / $1,000–1,200** ⊞ **HFA**

## Framing your picture

■ A frame should never overpower the picture. Never put a coloured plastic frame on a water-colour. A frame and mount should draw your eye into the picture.

■ Keep mounts and frames in proportion. A heavy frame requires a wider mount, a thin delicate frame a narrower one.

■ Hang watercolours away from direct sunlight. Never hang a glass-fronted picture opposite a door or window. The glass will reflect light and you will not see the picture. Use clear colour glass which eliminates the reflective rays.

▶ **John (Jack) Martin, RCA, OSA, CPE**
Canadian (1904–65)
An Artist's Table
Signed, oil on masonite
20 x 24in (51 x 61cm)
**£490–540 / $700–500** ↗ **WAD**

# Luke Martineau (b1970)

Luke Martineau was educated at Eton and Oxford and trained at Heatherley's School of Art, in London. Primarily a portrait painter, his professional reputation has been growing in recent years. He has a long waiting list of sitters and is sought out by the rich and fledgling famous – he has recently completed a portrait of Chanel model Candida Bond.

Martineau has also painted a series of views of the river Thames, recording life in London in the 21st century. His knowledge of and affection for his native London and its river is very evident in these paintings.

Luke Martineau can truly call himself a Young British Artist even though he represents an aspect of current British art that is not about unmade beds and pickled sharks. His work sells well because it is pleasant and easy to live with.

**Luke Martineau**
British (b1970)
Bella with a Flower in her Hair
Signed, oil on canvas
14 x 11in (35.5 x 28cm)
**£3,250–3,575**
**$4,700–5,250** ⊞ **P&H**

**Luke Martineau**
British (b1970)
St Mary's Abbot, W8
Signed, oil on board
17 x 7½in (43 x 19cm)
**£850–950**
**$1,250–1,400** ⊞ **P&H**

**Luke Martineau**
British (b1970)
Hungerford Bridge from Waterloo Bridge, Dusk
Signed, oil on canvas
30 x 40in (76 x 101.5cm)
**£3,250–3,575 / $4,700–5,500** ⊞ **P&H**

◄ **Luke Martineau**
British (b1970)
Breakfast at Valley Cottage
Signed, oil on canvas
30 x 24in (76 x 61cm)
**£1,500–1,700**
**$2,200–2,500** ⊞ **P&H**

**Luke Martineau**
British (b1970)
Albert Bridge, Dusk
Signed, oil on canvas
24 x 30in (61 x 76cm)
**£1,450–1,600 / $2,000–2,300** ⊞ **P&H**

**Luke Martineau**
British (b1970)
The Barle Valley, Exmoor from Withypool Hill
Signed, oil on canvas
42 x 48in (106.5 x 122cm)
**£5,500–6,000 / $8,000–8,700** ⊞ **P&H**

# Frank Henry Mason
# (1876–1965)

Frank Henry Mason was born at Seaton
Carew, County Durham in October 1876.
He trained as a marine engineer and whilst
with the Royal Navy became interested in
painting. To devote more time to his art he
returned to shore and studied under Albert
Strange at the School of Art in
Scarborough. He visited Whitby, Staithes,
Runswick Bay and other villages along the
east coast.

Mason was an extremely versatile painter
producing colourful scenes of fisherfolk as
well as some fine maritime scenes of shipping
and harbours. He also designed posters for
shipping and railway companies as well as
working for the Naval Directorate of
Camouflage during WWII. He exhibited at the
Royal Academy, Royal Institute of Painters in
Watercolours and many other institutions.

**Frank Henry Mason**
British (1876–1965)
The Custom House, Venice
Watercolour
9½ x 28½in (24 x 72.5cm)
**£2,600–3,000 / $3,800–4,500**  CAG

▶ **Frank Henry Mason, RI, RBA**
British (1876–1965)
Home from the Greenland Seas – Whitby
Signed and inscribed on various exhibition
labels verso, pencil, charcoal and
watercolour heightened with white
20 x 39in (51 x 99cm)
**£3,500–4,000 / $5,000–5,800**  B(L)
*This picture was exhibited at the Royal
Institute of Painters in Watercolours.*

**Frank Henry Mason, RI, RBA**
British (1876–1965)
A coastal scene at sunset with figures on a beach
A pair, signed, oil on panel
9¾ x 13¾in (25 x 35cm)
**£3,000–3,500 / $4,500–5,000**  B(L)

**Frank Henry Mason, RI, RBA**
British (1876–1965)
Waiting for the Evening Tide, Newlyn
Signed and dated 1944
Pencil and watercolour heightened with white
14 x 21in (35.5 x 53cm)
**£2,200–2,600 / $3,200–3,800**  B(L)

◀ **Frank Henry Mason**
British (1876–1965)
Along the Sands at Katwijk
Watercolour
6½ x 14in (16.5 x 35.5cm)
**£5,000–5,500 / $7,250–8,000**  HFA

◀ **Edward Masters**
British (19thC)
A Gathering along the Village Road
Signed, oil on canvas
20 x 30in (51 x 76cm)
**£9,000–10,000 / $13,000–14,500** ⊞ HFA

**Edwin Masters**
British (19thC)
Village Gathering
Oil on canvas
10 x 18in (25.5 x 45.5cm)
**£4,000–4,500 / $5,800–6,500** ⊞ HFA

◀ **Henri Matisse**
French (1869–1954)
Nue dans l'Atelier
Signed, pen and ink
9 x 11¾in (23 x 30cm)
**£19,000–21,000 / $28,300–30,500** 🖋 P
*This drawing was executed c1926–27.*

**Michael Matthews**
British (20thC)
The Clipper *Eleanor* Offshore
Oil
20 x 30in (51 x 76cm)
**£1,350–1,500 / $2,000–2,200** ⊞ Dr

**Edgard Maxence**
French (1871–1954)
Dame Pensive
Signed, oil on panel
13¾ x 10½in (35 x 26.5cm)
**£1,300–1,600 / $2,000–2,300** 🖋 SLN

**John Maxwell, RSA**
Scottish (1905–62)
The Archway
Signed, mixed media with pen and ink
19 x 22in (48 x 56cm)
**£2,700–3,200 / $4,000–4,700** ⚡ P(Ed)

*John Maxwell exhibited at the Arts Council, Scottish Committee 1960
and the Scottish National Gallery of Modern Art in 1963.*

**Paul Lucien Maze, DCM, MM**
French (1887–1979)
Horse Guards
Signed, watercolour
16 x 15in (40.5 x 38cm)
**£2,500–2,750 / $3,600–4,000** ⊞ P&H

*Maze was born at Le Havre, the son of Anglo-French parents.
He settled in Paris where he met Derain, de Segonzac and Edward
Vuillard. It was Vuillard who persuaded him to use pastels, the
medium for which Maze is perhaps best known. After exhibiting in
France, Maze was given his first solo exhibition at the Independent
Gallery in 1925, and after WWII settled in England, becoming friend and
painting adviser to Sir Winston Churchill. Maze exhibited regularly at a
number of major commercial art galleries in London, Paris and USA.*

**William Frederick (Fred) Mayor, IS**
British (1865–1916)
A Village Street, Winter Sunset
Signed, inscribed, pencil and watercolour
15½ x 19¼in (39 x 49cm)
**£2,000–2,500 / $3,000–3,600** ⚡ B(L)

# Denver Art Museum

■ 13th Avenue & Acoma, Downtown Denver, Colorado,
www.denverartmuseum.org

■ Modern and Contemporary collection of 4,500 works of
art from the 20thC.

**Ila Mae McAfee**
American (b1897–1995)
Juanita
A pair, signed, oil on board
5¾ x 3¾in (14.5 x 9.5cm)
**£5,000–5,800 / $7,000–8,500** ⚡ TREA

*McAfee was born in the small ranching community of Sargents,
southwestern Colorado. She studied at the Art Student's League and
the National Academy of Design in New York. McAfee was also an
illustrator and textile designer. In 1928 she married Elmer Turner,
another painter, and moved to Taos, New Mexico. She exhibited in
Texas, New Mexico, Oklahoma and Colorado and her work is included
in collections at the Denver Art Museum.*

◄ **For further information**
see Irish Art (pages 72–75)

◄ **Norman McCaig**
Irish (b1929)
Lough Corrib Fishing Boats, Connemara
Signed, oil on board
14 x 24in (35.5 X 61cm)
**£4,750–5,500 / $6,800–8,000 WrG**

*Norman McCaig was born in Bangor, Co Down and studied at Belfast College of Art and the Academy of Art, Vivan, Paris. He held his first exhibition in Paris in 1948 and went on to show his work in many galleries across the Republic and Northern Ireland, the USA and Australia. He is predominantly a landscape painter in the academic tradition and prefers marine subjects, painting loughs and harbours with great sensitivity.*

**Brett McEntagart, RHA**
British (b1939)
The Vegetable Garden, France
Signed, oil on panel
16 x 24in (40.5 x 61cm)
**£900–1,100 / $1,300–1,600** ↗ **WA**

**Norah McGuinness, HRHA**
Irish (1901–80)
From the Balcony
Gouache
7½ x 11in (19 x 28cm)
**£2,000–2,500 / $3,000–3,600** ↗ **JAd**

**Norah McGuinness, HRHA**
Irish (1901–80)
The Intruder
Signed, oil on canvas
15½ x 19¼in (39.5 x 49cm)
**£2,200–2,600 / $3,200–3,800** ↗ **JAd**

**William Bingham McGuinness, RHA**
British (1849–1928)
On the Thames near Abingdon
Signed, watercolour
14½ x 21in (37 x 53.5cm)
**£1,000–1,200 / $1,500–1,750** ↗ **WA**

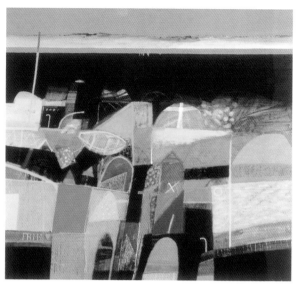

**Archibald Dunbar McIntosh, RSW, RGI**
Scottish (b1936)
Beach Symbols
Mixed media
32 x 31in (81.5 x 78.5cm)
**£2,600–3,000 / $3,800–4,400** ⊞ **P&H**

*Archie is one of the most original professional painters working in Scotland today. His very personal vision has brought many institutional awards and a worldwide following of private collectors. Glasgow born and trained, he exhibits at all the major Scottish Societies and his work can be found in the collections of the Scottish Arts Council, Glasgow Art Gallery and the Edinburgh Academy.*

**Sandy McIntosh, RSW**
Scottish (b1971)
Kite Maker's Table
Signed, mixed media
29 x 30in (73.5 x 76cm)
**£2,300–2,600 / $3,350–3,800** ⊞ **P&H**

*Although only recently graduated from Glasgow School of Art, Sandy has already established a formidable reputation. Winning the Alexander Graham Munro Travel Award in 1998, he visited Japan and his experiences there profoundly influenced his subsequent work. He exhibits regularly at the Royal Scottish Academy, the Royal Glasgow Institute and the Royal Scottish Society of Painters of Watercolours.*

◀ **Donald McIntyre**
British (b1923)
Evening Valley
Signed, oil on board
19¼ x 49¼in (49 x 125cm)
**£1,000–1,200 / $1,500–1,750** ✗ **AH**

**Donald McIntyre**
British (b1923)
Sunset Sea
Signed, oil on board
19¼ x 29½in (49 x 73.5cm)
**£800–900 / $1,200–1,300** ✗ **Bon**

**Donald McIntyre**
British (b1923)
Dunwich
Signed, oil on card
12½ x 16½in (32 x 42cm)
**£3,000–3,500 / $4,500–5,000** ✗ **B(Nor)**

**Hugh McNeil McIntyre, DA (Edin)**
Scottish (b1941)
Brazil
Signed, oil on canvas
20 x 24in (51 x 61cm)
**£1,650–1,800 / $2,400–2,600  CON**

*Hugh McIntyre studied at Rhode Island School of Design, USA and Edinburgh College of Art. His works are most typically outdoor scenes, enveloped in atmospheric overtones, and very much a continuing part of the long tradition of Scottish painting. He never works on fewer than three canvases at a time and by constantly changing from one canvas to another is able to see each with a fresh eye, thus he is able to produce the prodigious amount of work for which he is noted. He regularly returns to themes and knows his subject matter intimately. In recent years Hugh has travelled widely, working in Germany, France, Italy, Spain and Brazil. His works are held in many corporate collections, including those of the Bank of Scotland and Brunel University, USA.*

**Miller's is a price GUIDE not a price LIST**

**Graham H. D. McKean**
Scottish (b1962)
Swings and Roundabouts
Oil on canvas
40 x 50in
(101.5 x 127cm)
**£8,000–8,800
$11,500–12,500
 LGA**

▶ **Rosemary McLoughlin**
Australian (b1945)
Dreamer
Signed, pastel
18½ x 15in
(47 x 39.5cm)
**£950–1,100
$1,400–1,600
 WrG**

**Tony McNally**
Irish (b1953)
Wild Ponies on the Beach, West of Ireland
Signed, acrylic on canvas
12 x 16in (30.5 x 40.5cm)
**£950–1,000 / $1,350–1,500  WA**

**Arthur Meade, RBA, ROI**
British (1863–1948)
Robbers Bridge, Exmoor
Oil
28 x 34in (71 x 86.5cm)
**£3,800–4,200 / $5,500–6,200  Dr**

◄ **For further information**
see Marine Art (pages 130–133)

◄ **Arthur Joseph Meadows**
British (1843–1907)
Yarmouth Sands
Signed and inscribed, oil on canvas
10 x 14in (25.5 x 35.5cm)
**£11,000–12,000 / $16,000–17,500** ⊞ BuP

*Arthur Joseph Meadows, a painter of coastal scenes and marines, was greatly influenced by Clarkson Stanfield. Arthur Joseph is generally considered to be the best of the Meadows family of marine artists – he was the father of James Edwin and the brother of James Jnr.*

*Meadows painted harbour and coastal scenes in England, France and Holland. He exhibited mainly at Suffolk Street as well as the Royal Academy between 1863 and 1872, and the British Institute between 1863 and 1867. His paintings can be found in many museums and art galleries including the National Maritime Museum.*

# Reuben Mednikoff (1906–76)

Today Reuben Mednikoff may not be up there with the greats of Surrealism – Dali (1904–89), Man-Ray (1890–1976) and Meret Oppenheim (1913–86) but in 1930s he was according to the 'Pope' of Surrealism, Andre Breton, one of the most important figures in the British Surrealist movement. He was sadly omitted from a recent large Surrealist exhibition at the Tate Modern in London, however that show has awakened people to his talents.

Rueben Mednikoff's work is interesting as for the most part it is a collaboration between him as an artist and Freudian psychoanalyst, Doctor Grace Pailthorpe. She was twenty years older than him and although the pair became lovers, they never married. Pailthorpe considered adopting him as her son. Mednikoff changed his name to Ricky Pailthorpe.

Orgiastic Melody was painted in 1937 just before the pair left for the USA after an argument with E.L.T Mesens who ran the main surrealist gallery in Britain, The London Gallery. In America they were funded by Whitney Foundation to continue their psycho analytical research and painting. Encouraged by Mednikoff Grace Pailthorpe took up painting. They returned to Britain after the Second World War.

► **Reuben Mednikoff**
British (1906–76)
Orgiastic Melody
Signed, oil on board
21¼ x 15½in (54 x 39.5cm)
**£18,000–20,000 / $26,000–30,000** ⊞ JBG

◄ **Joseph Rusling Meeker**
American (1827–87)
Birches on Lake Pepin
Signed and dated 1873, oil on canvas
12 x 10in (30.5 x 25.5cm)
**£1,600–2,000 / $2,300–3,000** ⋏ SHN

► **Louis D. Meline**
American (1853–1905)
Hanging Game
Signed and dated 1884, oil on canvas
30 x 25in (76 x 63.5cm)
**£400–450 / $580–650** ⋏ SLN

◄ **William Mellor**
British (1851–1931)
On the Wharf, Bolton Woods, Yorkshire; and Falls on the Hugwy,
North Wales
A pair, signed, oil on canvas
18 x 14in (45.5 x 35.5cm)
**£9,000–10,000 / $13,000–14,500** ⊞ **Ben**

*Wiliam Mellor was born in Barnsley, Yorkshire, and painted
landscapes, working in Ilkley, Scarborough and Harrogate. He
travelled widely and was inspired by the landscapes of North Wales
and the north of England, particularly Yorkshire. His landscapes are
easily recognized and are generally scenes in summer or early autumn.
The most distinctive feature of Mellor's paintings is the meticulously
delicate rendering of trees and foliage, heightened by the rich English
sunlight that bathes the scene.*

*Mellor did not exhibit in London but his works frequently appear on
the market.*

► **Milton Menasco**
American
(1890–1974)
Greentree Farm's
Shut Out, A Chestnut
Racehorse
Signed, watercolour
on paper
13½ x 20½in
(34.5 x 52cm)
**£2,500–3,000**
**$3,600–4,400**
⚒ **S(NY)**

◄ **Bernard
Meninsky, NEAC, LG**
British (1891–1950)
Still life of flowers in
a green vase
Signed, oil on canvas
19½ x 15½in
(49.5 x 39.5cm)
**£3,000–3,500**
**$4,400–5,000**
⚒ **Bon**

◄ **Jack Merriott, RI, ROI, PS, SMA**
British (1901–68)
Polperro
Signed, watercolour
9½ x 13in (24 x 33cm)
**£1,100–1,200 / $1,600–1,750** ⊞ TBJ

◄ **Johan Hendrick Louis Meyer**
Dutch (1809–66)
An anchored merchantman offshore drying her sails, with barges in attendance
Signed, oil on panel
16 x 21in
(40.5 x 53.5cm)
**£1,700–2,000**
**$2,500–3,000**
🔨 Bon

**Johann Georg Meyer**
German (1813–86)
Listening at the Door
Signed, oil on mahogany panel
16½ x 10¼in (42 x 26cm)
**£7,000–7,700 / $10,000–11,250** ⊞ JC

*Johann Georg Meyer (known as Meyer von Bremen) was born in Bremen, Germany. He studied at the Academy in Dusselforf with Karl Sohn and William Schadow and became a member of the Academy of Arts in Amsterdam, where he won a medal in 1850. Examples of his work can be found in many museums and art galleries in Europe. He is popular in the USA and is well represented there.*

**William Henry Millais**
British (1814–99)
The Harbour Bar
Signed, inscribed and dated 1884, watercolour
11¼ x 20in (28.5 x 51cm)
**£750–900 / $1,100–1,300** 🔨 Bon
*This painting probably depicts the mouth of the River Torridge at Appledore, North Devon, with the Isle of Lundy in the distance.*

► **Frederick Miller**
British (19thC)
Tall Ship Setting Sail
Signed, watercolour
21 x 16in (53.5 x 40.5cm)
**£780–950**
**$1,100–1,400** 🔨 RBB

**Roy Miller**
British (b1938)
Risk of Thunder
Signed, oil on canvas
16 x 24in (40.5 x 61cm)
**£850–950 / $1,250–1,400** ⚒ S

**Maurice Millire**
French (b1871)
The Tennis Match
Signed, coloured drawing
34 x 26in (86.5 x 66cm)
**£420–500 / $600–720** ⚒ **TREA**
*Millire was well-known for this type of
subject. He also worked in oil and executed
several prints.*

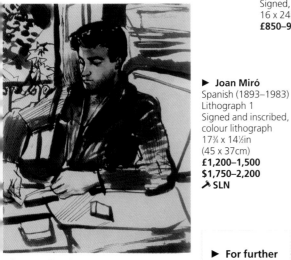

▶ **Joan Miró**
Spanish (1893–1983)
Lithograph 1
Signed and inscribed,
colour lithograph
17¾ x 14½in
(45 x 37cm)
**£1,200–1,500
$1,750–2,200**
⚒ **SLN**

**John Francis Minton, RBA, LG**
British (1917–57)
Young Man
Signed, pen and ink and wash
13½ x 10½in (34.5 x 26.5cm)
**£2,000–2,400 / $3,000–3,500** ⚒ **Bon**

▶ **For further
information**
see Limited
Edition Prints
(pages 104–107)

◀ **William Frederick Mitchell**
British (1845–1914)
The cruiser *Gladiator* in a snowstorm
Signed and dated 1908, pencil and watercolour heightened
with white
9½ x 15½in (24 x 39.5cm)
**£500–600 / $720–870** ⚒ **Bon**

**Carl Moll**
Austrian (1861–1945)
View of a Street
Signed and dated 1900, pencil on paper
8 x 6½in (20.5 x 16.5cm)
**£2,300–2,800 / $3,400–4,000** ⚒ DORO

► **Peder Monsted**
Danish (1859–1941)
A Garden in Summer
Signed and dated 1921, oil on canvas
14¼ x 20¼in (36 x 51cm)
**£6,500–7,200 / $9,500–10,500** ⊞ Bne

**William Monk, RE**
British (1863–1937)
The Grand Entrance, Irish International Exhibition 1907
Signed, watercolour
13 x 18in (33 x 45.5cm)
**£550–650 / $800–950** ⚒ WA

◄ **Carmel Mooney**
Irish (20thC)
Cattle and Sunlight
Signed, oil on canvas
10in (25.5cm) square
**£2,000–2,400**
**$3,000–3,500** ⚒ WA

**Barlow Moore**
British (1834–97)
A racing cutter in Portsmouth Harbour
Signed and dated 1894,
watercolour heightened with white
17 x 24½in (43 x 62cm)
**£3,500–4,200**
**$5,000–6,000** ⚒ Bon

► **Henry Moore, RA, RWS**
British (1831–1895)
Shoreline at Sunset
Signed and dated 1875,
oil on canvas
8 x 16in (20.5 x 40.5cm)
**£2,600–3,000**
**$3,800–4,500** ⚒ P(Ba)

**Sir Henry Moore, OM**
British (1898–1986)
Mother and Child on Seashore 1
Signed, pastel on paper
7¼ x 5¾in (18.5 x 14.5cm)
**£8,000–9,000 / $11,500–13,900** ⚒ DORO

**William J. Moore**
British (fl1885–92)
Cleric and Lady Playing Chess
Signed and dated 1884, oil on canvas
31 x 25in (78.5 x 63.5cm)
**£1,000–1,200**
**$1,500–1,750** ⚒ G(L)

◄ **Edward Percy Moran**
American (1862–1935)
The Happy Family
Signed, oil on canvas mounted
on board
14 x 20in (35.5 x 51cm)
**£1,800–2,200**
**$2,600–3,200** ⚒ JAA

► **Frederick Morgan, ROI**
British (1856–1927)
The Piggy-back Ride
Signed, watercolour heightened with
sponging out and scratching out
22½ x 13½in (57 x 34.5cm)
**£5,000–6,000**
**$7,250–8,750** ⚒ Bon

**Jenny Morgan**
British (20thC)
Dawn on the fishing grounds – the Grimsby trawler *Grimsby Town*
Signed, oil on canvas
24 x 36in (61 x 91.5cm)
**£1,800–2,000 / $2,600–3,200** ⚒ S(O)

**Jim Morgan**
American (20thC)
Morning Swim
Signed, oil on canvas
17 x 25½in (43 x 65cm)
**£1,350–1,600 / $2,000–2,300** ⚒ CdA

**R. F. Morgan**
American (b1929)
To Pull a Sneak
Signed, oil on canvas
24 x 36in (61 x 91.5cm)
**£5,300–6,000 / $7,700–8,700** ⚒ CdA

**George Morland**
British (1763–1804)
Moving in the Flock – Winter
Signed, oil on panel
10 x 12in (25.5 x 30.5cm)
**£12,000–14,000 / $17,500–20,000** ⊞ PLH

**Thomas William Morley**
British (1859–1922)
Street market in Bruges
Signed, watercolour
14 x 21in (35.5 x 53.5cm)
**£1,900–2,100 / $2,750–3,000** ⊞ TBJ

**Thomas William Morley**
British (1859–1922)
Shepherdess and flock in open landscape
Signed, watercolour
15½ x 23½in (39.5 x 59.5cm)
**£280–330 / $420–480** ⚒ G(L)

**Ken Moroney**
British (b1949)
On the Esplanade
Signed, oil on panel
23 x 35in (58.5 x 89cm)
**£6,500–7,200 / $9,500–10,500** ⊞ Bne

**Sir Cedric Morris**
British (1889–1982)
Landscape, Diana's Peak, St Helena
Signed and dated 1964, oil on canvas
28 x 36in (71 x 91.5cm)
**£4,800–5,500 / $7,000–8,000** ⚲ P

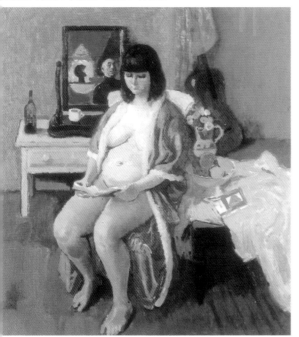

**Alberto Morrocco OBE, RP, RSW, RGI**
Scottish (1917–98)
Myself in the Studio, Bedford Mews
Oil on canvas
26 x 24in (66 x 61cm)
**£18,500–20,000 / $27,000–29,000** ⊞ P&H

**Jack Morrocco**
British (b1950)
Still Life with Violin
Signed, oil on canvas
32in (81.5cm) square
**£3,600–4,000**
**$5,000–5,800**
⊞ CON

## Wallace Collection

■ The Wallace Collection was bequeathed to the nation by Lady Wallace, widow of Sir Richard Wallace, in 1897.

■ Hertford House, Manchester Square, London W1M 6BN Tel: 020 7935 0687.  www.demon.co.uk/heritage/wallace

■ Open Mon–Sat 10am–5pm, Sun 2pm–5pm

■ Admission free

▶ **Anne Mortimer, RMS**
British (b1958)
And Tangerines? And Christmas Greens?
Watercolour
7in (18cm) square
**£600–700**
**$870–1,000** ⚲ Bon

◄ **Anna Mary Robertson 'Grandma' Moses**
American (1860–1961)
Home
Signed, dated 1944, numbered 1071, oil on Masonite
9¼ x 12in (23.5 x 30.5cm)
**£15,000–18,000 / $21,750–26,000** ⚒ S(NY)

*Anna Mary Robertson Moses became known to the world as Grandma Moses, and one of America's most noted folk artists. Most of her life was spent in Eagle Bridge, New York. The wife of a busy farmer, she did not begin to paint until she was in her 70s, when the farm no longer occupied her time. Moses' artistic rise began when a New York City collecter saw her paintings in the window of a local drugstore. In 1940 she received international acclaim for her one-woman show at the Galerie St Etienne in New York City.*

*Her paintings were popular because they depicted a nostalgic image of pre-industrial America. By the time of her death in 1961, Moses had created over 1,500 works of art.*

**Tom Mostyn, ROI, RWA, RCamA**
British (1864–1930)
Anstey's Cove, Devon
Signed, oil on canvas
20 x 27in (51 x 68.5cm)
**£1,000–1,200 / $1,500–1,750** ⚒ Bon

**Michael Mulcahy**
Irish (b1952)
At Dawn the Bailiffs
Signed, mixed media on paper
21 x 29in (53.5 x 73.5cm)
**£1,200–1,400 / $1,750–2,000** ⚒ WA

**William James Müller**
British (1812–45)
My Companion
Signed and dated 1836, oil on canvas
34 x 45½in (86.5 x 115.5cm)
**£800–950 / $1,200–1,400** ⚒ Bon

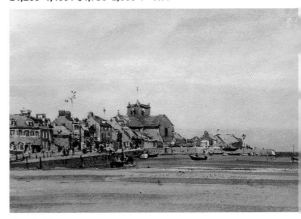

**Claude Muncaster**
British (1903–74)
Barfleur Harbour
Signed and dated 1959, watercolour
8½ x 13½in (21.5 x 34.5cm)
**£290–320 / $440–470** ⊞ LH

**Sir Alfred John Munnings, PRA**
British (1878–1959 )
In the Meadow
Signed, watercolour
12 x 16in (30.5 x 40.5cm)
**£18,000–21,000 / $26,000–30,000** ⚲ **GAK**

**Sir Alfred John Munnings, PRA**
British (1878–1959 )
Study of a horse and vignettes of horses heads
Signed, pencil sketch
7 x 19½in (18 x 49.5cm)
**£1,000–1,250 / $1,500–1,800** ⚲ **GAK**

**Sir Alfred John Munnings, PRA**
British (1878–1959)
Suffolk Pastoral – The River Dove with a Distant Clover Field
Signed and dated 1909, oil on canvas
20 x 24in (51 x 61cm)
**£20,000–24,000 / $30,000–35,000** ⚲ **B(Nor)**

▶ **Sir David Murray, RA, HRSA, RSW, RI**
Scottish (1849–1933)
The Greed Creek, Isle of Lewis – the Bay of Stornaway
Signed and dated 1919, oil on canvas
47½ x 71½in (120.5 x 181.5cm)
**£28,000–34,000 / $40,000–50,000** ⚲ **S**

**Scottish National Gallery of Modern Art**

■ Belford Road, Edinburgh EH4 3DR,
www.natgalscot.ac.uk

■ Houses a collection of 20th century Scottish
art including works by the Scottish Colourists
and members of the Edinburgh School.

◀ **Annie Feray Mutrie**
British (1826–93)
Still Lifes of Flowers
A pair, signed, watercolour
4½ x 8in (11.5 x 20.5cm)
**£4,800–5,300 / $7,000–7,700** ⊞ **HFA**

# Marine Art

The Dutch really popularized the notion of painting ships, and it was the 17th-century artist Van der Velde who inspired artists from the other important sea power, Great Britain. Willem Van de Velde was patronized by British government and royalty to paint galleons, tall ships and battle scenes. He influenced a whole generation of British artists such as Francis Swaine and Peter Monamy. These artists painted for a select few and prices for the work of Francis Holman, Dominic Serres, Nicholas Pocock and their contemporaries can be upwards of £50,000 ($72,500).

The 19th century saw a huge increase in the market for marine art and accordingly competent seascapes can be found from £2,000 ($3,000). William Lionel Wyllie is an important artist and on his death works remaining in his studio were acquired by the National Maritime Museum in Greenwich. His paintings and etchings have been fetching two to three times their saleroom estimates. Other Victorian artists to look out for are Thomas Bush Hardy and Henry Redmore.

During the early part of the 19th century, many of the American marine artists were British born. Robert Salmon emigrated from Liverpool during the 1840s and painted US coastal and harbour scenes and boat races, as did James Edward Buttersworth. The America's Cup yacht race along the Eastern seaboard began in 1851 and any images of the race are hugely valuable. The increasing industrialization of America saw the construction of huge ocean-going liners for nouveau riche men to travel the world. These became a popular subject to paint and liners in New York harbour by Antonio Jacobsen are very collectable.

The value of a seascape is much greater if the location can be identified. Bela Castle at the mouth of the River Tagus in Portugal is an ever popular and frequently painted view. British artist Norman Wilkinson's picture of the British fleet at Scapa Head during WWI was recently sold at auction for over £2,500 ($3,600). Works by British artist John Worsley of life on board WWII warships are increasing in price.

Today there are many artists painting scenes from what is perceived to be the golden age of British yacht racing, Cowes Regatta in the 1930s. A few are becoming sought after, particularly John Stephen Dews, born in 1929, and Stephen Renard.

**Frederick James Aldridge**
British (1850–1933)
Off Teignmouth
Signed, watercolour
6 x 9in (15 x 23cm)
**£620–700 / $900–1,000** ⚒ Bon

**David Brackman**
British (b1932)
*Britannia* and *Nyria* in tacking match off Cowes in 1920
Signed and dated 2001, oil on canvas
30 x 44in (76 x 112cm)
**£9,600–11,000 / $14,000–16,000** ⚒ S(O)

**James E. Buttersworth**
American (1817–94)
A Race Between *Volunteer* and *Thistle*
Signed and inscribed, oil on board
8 x 12in (20.5 x 30.5cm)
**£44,000–54,000 / $65,000–77,000** ⚒ S(NY)

◀ **John Steven Dews**
British (b1949)
*Endeavour I* racing *Velsheda* in the Solent
Signed, oil on canvas
30 x 40in (76 x 101.5cm)
**£60,000–70,000 $87,000–102,000** ⚒ Bon

**Thomas Bush Hardy**
British (1842–97)
Low Tide, Scherennigen, Holland
Signed and dated 1871, watercolour and gouache on heavy paper
20 x 28in (51 x 71cm)
**£650–750 / $950–1,100** ⚲ SLN

**Antonio Jacobsen**
American (1850–1921)
US Ship-of-the-Line
Signed, oil on board
14 x 23¾in (35.5 x 60.5cm)
**£12,500–14,500 / $18,000–21,000** ⚲ S(NY)

**Frank Henry Mason**
British (1876–1965)
Trawlers in Far Northern Waters
Signed and dated 1950, oil
20 x 29in (51 x 73.5cm)
**£2,000–2,500 / $3,000–3,600** ⊞ LH

---

**Further information**

Artists mentioned in the introduction may have works appearing elsewhere in this Guide. Consult the index for page numbers.

---

► **Frank Henry Mason**
British (1876–1965)
Clipper off Dover
Signed, oil
20½ x 29in
(52 x 73.5cm)
**£2,000–2,500
$3,000–3,600** ⊞ LH

**Antonio Jacobsen**
American (1850–1921)
SS Menzaleh Sail and Steam
Signed and dated 1887, oil on canvas
22¼ x 36in (56.5 x 91.5cm)
**£14,500–17,500 / $21,000–25,500** ⚲ SHN

**Martyn R. Mackrill**
British (b1961)
Britannia racing Shamrock V
Signed and dated 1986, oil on canvas
20 x 30in (51 x 76cm)
**£1,800–2,000 / $2,600–3,000** ⚲ P(S)

*Britannia was built in 1893 for King Edward VII when he was Prince of Wales. One of the most successful of all racing cutters, she achieved even greater celebrity when owned by King George V, and was a regular contender at Cowes for most of the inter-war years until she was scuttled after the King's death in 1936. Shamrock V was the last of Sir Thomas Lipton's five yachts with which he unsuccessfully challenged for the America's Cup between 1899 and 1930 and which, after Lipton's death, was bought by Mr T. O. M. 'Tommy' Sopwith.*

**Edward Moran**
American (1829–1901)
Around the Lighthouse
Signed, oil on canvas
18¼ x 36in (46.5 x 91.5cm)
**£48,000–55,000 / $70,000–80,000** ⚷ S(NY)

**Henry Redmore**
British (1820–87)
An Indiaman hove to off Dover for a pilot
Oil on canvas
20½ x 28½in (52 x 72.5cm)
**£29,500–32,500 / $42,000–47,000** ⊞ HFA

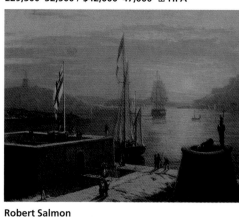

**Robert Salmon**
Anglo/American (1755–1844)
Vessels in a Harbour
Signed and dated 1839, oil on panel
9¾ x 12in (25 x 30.5cm)
**£36,500–43,500 / $53,000–63,000** ⚷ SK

*During 1839, Salmon's subjects varied greatly and included views of Boston and Nahant as well as the Isle of Bute and the River Clyde in the UK. It is generally believed that Salmon returned to England in 1840 and continued working there until 1844. This composition, although painted in America, probably depicts the Royal Naval Fort at Milford Haven, England.*

**Stephen J. Renard**
British (b1947)
*Britannia* and *Astra* off Cowes, 1929
Signed and dated 2001, oil on canvas
32 x 42in (81.5 x 106.5cm)
**£9,500–11,000 / $13,800–16,000** ⚷ S(O)

### National Maritime Museum

■ Greenwich, London
SE10 9NF (020 8858 4422).

■ Recorded information
line 020 8312 6565.

**Henry Scott**
British (b1911)
The Racing Yacht *Endeavour I*
Signed, oil on canvas
20 x 15in (51 x 38cm)
**£1,400–1,700**
**$2,000–2,500** ⚷ Bon

▶ **Pieter Van der Velde**
Flemish (1634–87)
Ship by a Southerly Harbour in a
Stormy Sea
Oil on canvas
25¼ x 32¼in (64 x 82cm)
**£5,000–6,000**
**$7,250–8,750** ⚷ DORO

**Theodore Walter**
British (19thC)
The legendary yacht *America* in the Solent
Signed, oil on canvas
13 x 17½in (33 x 44.5cm)
**£7,500–9,000 / $11,500–13,000** 🔨 **Bon**

*America's remarkable win at Cowes in the summer of 1851
guaranteed her a place in yachting history and established the race
that took her name and still awards as its prize one of the world's
most coveted sporting trophies.*

**Norman Wilkinson**
British (1878–1971)
Scapa Flow, Orkney
Signed and inscribed, oil on board
9¾ x 14in (25 x 35.5cm)
**£1,700–2,000 / $2,500–3,000** 🔨 **Bon**

*Scapa Flow, the principal anchorage of the Royal Navy in the 20th
century, is a vast expanse of sheltered water in the Orkney Isles, off
the north eastern tip of Scotland.*

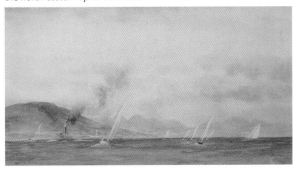

**William Lionel Wyllie, RA, RI, RE**
British (1851–1931)
A yacht race on the Clyde
Signed, watercolour
7 x 12¾in (18 x 32.5cm)
**£3,000–3,250 / $4,400–4,700** 🔨 **P(S)**

**John Worsley**
British (1919–2000)
Indian Ocean Convoy, 1942
Signed and dated 1942, oil on board
28 x 36in (71 x 91.5cm)
**£1,150–1,350 / $1,700–2,000** 🔨 **P(S)**

*This convoy included HMS Devonshire, New Amsterdam, Aquitania,
Queen Mary and Isle de France.*

**William Lionel Wyllie, RA, RI, RE**
British (1851–1931)
Beached Boats
Signed and dated 1878, watercolour
3½ x 8in (9 x 20.5cm)
**£850–950 / $1,250–1,400** 🔨 **Bon**

*Wyllie worked as a roving visual journalist for the illustrated weekly
newspapers, notably The Graphic and the Illustrated London News.
He exhibited at all the leading London exhibition venues including the
Royal Academy. He was a prolific artist and author, and his work is
represented in many public and private collections. The remnants of
his work was acquired in 1931 by the National Maritime
Museum, Greenwich.*

**William Lionel Wyllie, RA, RI, RE**
British (1851–1931)
Sailing Ship in the Medway
Watercolour
7½ x 20½in (19 x 52cm)
**£3,250–3,750 / $4,700–5,400** ⊞ **WrG**

# John & Paul Nash

Brothers John and Paul Nash were artists but it was Paul who became one of Britain's most influential landscape artists. His arresting and sometimes bleak views of the English countryside set him apart from the typical 'chocolate box' school of British landscape artists. He shows us a country-side full of energy rather than the quiet and dreamy place many 19th-century artists painted.

During the Great War he served with the Artists Rifles. He signed up in 1914 and was made a lieutenant in 1916, and fought near Ypres. An accident led to his repatriation in 1917 and he settled down to paint, from memory and the sketches he had made. It was his show 'Ypres Salient', showing war in an original and powerful light that led to his appointment as Official War Artist in 1917. As a middle-aged man he was again an Official War Artist during WWII. Paul Nash also taught photography and illustrated and edited books – the Shell Guide to Dorset being one of the most well known. John Nash had no intention of becoming a professional artist and started his career as a journalist. However, Paul believed in his talent as an artist and encouraged him to take up painting as a career. John also served in the Artist Rifles and became an Official War Artist in 1918. His landcapes are less dramatic than Paul's, and he also enjoyed drawing humorous subjects and still lives of flowers. John was also a teacher and taught at Ruskin School of Art and the Royal College of Art.

**John Nash, RA**
British (1893–1977)
Madame Pierre Oger
Signed, pencil and watercolour
15¾ x 10½in (40 x 26.5cm)
**£450–550 / $650–800** ⚒ P(Ba)

**John Nash, RA**
British (1893–1977)
Trees
Signed and dated 1961, oil on canvas laid on board
22 x 18in (56 x 45.5cm)
**£2,200–2,600 / $3,200–3,800** ⚒ Bon

**John Nash, RA**
British (1893–1977)
Iris Stylosa
Signed, inscribed and dated 1957, pencil with watercolour and crayon
13¾ x 12½in (35 x 32cm)
**£950–1,100 / $1,400–1,600** ⚒ P(Ba)

**Paul Nash**
British (1889–1946)
German Double Pill Box, Gheluvelt
Signed and dated 1918, lithograph on thin laid paper, titled and numbered 25 in pencil
18¼ x 14in (46.5 x 35.5cm)
**£1,300–1,500 / $2,000–2,300** ⚒ P

◀ **Paul Nash**
British (1889–1946)
Landscape Under Snow (Study 1)
Dated 1945, watercolour, pen, ink and pencil
11 x 15¼in (28 x 38.5cm)
**£3,800–4,500 / $5,500–6,500** ⚒ P

**Frances E. Nesbitt**
British (1864–1934)
Place des Cordeliers, Dinan, France
Signed, watercolour
13½ x 10in (34.5 x 25.5cm)
**£580–680 / $850–1,000** ⊞ LH

**Kate Nessler**
American (20thC)
Snowdrops and Miniature Iris
Watercolour and bodycolour on vellum
9½ x 11in (24 x 28cm)
**£5,000–5,500 / $7,250–8,000** ⊞ PWG

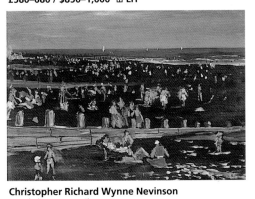

**Christopher Richard Wynne Nevinson**
British (1889–1946)
The Beach
Signed, oil on panel
12 x 16in (30.5 x 40.5cm)
**£2,800–3,200 / $4,000–4,650** ⚒ P

**Mary Newcomb**
British (b1922)
The Dahlia Show
Signed and dated 1985, oil on board
21 x 32in (53.5 x 81.5cm)
**£13,000–15,000 / $19,900–22,500** ⚒ P

◄ **Mary Newcomb**
British (b1922)
Sheep in the Frost
Signed and dated 1977, oil on board
7 x 14¼in (18 x 36cm)
**£11,500–13,500 / $16,750–19,500** ⚒ P

**Algernon Newton, RA**
British (1880–1968)
Winter Sunset, Beckhole, Yorkshire
Signed and dated 1945, oil on canvas
24 x 35¾in (61 x 91cm)
**£7,500–9,000 / $11,000–13,000** ⚒ S(O)

**Andrew Nicholl, RHA**
British (1804–86)
The Lower Lake Killarney
Signed and inscribed, watercolour with scratching out
13 x 20in (33 x 51cm)
**£2,000–2,300 / $3,000–3,400** ⚒ B(L)

◀ **Bertram Nicholls**
British (1883–1974)
View from the Piazza, Malcesine
Signed and dated 1929, oil on canvas
16 x 32in (41 x 81.5cm)
**£1,800–2,200 / $2,600–3,200** ⚒ P

**Charles Wynne Nicholls, RHA**
Irish (1831–1903)
The Light of the Harem
Signed, oil on canvas
30 x 24¾in (77 x 63cm)
**£24,000–28,000 / $35,000–40,000** ⚒ P

◀ **Dale Nicholls**
American (1904–98)
Evening in Antigua
Signed, inscribed and dated 1969, oil on canvas
20 x 24in (51 x 61cm)
**£800–1,000 / $1,200–1,500** ⚒ SLN

# The Nicholson Family

The Nicholsons can truly be called a painting dynasty. Founded by Victorian painter William, his son Ben (1894–1982) married painter Winifred Roberts (1893–1981) who always worked under the name of Nicholson although they were divorced for many years. Kate (b1929) was their only daughter. Ben Nicholson then married sculptress Barbara Hepworth (1903–75) and produced two painter children, Simon and Rachel.

Ben lived all over the world including St Ives in Cornwall but he spent the latter part of his life in Switzerland. Ben's work covers a huge stylistic spectrum from the figurative to the abstract. His influences ranged from näive artist Alfred Wallis to Picasso and abstract artist, Piet Mondrian (1872–1944).

Winifred on the other hand, lived most of her life in Bankshead, Cumbria, and the majority of her work is still lifes and landscapes in both watercolour and oil. Recently a new record for the artist was set when Window Still Life with Conch Shell was sold for £52,000 ($75,000) followed by the sale of her portrait of Ben for £100,000 ($145,000).

Kate Nicholson was born at Bankshead, Cumbria and like her mother, specialized in still lifes and flower pieces. She moved to St Ives in the 1960s but regularly visited Greece and Cumbria to paint.

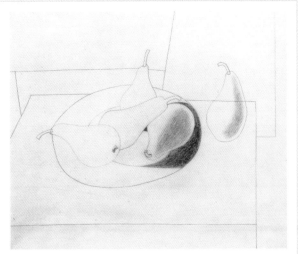

**Ben Nicholson, OM**
British (1894–1982)
1948 (Plate of Pears)
Signed and dated Sept 48, pencil
12¼ x 14¾in (31 x 37.5cm)
**£12,000–14,000 / $17,400–20,000**  ⚒ S

**Ben Nicholson, OM**
British (1894–1982)
Banks Head, 1925
Signed, oil on canvas
22 x 24in (56 x 61cm)
**£60,000–70,000 / $87,000–102,000**  ⚒ P

**Kate Nicholson**
British (b1929)
Solitude
Signed and dated 1956, oil on canvas
16 x 29in (41 x 74cm)
**£8,500–9,000 / $12,300–13,000**  ⊞ NZ

▶ **Winifred Nicholson**
British (1893–1981)
Periwinkles
Watercolour
21 x 15in
(53.5 x 38cm)
**£34,000–38,000
$50,000–55,000**
⚒ NZ

◀ **Winifred Nicholson**
British (1893–1981)
Children's Bunches
Oil on board
18 x 27¾in
(45.5 x 70.5cm)
**£24,000–28,000
$35,000–40,500**
⚒ P

**Basil J. Nightingale**
British (1864–1940)
A Water Jumper
Signed and dated 1905, pastel
14½ x 21½in (37 x 54.5cm)
**£650–750 / $950–1,100** ⚒ G(L)

**John Bates Noel**
British (fl1893–1909)
The Passing of Summer
Oil on canvas
18 x 24in (45.5 x 61cm)
**£3,750–4,250 / $5,500–6,000** ⊞ Dr

**Lesley Ninnes**
British (20thC)
Cornish Palm
Signed and dated, oil on canvas board
29¼ x 34¼in (74.5 x 87cm)
**£450–550 / $650–800** ⚒ Stl

**Sidney Nolan**
Australian (1917–92)
Bow Tie and Broom Moustache
Signed and dated 1949, ripolin and ink on glass
12¼ x 10in (31 x 25.5cm)
**£8,000–9,000 / $11,500–13,000** ⚒ P(Sy)

◀ **Sidney Nolan**
Australian (1917–92)
A Man Feeding a Horse
Oil on paper
20 x 24¾in (51 x 63cm)
**£5,750–7,000 / £8,500–10,000** ⚒ S

**G. Parsons Norman**
British (1840–1914)
Broadland scene with fisherman and rowing boat
Signed, watercolour
9 x 12in (23 x 30.5cm)
**£100–125 / $145–180** ⚘ **GAK**

◄ **Elizabeth Nourse**
American (1859–1938)
At the Oasis, Algers
Signed, watercolour laid down on board
19¼ x 13½in (49 x 34.5cm)
**£2,200–2,600 / $3,200–3,800** ⚘ **SHN**

**Willian Edward Norton**
American (1843–1916)
Dieppe Lighthouse
Signed, oil on canvas
26 x 40in (66 x 101.5cm)
**£2,200–2,600**
**$3,200–3,800** ⚘ **JAA**

**Friis Nyboe**
Danish (1869–1929)
Woman in an Interior
Signed, oil on canvas
23 x 24in
(58.5 x 61cm)
**£600–700**
**$870–1,000** ⚘ **TREA**

## National Museum of Fine Art

■ Solvgade 48–50, 1307 Copenhagen, Denmark, www.aok.dk

■ The art collections date back to the 16th century when the Danish royal family began to build up their own private collection. The current museum was built and opened in 1896 and houses 8,000 paintings and sculptures covering a wide range of Danish and International art from the 16th century to the present day.

◄ **Edgar Nye**
American (1879–1943)
Rural Landscape
A pair, signed, oil on board and oil on canvas
20 x 24in (51 x 61cm)
**£350–400**
**$500–600** ⚘ **SLN**

# Nudes

The Victorians loved nudes. They may have covered up their piano legs and ankles and deleted references to sex in literature but they had a healthy appetite for the naked body in art. Queen Victoria and Prince Albert loved to give each other little nude drawings, indulging their fantasies by putting the nude in a legendary or classical setting. One wonders whether it was strictly true to the legend to have quite so many females naked or clad only in diaphanous veils. A recent exhibition celebrating The Victorian Nude at the Tate Britain has made us appreciate the nude again.

The English may have been coy about the naked body in 19th century but life drawing classes flourished, whereas in continental Europe it was difficult to find models who would pose naked. Young girls came from Italy to work in England and were the most sought after models.

The most well known Victorian painter of nudes was William Etty who was patronized by the new wealthy industrialists, such as soap magnate Lord Leverhulme, who wanted to commission English painters to depict romantic and classical scenes. Lord Leighton was such an esteemed painter of scenes from legend and mythology, that he was knighted. Both Etty and Leighton were influenced by the arrival of the Elgin Marbles at the British Museum. Their depictions of women are not really sensuous figures in the manner of François Boucher (1703–70), but smooth and as pale as marble.

Henry Scott Tuke was a painter collected by the Victorian gay market. He lived in Cornwall and was primarily a marine painter. He not only painted deck hands and sailors but also naked boys. In accordance with the spirit of the age they are shown having no body hair or genitalia – the Renaissance Italians at least gave them their 'private parts'. Tuke got around Victorian prudery and homosexual prejudice by taking the healthy living angle. Although one of the boys in The Sunbathers looks post-coital ostensibly they are just enjoying a healthy swim – his boys are always bathing outdoors. Tuke is always collectable although pictures of clothed boys fetch more than naked ones. The record for a Tuke is £200,000 ($300,000).

Ethel Walker was really a portrait painter but was commissioned to paint a series of decorative panels, of which the series of imagined and creation myths Decoration: Evening, is part.

French Impressionists, particularly Renoir and Cézanne celebrated the body as a fleshy physical presence rather than an as something in a mythological vision. Their influence was immense on British, Australian and North American artists who all studied, and were influenced by, French art at the beginning of 20th century. Australian Janet Cumbrae Stewart portrays her nudes in a more naturalistic view. Cumbrae Stewart is one of the few women painting female nudes and critics have suggested that she concentrated on the nude to express female sexuality although she looked no further than the traditional image. Her nudes are both sexual and innocent at the same time.

However in Britain the legacy of Victorian morals were hard to throw off and many painters were not so at ease with the nude as early 20th-century French artists. Compare Henri Matisse with Harold Knight who are roughly contemporary; Harold Knight's nudes often look as if they long to put their clothes back on whereas Matisse's figures have no problem with being naked. Laura Knight's nudes are happier than her husband's.

Many 20th-century European and American artists took nude images from folk art. We know Picasso borrowed from ancient cultures. Mexican-born Diego Rivera (1886–1957) met Picasso and studied Cézanne, and was also interested in pre-Columbian art from South America.

**Janet Agnes Cumbrae-Stewart**
Australian (1883–1960)
Study of a Female Nude
Signed, pastel
19¾ x 29½in (50 x 75cm)
**£8,500–10,000 / $12,300–14,500** 🔨 S

**Further information**
Artists mentioned in the introduction above may have works appearing elsewhere in this Guide. Consult the index for page numbers.

▶ **William Etty, RA**
British (1787–1849)
The Rose of Love
Inscribed, oil on panel
20 x 13¾in (51 x 35cm)
**£36,000–43,000**
**$52,000–62,000** 🔨 S

**William Etty, RA**
British (1787–1849)
The Bather
Oil on board
9½ x 18½in (24 x 47cm)
**£11,500–13,500 / $16,700–19,500** ⚒ S

**Harold Knight, RA**
British (1874–1961)
The Maiden
Signed, oil on canvas
30¾ x 25in (78 x 63.5cm)
**£3,600–4,300 / $5,200–6,200** ⚒ B

**Henry Scott Tuke, RA**
British (1858–1929)
The Sunbathers
Signed, oil on canvas
21½ x 25¼in (55 x 64cm)
**£30,000–36,000 / $43,500–52,000** ⚒ P

**Attributed to Frederic Lord Leighton, PRA**
British (1830–96)
The Bather
Oil on canvas
30 x 17in (76 x 43cm)
**£24,000–28,000 / $35,000–40,000** ⚒ S

*The style of* The Bather *and the nature of its
composition suggest that, if painted by Lord
Leighton, it dates from the mid-1850s. This is
the period of Leighton's transformation from
a student, working in a predominantly
German idiom, to a fully-fledged artist
who had absorbed the influences of
contemporary Italian and French schools.
During this period Leighton becomes
increasingly interested in painting the nude
which foreshadows the great paintings of
the 1860s,* Salome, Venus Disrobing *or*
Actaea. *The model herself in the* The Bather,
*with her carefully coiled hair, also reflects
contemporary fashion of the mid-1850s.*

**Diego Rivera**
Mexican (1886–1957)
Nude with Long Hair
Signed and numbered 50/100, lithograph
printed on Umbria Italia wove paper
16½ x 9½in (42 x 24cm)
**£7,200–8,600 / $10,500–12,500** ⚒ S(NY)

▶ **Ethel Walker, ARA**
British (1861–1951)
Decoration: Evening
74 x 50in (188 x 127cm)
**£22,000–26,500 / $32,000–38,000** ⚒ PN

▶ **Séamus Ó Colmáin**
Irish (1925–90)
Shadows
Oil on canvas board
27 x 36in
(68.5 x 91.5cm)
**£1,200–1,500**
**$1,750–2,200** ⚒ WA

◀ **Octavius Oakley, RWS**
British (1800–67)
Taking Shelter
Watercolour
22 x 16½in
(56 x 42cm)
**£820–1,000**
**$1,200–1,500**
⚒ Bea(E)

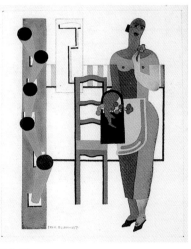

**Helen O'Hara**
Irish (fl1881–1908)
Waves breaking, with a view of cliffs in distance
Signed, watercolour
14 x 20in (36 x 51cm)
**£600–700 / $870–1,000** ⚒ WA

**John O'Connell**
British (b1935)
Rough Sea, Cill Rialaig, County Kerry
Signed, oil on panel
24 x 30in (61 x 76cm)
**£2,750–3,250 / $4,000–4,700** ⊞ WrG
*Born in Londonderry, John studied at St Mary's College, Belfast between 1953 and 1957. He went on to teach at Our Lady and St Patrick's College, Belfast. Since 1975, he has shown with the Royal Ulster Academy and from 1983, with the Royal Hibernian Academy. He has exhibited extensively including many one-man shows in Ireland and his work is held in numerous private collections worldwide.*

▶ **Claes Oldenburg**
Swedish (b1929)
Study For Standing Mitt
Signed in pen and numbered 47/50,
offset lithograph on Hammermille paper
28 x 21½in (71 x 54.5cm)
**£500–600 / $720–870** ⚒ BUK

**Erik Olson**
Swedish (1901–86)
Flower Girl
Signed and dated 1927, gouache
9¾ x 8in (25 x 20.5cm)
**£3,000–3,500 / $4,400–5,000** ⚒ SK

**Jane O'Malley**
Irish (b1944)
La Coruna from Marquez, Lanzarote
Signed and dated 1988, watercolour, gouache and ink
5 x 7in (12.5 x 18cm)
**£250–300 / $360–440** ↗ **WA**

**Sandra Oppegard**
American (b1941)
Going to the Track, Keeneland (Study 1)
Signed, watercolour on paper
7½ x 11in (19 x 28cm)
**£1,200–1,400 / $1,750–2,000** ↗ **S(NY)**

▶ **For further information**
see Irish Art
(pages 72–75)

◀ **James Orr**
British (b1931)
The Tent
Acrylic on board
20 x 22in
(51 x 56cm)
**£1,550–1,850**
**$2,200–2,600**
⊞ **WrG**

**Fergus O'Ryan, RHA, ANCA, ATC**
Irish (1911–89)
Annamoe Bridge, Autumn
Signed, oil on board
20 x 22¾in (51 x 58cm)
**£1,600–2,000 / $2,300–3,000** ↗ **JAd**

**Denis Osborne, ARUA**
British (b1919)
Canadian Village
Signed, watercolour
12 x 20in (30.5 x 51cm)
**£325–375 / $470–570** ↗ **WA**

*Denis Osborne was born in Portsmouth but emigrated to Canada in
1952. He was based at St Catherine's in Ontario where he taught art
and exhibited with the Ontario Society of Artists. In 1959 he moved
to Northern Ireland and now lives at Newtownards. His work regularly
appears at the Royal Ulster Academy.*

**Samuel W. Oscroft**
British (1834–1924)
Shepherd and sheep in a moorland lane
Signed and dated, watercolour
9½ x 13in (24 x 33cm)
**£350–450 / $500–650** ↗ **GAK**

# Outsider Art

The French writer and artist Jean Dubuffet (1901–85) championed Outsider Art or Art Brut. Writing in the 1940s, he contended that art by establishment artists with art school training was lifeless by virtue of the praise heaped upon it. He maintained that true art was to be found in unlikely places such as psychiatric hospitals and prisons, among people distanced from high culture by their lack of education, and in children whose art is uninhibited. The Russian-born painter and writer on art, Wassily Kandinsky (1866–1944), found children's art inspiring and amassed a large collection. Americans Keith Haring (1958–90) and Jean Michael Basquiat (1960–88) also collaborated with children. If Dubuffet were alive today he would be dismayed to see Outsider Art becoming part of the art establishment with an annual Outsider Art Fair in New York.

Most Outsider Artists cannot afford expensive oil paints and canvas, much of their work is in pencil or crayon on scraps of paper. Many of their subjects are expressions of personal feelings.

British-born outsider artist Scottie Wilson (1888–1990) worked as a scrap dealer in Canada and produced intricate crayon and watercolour drawings of an inner world populated by trees, animals and people enacting battles between good and evil.

Madge Gill produced thousands of intricate drawings, many of women with flowing hair, which were created by candlelight. They reflect her troubled life – the death of a son and the birth of a stillborn daughter, as well as her own partial blindness.

Outsider artists have always achieved greater respect in the United States than in Britain. The American Visionary Museum in Baltimore is devoted entirely to Outsiders, no substantial collection exists in a British museum. This of course can make some of the artist's work self conscious because once discovered they become aware that they are 'artists'.

That cannot be said of Malcolm McKesson, a recluse who although married for a short time, never had a sexual relationship. His work only came to public attention in his eightieth year.

Henry Darger (1892–1973) spent some of his childhood years in a psychiatric institution. Devastated at the death of his sister, he tried unsuccessfully to adopt a child. He produced a huge volume of work featuring a fantasy world ruled by children, which only came to light shortly before his death.

Dwight Mackintosh was considered to be mentally retarded and did not see himself as an artist. He started to draw in 1978 having spent 56 years in institutions. He became obsessed by drawing, often falling asleep during his work and on waking he would just continue to draw. However, once he had finished a picture he lost interest in it. His main subjects were male figures, although animals and methods of transport have been spotted in his work. Whereas Ody Saban, born nearly fifty years later in 1906, is articulate about her talent. 'My art is magic art, I am a shaman, a seer', she has said. Albert Louden (b1942) has been rejected by some Outsider purists because he nursed artistic ambition and had the temerity to approach an art dealer rather than wait 'to be discovered'.

Outsider Art has become extremely fashionable in recent years, collected by celebrities so expect to see prices rise for the big names mentioned here. British art dealer Henry Boxer puts the interest down to 'a reaction against the hype surrounding today's media manipulative artists who belong to the elite art world'.

**Thornton Dial**
American (b1928)
Nude
Signed, charcoal and watercolour on paper
30 x 22in (76 x 56cm)
**£1,700–1,800**
**$2450–2,600** ⚡KMS

**Rev Howard Finster**
American (b1916)
Franklin D Roosevelt
Paint on panel
10¼ x 9¼in (26 x 23.5cm)
**£100–120 / $145–175** ⚡KMS

**Madge Gill**
British (1882–1961)
Sarah Bernhardt
Pen and ink
14 x 10in (35.5 x 25.5cm)
**£1,800–2,000 / $2,500–3,000** ⊞ BOX

◄ **Keith Haring and Andy Warhol**
American (1958–90 and 1928–87)
Andy Mouse
Four, signed by both artists, dated 1986 and numbered 24/30, screenprint in colours
38in (96.5cm) square
**£36,000–43,000**
**$52,000–62,000** ⚒ S(NY)

► **Bessie Harvey**
American (b1929)
Bird of Paradise
Markers on paper
18 x12in (45.5 x 30.5cm)
**£155–170 / $225–250** ⚒ KMS

**Miller's is a price GUIDE not a price LIST**

**Clementine Hunter**
American (1885–1988)
Untitled
Paint on panel
16 x 24in (40.5 x 61cm)
**£1,800–2,000 / $2,600–3,000** ⚒ KMS

*Born at Hidden Hill Plantation she is reported to have begun her career in her 50s with discarded paints and brushes left by a visitor to the Melrose Plantation where she worked for almost 75 years.*

**Matt Lamb**
American (b1932)
Untitled
Oil on canvas
36in square (91.5cm)
**£3,000–3,500 / $4,500–5,000** ⊞ MLM

◄ **Albert Louden**
British (b1942)
Whistling in the Wind
Oil on canvas
135in (343cm) square
**£8,000–8,800**
**$11,600–13,000**
⊞ WHI

► **Dwight Mackintosh**
American (1906–99)
Untitled (Orange vehicle)
Pencil and tempera on paper
23 x 25in
(58.5 x 63.5cm)
**£5,000–5,500**
**$7,250–8,000** ⊞ RMG

◀ **Malcolm McKesson**
American (1909–99)
Croquet
Pen and ink
4 x 6in (10 x 15cm)
**£1,200–1,350 / $1,750–2,000 ⊞ BOX**

**Reginald Mitchell**
American (b1961)
French Quarter
Paint on Formica
15½ x 11½in (39.5 x 29cm)
**£155–170 / $225–250 ↗ KMS**

**Ody Saban**
Turkish (b1953)
Kiss Me
Watercolour
22 x 36in (56 x 91.5cm)
**£1,800–2,000 / $2,500–3,000 ⊞ BOX**

**Reverend B.F. Perkins**
American (1904–93)
10 Commandments For Successful Daily Living
Signed, paint on canvas
41 x 34in (104 x 86.5cm)
**£700–750 / $1,000–1,100 ↗ KMS**

*Reverend Benjamin Perkins served in the Marine Corps from
1921 to 1925 and became a minister in 1940. He often
illustrated stories from the Bible and frequently included the
American flag and the Statue of Liberty.*

▶ **Bernice Sims**
American (b1926)
First St John Baptist Church
Signed, paint on canvas
18 x 24in (45.5 x 61cm)
**£240–250 / $350–360 ↗ KMS**

*Bernice Sims started painting after a visit to Mose Tolliver's
house in Alabama. Churches are often a backdrop in many
of her works, but she also depicts the daily routine of
southern life and scenes of playgrounds and children.*

**Jimmy Lee Sudduth**
American (b1910)
Untitled
Paint on canvas
30 x 20in (76 x 51cm)
**£800–850**
**$1,150–1,250 ↗ KMS**

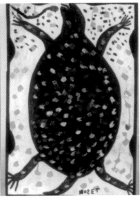

**Mose Tolliver**
American (b c1920)
Turtle
Signed paint on panel
30 x 20½in (76 x 52cm)
**£100–110 / $150–160** ⚒ **KMS**

*Mose Tolliver was born into a sharecropping family in rural Alabama around 1920 and is the youngest of twelve children. He was injured while working when a crate of marble fell on him. During a period of depression he was encouraged to take up painting by his former boss. His subject matter covers a wide range and he favours single images, painting on many different surfaces including cardboard, scraps of wood, metal trays and old furniture. He attaches tab openers from aluminium cans to the backs of his paintings as hangers.*

**Mose Tolliver**
American (b c1920)
Loving Woman Mary Ann
Signed, paint on canvas
32 x 26in (81.5 x 66cm)
**£190–200 / $275–320** ⚒ **KMS**

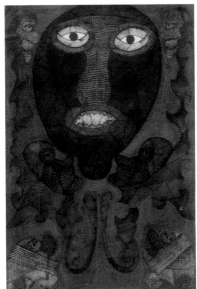

**Scottie Wilson**
British (1888–1972)
Untitled
Signed, ink and crayon
22 x 10in (56 x 25.5cm)
**£3,500–4,000 / $5,000–5,800** ⊞ **BOX**

◄ **Scottie Wilson**
British (1888–1972)
Untitled
Signed, ink and crayon
15 x 10in (38 x 25.5cm)
**£2,400–2,650 / $3,500–3,800** ⊞ **BOX**

**Scottie Wilson**
British (1888–1972)
Masquerade
Signed, Ink and crayon
11 x 7in (28 x 18m)
**£2,500–2,750**
**$3,600–4,000** ⊞ **BOX**

▶ **Purvis Young**
American (b1943)
Horses in Register
Mixed media on wood
96 x 34in (244 x 86.5cm)
**£4,000–4,500 / $5,800–6,500** ⊞ **RMG**

**Harry Sutton Palmer, RI, RBA**
British (1854–1933)
Wargrave on Thames
Signed and dated
1878, watercolour
12 x 19½in
(30.5 x 49.5cm)
£3,000–3,300
$4,400–4,800 ⚒ Bon

▶ **Morris Hall
Pancoast**
American
(1877–1963)
Harbour Scene
Signed, oil on masonite
12 x 16in
(30.5 x 40.5cm)
£2,400–3,000
$3,500–4,400
⚒ SHN

**E. Pale**
French (20thC)
Cottages by a River
Signed, oil on canvas
38 x 27in (96.5 x 68.5cm)
£500–550 / $720–800 ⚒ TREA

# John Anthony Park (1880–1962)

Originally from Lancashire, Park moved to St Ives at the age of 18 and became probably the best known of the early St Ives painters. He studied under Julian Olsson who encouraged him to study in Paris. From 1905 he attended the Atelier Colarossi where he was a contemporary of Modigliani.

Strongly influenced by the French Impressionists, Park's work is always brightly coloured and spontaneous. He exhibited coastal and fishing scenes at the Royal Academy, the Paris Salon and St·Ives Society of Artists. His work is held in the public collections of Manchester City Art Gallery, Salford Art Gallery and the Tate.

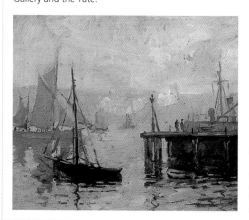

◀ **John Anthony
Park, ROI, RBA**
British (1880–1962)
Shipping by a jetty,
a bay beyond
Signed and
indistinctly dated,
oil on canvas board
12½ x 16¼in
(32 x 41cm)
£4,000–4,400
$5,800–6,500
⚒ P(NW)

**John Anthony Park,
ROI, RBA**
British (1880–1962)
St Ives Harbour
Signed, oil on panel
16in (40.5cm) square
£4,200–4,600
$6,000–6,600 ⚒ P

**Alfred William Parsons, RA, RI**
British (1847–1920)
The Meeting of the Waters
Signed, oil on canvas
14½ x 21½in (37 x 54.5cm)
£5,750–6,200 / $8,400–9,000 ⊞ Bne

**Henry Hillier Parker**
British (1858–1930)
Cattle Watering on a Riverbank
Signed, oil on canvas
24 x 40in (61 x 101.5cm)
£4,600–5,200 / $6,500–7,500 🗡 Bon

▶ **Frederick Henry Partridge**
British (fl.1919)
Two views at Blakeney Point
A pair, signed and dated, watercolour
14 x 50in (35.5 x 127cm)
£2,000–2,400 / $3,000–3,500 🗡 GAK

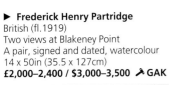

◀ **Frederick Henry Partridge**
British (fl.1919)
Sea Lavender at Blakeney Creek
Signed and dated 1919, watercolour
19 x 28in (48.5 x 71cm)
£850–1,000 / $1,250–1,500 🗡 GAK

**Charles Henry Passey**
British (fl1870–85)
The Corn Harvest
Signed and dated 1876, oil
29½ x 49½in (75 x 125.5cm)
£920–980 / $1,325–1,400 🗡 Bea(E)

◀ **Frank Paton**
British (1865–1909)
The Recital, three kittens
listening to a canary
Signed and dated 1893,
oil on canvas
17 x 21in (43 x 53.5cm)
£10,500–12,500
$15,250–18,250 🗡 Bon

**Cats**

Cat pictures are internationally popular and can command very impressive prices. Many of the artists and buyers are women.

**Léon du Paty**
French (19thC)
Bringing in Supplies
Signed, oil on panel
7½ x 9¾in (19 x 25cm)
**£1,000–1,200 / $1,500–1,750** 🔨 Bon

**Joseph Paul**
British (1804–87)
A river scene with thatched cottage
Oil
10½ x 14in (26.5 x 35.5cm)
**£500–600 / $720–870** 🔨 GAK

**Vladimir Pavlosky**
Russian/American (1884–1944)
Mending the Nets
Signed, oil on canvas,
28 x 34½in (71 x 88.5cm)
**£6,000–7,000 / $8,700–10,200** 🔨 SK

**Vladimir Pavlosky**
Russian/American (1884–1944)
Sunny mornings on the harbour
Signed and dated 1930, watercolour on paper
16¼ x 21½in (41.5 x 54.5cm)
**£950–1,200 / $1,400–1,750** 🔨 SK

▶ **Charles Johnson Payne (Snaffles)**
British (1884–1967)
The Rivals
Signed, pencil and watercolour heightened
with white
10¾ x 15in (27.5 x 38cm)
**£2,800 / $4,000** 🔨 B(WM)

*Charlie Johnson Payne was born in
Leamington Spa, Warwickshire, the fourth of
eight children. His interest in horses and the
military was influenced by childhood
memories of the parades through Warwick
of the Warwickshire Yeomanry Cavalry, and
stories of the Crimean War told to him by a
great uncle.*

**Edgar Payne**
American (1883–1947)
Sierra Landscape
Signed, oil on masonite
14 x 18in (35.5 x 45.5cm)
**£6,000–6,500 / $8,700–9,400** ↗ **TREA**

*Edgar Payne first arrived in California in 1909, eventually establishing a home and studio in Laguna Beach in 1918. He was a member of the Laguna Beach Art Association, California Art Club, Ten painters of Los Angeles, Chicago Society of Artists and the Salmagundi Club. Payne was known for his scenes of the Sierra Nevada.*

**William Payne**
British (1760–1830)
Crossing a West Country Bridge
Signed, watercolour
8 x 11½in (20.5 x 29cm)
**£2,000–2,200 / $3,000–3,200** ⊞ **BG**

**Philip Pearlstein**
American (b1924)
Halloween
Signed, oil on canvas
20 x 24in (51 x 61cm)
**£2,000–2,200 / $3,000–3,200** ↗ **NOA**

**Eugène Pechaubes**
French (1890–1967)
Racing at Longchamp; Racing at Auteuil
A pair, signed and titled, oil on canvas
17¾ x 21½in (45 x 54.5cm)
**£800–1,000 / $1,200–1,500** ↗ **B**

◄ **Fred Penney**
American (1900–88)
Western Scene
Signed, oil on board
26 x 34in (66 x 86.5cm)
**£380–450 / $550–650** ↗ **TREA**

*Fred Penney studied at the Art Insitute of Chicago before moving to Los Angeles. He spent the greater part of 30 years painting the Coachella Valley near Palm Springs. He exhibited at the California Art Club and the California Watercolour Society.*

## Louvre Museum

■ 36 Quai du Louvre, 75058 Paris, www.louvre.fr

■ Divided into seven departments, the Louvre Museum houses more than 6,000 European paintings dating from the end of the 13th century to the mid-19th century.

**Herbert Sidney Percy**
British (fl1880–1903)
At Porlock Weir, Somerset
Signed, oil on canvas
11 x 17in (28 x 43cm)
**£3,000–3,500 / $4,400–5,000** ⊞ Ben

**Arthur Perigal Jnr**
British (1816–84)
The Grand Canal, Venice, looking towards Sante Maria Della Salute
Signed, inscribed and dated 1872, oil
28 x 44½in (71 x 112.5cm)
**£6,400–7,700 / $9,300–11,300** ⚒ AH

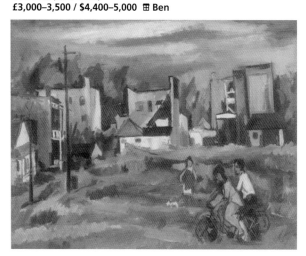

◄ **Frank Perri**
American (fl.1940–45)
Chicago Scene
Oil on canvas
24 x 30in (61 x 76cm)
**£560–600**
**$800–1,300** ⚒ TREA

*Frank Perri emigrated from Italy to Chicago c1930. He exhibited at the Carnegie Insitute of Art and the Art Institute of Chicago and was President of the Oak Park Artists League. He travelled to Mexico in the late 1930s. He specialized in figurative works and urban scenes of Chicago.*

**John W. Ross Perrin**
British (19thC)
Roses in Vase
Signed, oil
20½ x 14in (52 x 35.5cm)
**£670–800**
**$1,000–1,150** ⊞ LH

**Jane Peterson**
American (1876–1965)
Central Florida Scene
Signed, watercolour
14 x 21½in (35.5 x 54.5cm)
**£2,800–3,000 / $4,000–4,500** ⚒ SHN

**William Pettingale**
British (19thC)
Near Mickleover
Oil
12 x 18in (30.5 x 45.5cm)
**£1,275–1,400 / $1,800–2,000** ⊞ DR

**Glyn Philpot, RA**
British (1884–1937)
Portrait of Dorothy Warrren
Oil on canvas
21 x 17in (53.5 x 43cm)
**£2,000–3,000**
**$3,000–4,500** ⚒ P

**Francis Picabia**
French (1878–1953)
At the Park Bench
Signed, pen and ink
11¾ x 9in (30 x 23cm)
**£1,000–1,200**
**$1,500–1,750** ⚒ BUK

▶ **Pablo Picasso**
Spanish (1881–1973)
Original etching
Signed, limited
edition of 303
14½ x 11¾in (37 x 30cm)
**£12,000–14,000**
**$17,500–20,000**
⚒ WO

◀ **Franz Xavier
Pieler**
Austrian (1879–1952)
A Still Life of Flowers
in Bowl
Signed, oil on board
11¾ x 10in
(30 x 25.5cm)
**£600–700**
**$870–1,000**
⚒ P(Ba)

**William Henry Pike, RBA**
British (1846–1908)
Windmill Park, Tamerton Foliot, Devon
Signed, oil on board
10 x 16in (25.5 x 40.5cm)
**£2,000–2,200 / $3,000–3,200** ⊞ JC
*William Henry Pike became a member of the Royal Society of British
Artists in 1889 and exhibited regularly at leading London galleries.
His work may be found at the British Museum and the Royal Albert
Museum, Exeter.*

# John Piper (1903–92)

It was not until the death of his father in 1926 that John Piper took up the study of art, firstly at the Richmond School of Art and then at the Royal College of Art. From 1928 to 1933 he was an art critic for *The Listener* and was among the first to recognize such contemporaries as William Coldstream, Ivon Hitchens and Ceri Richards. By the mid-1930s he was one of the leading British abstract artists but by the end of the decade had become disillusioned with non-representational art and reverted to naturalism. He concentrated on landscape and architectural views and then became an Official War Artist, painting bomb-damaged buildings. He published a best-selling monograph *English Romantic Artists*, and illustrated and wrote many of Shell's Guidebooks to Great Britain. Piper also worked as a stage designer and designer of stained glass (notably at Coventry Cathedral) and was also a prolific printmaker.

**John Piper, CH, LG**
British (1903–92)
Three Towers: Backwell; Leigh on Mendip; Weston Leyland
Three, titled, gouache, coloured chalk and pen and ink
24 x 10in (61 x 25.5cm)
**£10,000–12,000 / $14,500–17,500** ⚒ P

**John Piper, CH, LG**
British (1903–92)
St Kew, Cornwall
Signed, titled and dated October 1962, watercolour, bodycolour and black ink
14 x 20in (35.5 x 51cm)
**£12,000–13,200 / $17,500–19,000** ⊞ NZ

**John Piper, CH, LG**
British (1903–92)
Mont St Victoire
Signed, titled on verso, gouache, pen and ink
15 x 23in (38 x 58.5cm)
**£4,200–5,000 / $6,000–7,250** ⚒ P

**John Piper, CH, LG**
British (1903–92)
South Midlands Landscape
Pen brush, black ink, watercolour and bodycolour on paper
22 x 30in (56 x 76cm)
**£9,500–11,000** ⊞ MJFA

**John Piper, CH, LG**
British (1903–92)
Dryslwyn Castle
Watercolour
14 x 19in (35.5 x 48.5cm)
**£8,500–10,000 / $12,500–14,500** ⊞ P&H

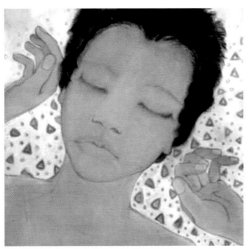

**Orovida Camille Pissarro**
British (1893–1968)
Samoan Boy
Watercolour on linen
10 x 10in (25 x 25cm)
**£6,000–6,500**
**$8,700–9,400** ⊞ NZ

▶ **Roland Vivian Pitchforth**
British (1895–1982)
Untitled coastal scenes
Four, signed, watercolours
17½ x 23in (44.5 x 59cm)
**£1,880–2,000**
**$2,700–3,000** ⚒ S(O)

▶ **Geoffrey Buckingham Pocock**
British (b1879)
Female Nude
Signed and dated 1900, oil
13½ x 8in (34.5 x 20.5cm)
**£1,150–1,350**
**$1,700–2,000** ⊞ LH

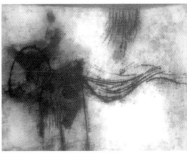

**Douglas Portway**
South African (1922–93)
Palma No. 5
Signed, dated 1961 and inscribed, oil on canvas
35 x 45½in (89 x 114.5cm)
**£2,300–2,500 / $3,400–3,600** ⚒ P

John Piper 'Dungeness Lighthouse' (detail) collage, ink and watercolour

# Moila Powell (1895–1994)

As is the fate of so many disciples of famous artists, Moila Powell's name will always be synonymous with that of her teacher, mentor and close friend, Norah McGuinness. Moila was the only pupil of Norah McGuinness and became a professional artist, establishing a long list of credits to her name with works exhibited in Yorkshire, London and Paris.

Powell was born in India and began her painting career as a miniaturist. She married Dr William Jackson Powell, a colonel in the Indian army and lived for periods in India, England and Ireland. It was in Nagpur, India in 1930 that she met Norah McGuinness, who was then escaping a broken marriage. Under Norah's tutelage, Moila adopted a more Expressionist style, delighting in freely mixing media – oil, gouache, wax crayon, pastel and watercolour. Returning to England Moila continued her studies with her teacher but she also travelled extensively, particularly to continental Europe, Canada and Australia, where she would spend six months at a time painting the landscape. She continued to paint well into her nineties, dying in her 100th year.

**Moila Powell**
British (1895–1994)
Norah McGuinness painting
Signed, gouache and coloured chalks on paper
14½ x 21in (37 x 53.5cm)
**£740–800 / $1,100–1,200** ⚒ WA

**Harold Septimus Power**
New Zealander (1878–1951)
The Harvest Team's Rest
Signed, oil on canvas
22 x 32in (56 x 81.5cm)
**£16,500–18,000 / $24,000–26,000** ⊞ CG

**Miller's is a price GUIDE not a price LIST**

**Levi Wells Prentice**
American (1851–1935)
Red Currants
Signed, oil on canvas
12½ x 10¼in (32 x 26cm)
**£25,000–30,000 / $36,000–44,000** ⚒ S(NY)

◄ **Harry Prest**
British (20thC)
North Cornish Coast
Signed, oil on board
16 x 30in (40.5 x 76cm)
**£400–450 / $580–650** ⊞ Stl

► **George Thompson Pritchard**
American (1878–1962)
Along the Coast
Signed, oil on canvas
25 x 30in (63.5 x 76cm)
**£520–625/ $750–900** ⚒ TREA

*George Thompson Pritchard was born in New Zealand and studied at the Auckland Academy of Art before travelling to Paris to attend the Academie Julian. He later worked in California and specialized in landscapes and marines executed in a tonalist aesthetic.*

◄ **Alfred Priest**
British (1874–1929)
Extensive seascape with sailing barge and distant view of shipping
Oil on canvas
19½ x 35in (49.5 x 89cm)
**£1,000–1,200 / $1,500–1,750** ⚒ GAK

**Aleksandr Pushnin**
Russian (1921–89)
Untitled
Pen and wash
22¾ x 17in (58 x 43cm)
**£950–1,150 / $1,400–1,700** ⊞ B&B

◄ **James Baker Pyne**
British (1800–70)
Distant View of Rouen
Signed, dated 1838 and inscribed, watercolour
7¾ x 12in (19.5 x 30.5cm)
**£900–1,000**
**$1,300–1,500**
⚒ S(O)

► **Alphonse Quizet**
French (1885–1955)
Vue de la Seine
Signed, oil on board
14¼ x 17½in (36 x 44.5cm)
**£5,200–6,200 / $7,500–9,000** ⚒ P

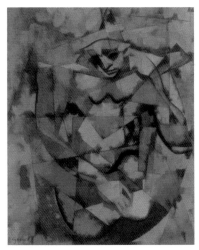

**S. Ravel**
American (20thC)
Cubist Figure
Signed, oil on canvas
36 x 29in (91.5 x 73.5cm)
**£600–700 / $870–1,000** ↗ **TREA**

**Igor Razdrogin**
Russian (b1923)
Untitled
Signed, pencil
26 x 17¾in (66 x 45cm)
**£850–1,000**
**$1,250–1,500** ↗ **B&B**

**Charles Reddington**
American (b1929)
A King's Ransom
Signed, dated 1994 and inscribed, oil on canvas
60 x 37in (152.5 x 137cm)
**£3,000–3,700 / $4,500–5,500** ↗ **P(Sy)**

*Born in Chicago Charles Reddington has been resident in Australia since 1996. He trained at the School of Art Institute of Chicago during the 1950s and moved to Australia in 1959, where he taught at the Royal Melbourne Institute of Technology. In 1960, he moved to Adelaide to set up a painting studio and consequently was appointed Lecturer of Painting at the South Australian School of Art, establishing a School of Contemporary Painting. He moved to Sydney in 1966 to establish an art studio but a year later was forced to return to the USA because of visa restrictions.*

*Between 1970 and 1992 Reddington taught as Professor at Indiana State University in Terre Haute, Indiana, in charge of graduate painting, and from 1992 to 2001 he took up Artist in Residency throughout Europe, Australia and the USA. Charles Reddington was appointed Professor Emeritus and Artist in Residence at the Art Museum of La Trobe University, Melbourne and now lives in New South Wales.*

**H. W. Reed**
British (19thC)
Landscape with figure, stream and cottage, near Wixford, Bideford on Avon
Signed, oil on canvas
19½ x 29½in (49.5 x 75cm)
**£450–550 / $650–750** ⊞ **RBB**

▶ **Isobelle Chestnut Reid**
Canadian (b1899)
A Woman in a Hat
Signed, oil on board
20 x 16in
(51 x 40.5cm)
**£700–800**
**$1,000–1,200**
↗ **WAD**

◀ **Leonard Reedy**
American
(1899–1956)
Indians outside a Teepee
Signed, watercolour
8¼ x 12in (21 x 30.5cm)
**£300–350**
**$440–500** ↗ **TREA**

**Robert Reid**
American (1862–1929)
New England Autumn Landscape with Church
Signed, oil on board
14 x 16in (35.5 x 40.5cm)
**£2,400–2,800 / $3,500–4,000** ↗ **NOA**

**Walter Newton Reinsel**
American (1905–79)
The Catch
Signed, oil on canvas
26 x 40in (66 x 101.5cm)
**£550–600 / $800–870** ↗ **TREA**

# Frederick Remington

Remington, the son of a newspaper publisher, was born in Canton, New York. He attended a Massachusetts military academy from 1876 to 1878, followed by the then newly-formed Yale University Art School in New Haven, Connecticut.

In 1883 he bought a sheep ranch in Kansas where he sketched horses, cavalrymen, cowboys and Indians. He sold the ranch in 1884 and established a studio in Kansas City, Missouri.

Remington returned to New York in 1885 and quickly became a successful illustrator. He began writing and illustrating his own books, giving eastern America what became the accepted version of the American West. In 1886 he studied at the Art Students League in New York City and began submitting his paintings to exhibitions. In 1895 Remington produced his first bronze sculpture, *The Bronco Buster*, which was followed by 24 other bronzes.

In 1905 Remington began to experiment with impressionism, but never really ceased to be a realist. During his lifetime he produced more than 2,750 paintings and drawings and 25 sculptures from which multiple casts were made, wrote eight books and numerous articles about the American West and served in the Spanish/American war as a war correspondent. His work is a valuable record of the now vanished Western frontier.

▶ **Frederick Remington**
American (1861–1908)
Mexican Labourer
Signed and dated 1889, watercolour, gouache and ink on paper
16¼ x 10in (41.5 x 25.5cm)
**£12,500–14,500 $18,000–21,000** ↗ **S(NY)**

◀ **A. Renoux**
French (20thC)
Paris Street Scene
Signed and dated 1952, oil on canvas
11 x 14in (28 x 35.5cm)
**£650–750 $900–1,100** ↗ **TREA**

**Oscar Ricciardi**
Italian (1864–1935)
The *Faraglioni*, Capri; Coastal Scene, Sorrento; Fishing Boats at Sea; A Beach Scene
Four, two signed, oil on panel
Two 5½ x 10in (13.5 x 25.5cm) and two 10¼ x 6in (26 x 15cm)
**£1,000–1,300 / $1,500–2,000** ↗ **Bon**

**Michael Richardson**
British (b1933)
Lane in Blossom
Signed, oil on panel
16 x 12in (40.5 x 30.5cm)
**£400–450 / $580–650 ⊞ Dr**

**Ray Richardson**
British (b1964)
The Italian Job
Original etching
4 x 11½in (10 x 29cm)
**£300–350**
**$450–500 ⊞ WO**

## Abbreviations

Letters after the artist's name denote that the artist has been awarded the membership of an artistic body. See page 233 for the explanation of abbreviated letters.

◀ **Thomas Miles Richardson, Snr**
British (1784–1848)
Bamburgh Castle
Signed and dated 1829, watercolour
10 x 14½in (25.5 x 36.5cm)
**£700–800**
**$1,000–1,150**
**⤴ S(O)**

◀ **Herbert Davis Richter, RI, RSW, ROI, RBA, RBc, PS**
British (1874–1955)
The Shimmer of Silver, (Polyanthus and Roses)
Signed, oil on canvas
20 x 24in (51 x 61cm)
**£6,000–7,000**
**$8,700–10,200 ⊞ JC**

*Herbert Davis Richter was born in Brighton, Sussex. He exhibited at the Royal Academy from 1906 and became a Member of the Royal Society of British Artists in 1910. Richter exhibited in the provinces as well as the leading London galleries, including one-man exhibitions at the St George's Gallery in 1923, and the Leicester Gallery in 1925.*

◀ **Philip Rickman**
British (1891–1982)
Garganeys rushing after Water Beetles
Signed and dated 1917, watercolour
14¼ x 12½in (36 x 54.5cm)
**£600–700**
**$870–1,000 ⤴ Bon**

**Claudio Rinaldi**
Italian (19thC)
Grandmother and Grandchildren
Signed, dated 1886 and inscribed, oil on canvas
31¾ x 23¾in (81 x 61.5cm)
**£2,800–3,400**
**$4,000–5,000 ⤴ SLN**

◀ **For further information**
see Irish Art (pages 72–75)

◀ **Elizabeth Rivers**
Irish (1903–64)
Sketch of Cows in Pasture, Aran
Oil on canvas board
10 x 14in (25 x 36cm)
**£700–800**
**$1,000–1,150** ⚷ WA

▶ **David Roberts**
British (1796–1864)
Rouen
Signed and dated
1858, watercolour
17 x 11in
(43 x 28cm)
**£500–550**
**$720–800** ⚷ GAK

◀ **James Roberts**
French (c1800–67)
The interior of a sitting room, possibly Paris
Signed and dated 1843, pencil and watercolour heightened with
bodycolour and gum arabic
10¾ x 14in (27.5 x 35.5cm)
**£4,500–5,000 / $6,500–7,250** ⊞ CW

## Markey Robinson (1918–99)

Markey Robinson at first resisted becoming a professional artist. His talent for painting
was spotted early on in life by a teacher who felt he should be formally trained. However,
on leaving school he became a welder, then went on to be a boxer, toy maker, glass
decorator and merchant seaman. In the late 1940s he attended Belfast College of Art and
later had studios in Belfast and Dublin, exhibiting extensively in both cities. The influence
of his travels to Europe, Africa and South America can be clearly seen, particularly the Incas
and the Aztecs, as portrayed in the authentic style of bold brush work. However, once he
had become a recognized artist he was prolific.

**For further
information**
see Irish Art
(pages 72–75)

◀ **Markey
Robinson**
Irish (1918–99)
Irish Lakeside
Oil on board
4 x 5in (10 x 12.5cm)
**£2,000–2,200**
**$3,000–3,300**
⊞ WrG

**Markey Robinson**
Irish (1918–99)
Bread and Grapefruit
Signed, gouache on board
21 x 14in (53.5 x 35.5cm)
**£950–1,150**
**$1,400–1,750** ⚷ WA

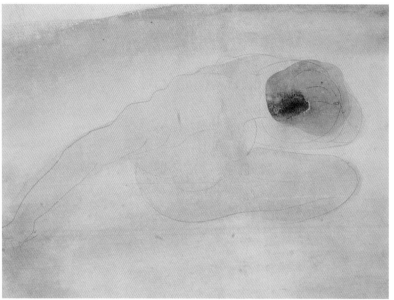

**Francois Roeder**
French (19thC)
La Raccomodeur de Parapluies
Signed and dated 1879, oil on panel
26¼ x 20¼in (66.5 x 51.5cm)
**£7,500–8,500 / $11,000–12,500** ⊞ **Bne**

**Auguste Rodin**
French (1840–1917)
Crouching Nude
Signed, pencil and watercolour
on paper
9¼ x 12¼in (23.5 x 31cm)
**£10,000–12,000**
**$14,500–17,500** ➹ **Bon**
*This artist is more famous for
his sculptures.*

**Mick Rooney, RA**
British (b1944)
Boy with Bird
Signed, oil on panel
10 x 8in (25.5 x 20.5cm)
**£1,100–1,300 / $1,600–1,900** ⊞ **BRG**

▶ **Marcel Ronay**
German (b1910)
Nude, 1937
Ink and gouache
10 x 8in (25.5 x 20.5cm)
**£500–550 / $720–800** ⊞ **JDG**

◀ **Ernest T. Rosen**
American (1877–1926)
The Boudoir
Signed, oil on canvas
61½ x 41in (156 x 104cm)
**£5,300–5,800 / $7,500–8,500** ➹ **S(O)**

▶ **Leonard Rosoman**
British (b1913)
Runners in the Snow
Signed, gouache over pen
and ink
8½ x 10¼in (21.5 x 26cm)
**£650–750 / $900–1,100** ➹ **P(Ba)**

**Samuel Rothbort**
American (1882–1971)
Figures in a Park
Oil on board
48 x 36in (122 x 91.5cm)
**£350–400 / $500–580** ⚡ **TREA**
*Samuel Rothbort was born in Wolkovisk, Russia and moved to the USA in 1904. He is well known for his scenes of New York City life, executed in heavy impasto. Rothbort exhibited between 1920 and 1960 at the Salons of America, Pratt Institute, Brooklyn Museum and the Rockefeller Centre.*

**George Rouault**
French (1871–1958)
Christ et Sainte Femme, from the Passion series
Signed and dated 1936, aquatint
12½ x 8¼in (32 x 21cm)
**£1,100–1,300 / $1,600–2,000** ⚡ **SLN**

**Michael Rothenstein, RA**
British (1908–93)
Fallen Sunflower
Signed, watercolour over pen and ink
14½ x 22in (37 x 56cm)
**£1,900–2,300**
**$2,750–3,350** ⚡ **P**

▶ **Frank Rousse**
British (fl1897–1915)
Continental Sea Shore Scenes
A pair, signed, watercolour
10½ x 14½in (26.5 x 37cm)
**£850–1,000**
**$1,250–1,500**
⚡ **GAK**

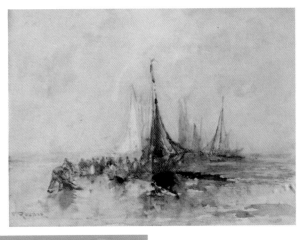

◀ **Charles Rowbotham**
British (1856–21)
Positano, Gulf of Salerno, Italy
Signed, watercolour and bodycolour
4¾ x 7¾in (12 x 19.5cm)
**£1,000–1,200**
**$1,500–1,750** ⚡ **Bon**

▶ **Tom Rowden**
British (1842–1926)
Dartmoor, near Two Bridges, Sheep and Drover
Signed and dated 1898, watercolour
12 x 22in (30.5 x 56cm)
**£650–750**
**$950–1,100** ⊞ **LH**

**Ernest Arthur Rowe**
British (1862–1922)
Vesuvius and the Bay of Naples from Sorrento
Signed and inscribed, watercolour
10 x 14in (25.5 x 35.5cm)
**£4,000–5,000 / $5,800–7,250 ⊞ JSp**

*Ernest Arthur Rowe was an important late Victorian garden painter. He lived most of his life in Kent, painting many great English gardens. He also worked for English expatriates in Italy and France.*

**George Derville Rowlandson**
British (b1861)
A Coaching Scene
Signed, oil on canvas
23 x 35in (58.5 x 89cm)
**£2,200–2,600 / $3,200–3,800 ↗ GAK**

**George Ruff, Snr**
British (fl1880–86)
Landscape, near Balcombe, East Sussex
Signed, oil on board
6½ x 11¾in (16.5 x 30cm)
**£180–220 / $260–320 ↗ G(L)**

**Herbert Royle**
British (1870–1958)
Haymaking, Nesfield, Ilkley
Signed, oil on canvas
19¾ x 23½in (50 x 59.5cm)
**£9,500–10,500 / $14,000–15,250 ↗ AH**

▶ **Carl Rungius**
American/German (1869–1959)
Moose Head
Signed, oil on canvasboard
9 x 11in (23 x 28cm)
**£30,000–35,000 / $43,500–50,000 ↗ S(NY)**

*A native of Germany, Carl Clemens Moritz Rungius studied art at several academies where he found himself drawn to the work of European animal artists. In 1894, Rungius visited an uncle in the USA and immigrated a year later. He was an avid sportsman and from his base in New York he made frequent hunting and sketching trips to Maine and New Brunswick and eventually to the Rocky Mountain region. At a time when wilderness was fast disappearing, Rungius presented an image of the wild and the West which appealed to the early conservationists.*

# Charles M. Russell (1864–1926)

They may not make Western films any more but the market in cowboy paintings goes from strength to strength. It's not just the Americans but also Europeans who romanticize scenes of the Wild West, and appreciate the noble beauty of Indian chiefs and squaws.

Charles Marion Russell is one of the most collectable of cowboy artists working at the end of the 19th century. Born in St Louis, Missouri he grew up dreaming of being a cowboy. He persuaded his parents to send him on a trip to Montana for his sixteenth birthday where he worked on a ranch as a horse wrangler on cattle drives. During the 1880s he saw the change in the cowboy's traditional way of life due to the expanding railroads and increasing numbers of settler farmers from the East coast.

Russell frequently came into contact with the Kootenai, Arapho and Crow tribes and in 1888 travelled to Canada where he lived among a tribe of Blackfoot Indians learning their customs and language. He was sensitive to their plight and portrayed their way of life sympathetically. He is appreciated by Western writer Arthur Hoeber because 'he paints the West from a personal intimate knowledge of it all and he has the tang of its spirit in his blood.'

▶ **Charles M. Russell**
American (1864–1926)
Kootenai Lodge Bear
Signed, dated 1926 and inscribed, gouache
7½ x 5in (19 x 12.5cm)
**£21,000–26,000 / $31,000–38,000** ↗ CdA

**Charles M. Russell**
American (1864–1926)
The Frontiersman
Signed, pen and ink
17 x 12¾in (43 x 59cm)
**£23,000–32,000 / $33,000–40,000** ↗ CdA

◀ **Charles M. Russell**
American (1864–1926)
Indians on Horseback
Signed and dated 1900, pen and ink on paper
8¼ x 12¼in (21 x 31cm)
**£26,000–30,000 $38,000–44,000** ↗ S(NY)

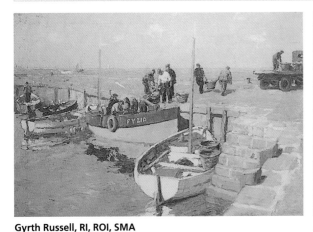

**Gyrth Russell, RI, ROI, SMA**
Canadian (1892–1970)
St Ives, Unloading the Catch
Signed, oil on canvas
21 x 30in (53.5 x 76cm)
**£5,000–5,500 / $7,250–8,000** ↗ Bon

**John Russell**
British (19thC)
A Good Catch
Oil on canvas
28 x 36in (71 x 91.5cm)
**£3,000–3,500 / $4,500–5,000** ↗ P(L)

**Richard Sale**
British (20thC)
In the Park
Oil on canvas
20 x 24in (51 x 61cm)
**£1,500–2,000 / $2,200–3,000** ⊞ MP

## National Cowboy & Western Heritage Museum

■ 1700 N.E. 63rd Street, Oklahoma City, Oklahoma 73111, www.cowboyhalloffame.org

■ Opened in 1965, the Museum was originally conceived as a dream of Chester A. Reynolds, a Kansas City businessman, as a tribute to the men and women who helped establish the West as an integral part of America's cultural heritage.

**James Salt**
British (1850–1903)
A Venetian Caprizzio
Signed, oil on canvas
24 x 37in (61 x 94cm)
**£5,000–6,000 / $7,250–8,000** ⊞ Ben

**Tom Sander**
American (b1938)
Bald Eagles in Glacier
Signed, oil on board
30 x 48in (76 x 122cm)
**£3,600–4,400 / $5,200–6,200** ⚲ CdA

### Buying at galleries

Even the smartest galleries will have more affordable works by famous names tucked away out of sight. Gallery owners will be only too happy to share their enthusiasm and knowledge so do not be afraid to ask questions.

◄ **John Singer Sargent**
American (1856–1925)
The Simplon: Large Rocks
Watercolour and pencil on paper
10 x 14in (25.5 x 35.5cm)
**£28,000–34,000**
**$41,000–48,000** ⚲ S(NY)

**David Sawyer**
British (b1961)
Ponte dei Sospiri
Oil on board
16 x 12in (40.5 X 30.5cm)
**£875–975 / $1,250–1,400** ⊞ **P&H**

▶ **Frank William Scarborough**
British (1896–1939)
Sunset, Pool of London
Signed and inscribed, watercolour heightened with white
9½ x 13½in (24 x 34.5cm)
**£3,700–4,400 / $5,500–6,500** ⚒ **B**

**Richard Allen Schmid**
American (b1934)
Snow Shadows
Signed, oil on canvas
18 x 28in (45.5 x 71cm)
**£4,000–4,500 / $5,800–6,500** ⚒ **JAA**

**Lilian D. Sawyers**
British (b1904)
Sunset: Aldrington Basin, Sussex
Oil on canvas
30 x 40in (76 x 101.5cm)
**£3,500–4,500 / $5,000–6,500** ⊞ **Ben**
*Lilian Sawyers won the Turner Gold Medal in 1927 and exhibited at the Royal Academy in 1928.*

**J. G. Schmiedel**
German/Russian (19thC)
Difficult Travel
Signed and dated, oil on canvas
18 x 26in (45.5 x 66cm)
**£850–1,000 / $1,250–1,500** ⚒ **TREA**

# Charlotte Mount Brock Schreiber (1834–1922)

Charlotte Mount Brock Schreiber (née Morrell), is one of Canada's prominent early women painters. She was the first woman member of the Royal Canadian Academy of Arts, a member of the Ontario Society of Artists and founding member of the Women's Art Association of Canada.

Charlotte was the only woman on the council of the Ontario School of Design in Toronto. She also exhibited in the Fine Art section of the Toronto Industrial Exhibition and the Montreal Museum of Fine Arts in the 1870s and 1880s. Chiefly known for her paintings of local landscapes, painted on site, portraits and genres from life for her friends, family and charitable causes, Schreiber was also a celebrated photographer and illustrator of children's books and literary publications.

Born in Essex, England, Charlotte trained under the notable painter of the day, J. R. Herbert and at Mr. Carey's School of Art, London, where she took private lessons in anatomy and figure painting. In 1855, she began exhibiting at the Royal Academy, London. Arriving in Canada in 1875, she was fully trained in the English Academic Tradition. The Schreiber's family residence, Lislehurst, Ontario, was purchased by the University of Toronto in 1962 and is now the residence of the Principal of Erindale College.

**Charlotte Mount Brock (Morrell) Schreiber, RCA, OSA**
Canadian (1834–1922)
Portrait of one of the Grahame daughters with canary
Inscribed, oil on board
12 x 9½in (30.5 x 24cm)
**£1,500–1,800 / $2,200–2,600** ⤴ WAD

**Charlotte Mount Brock (Morrell) Schreiber, RCA, OSA**
Canadian (1834–1922)
Springfield Rabbits
Oil on canvas
25 x 35in (63.5 x 89cm)
**£3,500–4,200 / $5,000–6,000** ⤴ WAD

**Charlotte Mount Brock (Morrell) Schreiber, RCA, OSA**
Canadian (1834–1922)
St Martins, NB
Signed, oil on canvas
8 x 15in (20.5 x 38cm)
**£110–135 / $160–200** ⤴ WAD

**Charlotte Mount Brock (Morrell) Schreiber, RCA, OSA**
Canadian (1834–1922)
Portrait of one of the Grahame daughters
Inscribed, oil on board
12 x 9½in (30.5 x 24cm)
**£2,600–3,200 / $3,800–4,600** ⤴ WAD

**George F. Schultz**
American (1869–1934)
Marine Scene with Schooners
Signed, watercolour with gouache on paper
14 x 20in (35.5 x 51cm)
**£700–850 / $1,000–1,250** ⚒ JAA

**Andrew T. Schwartz**
American (1867–1942)
View of the Hudson River Valley
Signed, oil on canvas
32 x 36in (81.5 x 91.5cm)
**£4,800–5,500 / $7,000–8,000** ⚒ NOA

**John Schwatschke**
Irish (b1943)
Between Ourselves
Signed with monogram, oil on canvas
30 x 24in (76 x 61cm)
**£1,100–1,300 / $1,600–1,900** ⚒ WA

**Kurt Schwitters**
German (1887–1948)
Porträt Des Herrn C. Cohen
Signed and dated, oil on board
17½ x 16in (44.5 x 40.5cm)
**£2,200–2,400 / $3,200–3,500** ⚒ P

▶ **Henry Scott**
British (fl1950–66)
Evening Glow off
the Lizard
Signed, oil on canvas
20 x 30in
(51 x 76cm)
**£2,000–3,000**
**$3,000–4,500** ⚒ S(O)

## Abbreviations

Letters after the artist's name denote that the artist has been awarded the membership of an artistic body. See page 233 for the explanation of abbreviated letters.

**Michael Scott**
British (b1940)
Little Neptune
Signed, oil on canvas
30in (76cm) square
£4,800–5,300 / $7,000–7,700 ▦ CON

**Sir Peter Scott**
British (1909–89)
Pintail in Flight
Signed and dated 1948, oil on canvas
18 x 14½in (45.5 x 37cm)
£1,150–1,350 / $1,600–2,000 ➶ P(Ba)

▶ **Sir Peter Scott**
British (1909–89)
A skein of geese over wetlands
Signed and dated, oil on canvas
25½ x 67in (64.5 x 170cm)
£4,000–5,000 / $5,800–7,200 ➶ P(Ba)

◀ **Samuel Scott**
British (1703–72)
The Thames at Westminster Bridge looking east
Oil on canvas
36½ x 55½in (92.5 x 141cm)
£34,000–38,000 / $48,000–55,000 ➶ P

*Samuel Scott played an important part in the development of marine painting in England. By the end of the 1730s he was receiving regular commissions for marine subjects. His early seapieces are closely based on those of Willem Van de Velde II. By the mid-1740s he had introduced buildings into his pictures and was working on a series of topographical views of London and the Thames. In 1746, when Canaletto arrived in London, Scott was encouraged to paint more detailed riverscapes with a Venetian flavour. Among his favourite views along the Thames are Westminster Bridge and Old London Bridge. This historically interesting painting is an accurate geographical record of London as it was contemporary to Scott, before the Houses of Parliament had been built.*

**William Scott, RA**
Scottish (1913–89)
Red Ground with Off-White Forms
Oil on canvas
45 x 66in (114.5 x 167.5cm)
**£44,000–54,000 / $65,000–79,000** 🔨 S

**Septimus Scott**
British (fl1839)
Spring Lambs on the Downs
Signed, oil
18 x 14in (45.5 x 35.5cm)
**£2,800–3,000** ⊞ **Dr**
**$4,000–4,400**

▶ **William Scott, RA**
Scottish (1913–89)
Summer Suite with Green Predominating
Lithograph, 1976, one of an edition of
40, from a series of three lithographs
22¼ x 30¼in (56.5 x 77cm)
**£2,250–2,500 / $3,300–3,600** 🔨 **JLX**

## National Gallery of Scotland
■ The Mound, Edinburgh EH2 2EL, www.nationalgalleries.org

■ Home to Scotland's greatest collection of European
paintings and sculpture, from the Renaissance to Post-
Impressionism. The gallery also has a comprehensive
collection of Scottish art.

**Sean Scully**
Irish/American (b1945)
Untitled
Signed and dated 1972, acrylic on paper
24 x 35¾in (61 x 91cm)
**£2,350–2,800 / $3,200–4,000** 🔨 **S(O)**

**Elliot Seabrooke**
British (1886–1950)
Fruit on a White Dish
Signed and dated 1938, oil on canvas
20¼ x 24in (51.5 x 61cm)
**£800–950 / $1,200–1,400** 🔨 **P**

# Edward Brian Seago (1910–74)

Edward Seago was a British Post Impressionist who never achieved the critical acclaim of his European counterparts. However, he has a loyal band of collectors and a wide public following, who regard his oils and watercolours of land and seascapes as reminiscent of Turner because his work is often bathed in a shimmering light, giving that blurred Turner-like feel. Seago was a very competent draughtsman and still life artist.

His parents wanted him to get a 'proper job' and tried to dissuade him from becoming an artist. Despite their opposition and his ill health he persevered with his painting and won a Royal Drawing Society prize when he was only fourteen years of age. Seago was self taught although he did receive some instruction from Royal Academician Bertram Priestman.

Seago grew up in East Anglia and his early work was mostly in watercolour of the Norfolk Broads and sailing boats. His first one-man show in 1933 depicted life in the Circus. As his popularity grew he began to paint in Italy, France and in old age, Sardinia, where he bought a villa. His exhibitions in USA and Canada were very successful.

**Edward Brian Seago, RWS, RBA**
British (1910–74)
Stormy Afternoon, Ostend
Oil on board
8½ x 10½in (21.5 x 26.5cm)
**£7,000–7,700 / $10,000–11,000** ⊞ **P&H**

**Edward Brian Seago, RWS, RBA**
British (1910–74)
October Morning, Ranworth Creek
Signed, oil on board
10 x 14in (25.5 x 35.5cm)
**£4,600–5,600 / $6,700–8,300** ⚒ **P**

**Edward Brian Seago, RWS, RBA**
British (1910–74)
High Pasture
Watercolour
11 x 15in (28 x 38cm)
**£4,500–5,000 / $6,500–7,250** ⊞ **P&H**

**Edward Brian Seago, RWS, RBA**
British (1910–74)
Cow Parsley, Norfolk
Signed, inscribed on reverse, oil on board
14 x 20in (35.5 x 51cm)
**£9,000–10,500 / $13,000–15,000** ⚒ **B(EA)**

**Edward Seago**
British (1910–74)
The Mill at Thurne
Signed, oil on panel
8½ x 10½in (21.5 x 26.5cm)
**£13,000–14,500 / $18,800–21,000** ⊞ **BuP**

**Frederick Seeth**
American (1845–1929)
Crashing Waves
Oil on canvas
14 x 20in (35.5 x 51cm)
**£650–800 / $950–1,150** SLN

**Mark Senior, NPS**
British (1862–1927)
The Milk Maid
Signed and dated 1900,
oil on canvas
12¼ x 16¼in (31 x 41.5cm)
**£3,400–4,000 / $5,000–5,800** B(L)

## Pairs
Unless otherwise stated, any description which refers to
'a pair' includes a guide price for the pair, even though the
illustration may show only a single picture.

**Joseph van Severdonck**
Belgian (1819–1905)
Cocks and Hens
A pair, signed, oil on panel
5¾ x 7¾in (14.5 x 19.5cm)
**£1,400–1,700 / $2,000–2,500** SHN

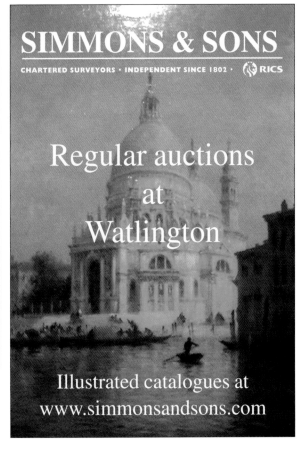

**George Shalders**
British (1826–73)
A Roadside Chat
Watercolour
10¾ x 18¾in (27.5 x 47cm)
**£9,000–10,000 / $13,000–14,500** ⊞ HFA

**Dorothea Sharp**
British (1874–1955)
Still life of flowers in a vase
Signed, oil on board
18 x 15in (45.5 x 38cm)
**£1,000–1,200 / $1,500–1,750** ⚒ G(L)

◄ **Joseph Henry Sharp**
American (1859–1953)
Breakers at Waikiki Beach
Signed, oil on board
6 x 8¾in (12.5 x 22cm)
**£3,000–3,600 / $4,400–5,000** ⚒ CdA

## Prices

■ The first consideration when pricing a work is the artist and the subject matter.

■ On a decorative level oils are generally more expensive than watercolours, and watercolours generally more expensive than pencil drawings.

■ An artist's work which is out of character, ie a notable landscape artist producing a portrait, will command less.

■ Work completed during the established peak of an artist's career will cost more.

**Walter Shaw**
British (1851–1933)
Waves
Signed, oil on canvas
30½ x 50¾in (77.5 x 129cm)
**£12,000–13,000 / $17,500–19,500** ⊞ BuP

► **William Shayer**
British (1787–1879)
A Passing Conversation
Signed, oil on canvas
16 x 24in (40.5 x 61cm)
**£2,000–2,400 / $3,000–3,500** ⚒ P(Ba)

**David Shepherd**
British (b1931)
Bull Elephant
Signed, oil on canvas
24 x 36in (61 x 91.5cm)
**£45,000–50,000 / $65,250–72,500** ⊞ HFA

**Daniel Sherrin**
British (1868–1940)
The Still of Evening
Signed, oil on canvas
30 x 50in (76 x 127cm)
**£2,000–2,200 / $3,000–3,200** ⚒ P(S)

▶ **Frank Sherwin, RI, RSMA**
British (b1896)
Summer by the River
Signed, watercolour
12 x 16in (30.5 x 40.5cm)
**£320–380 / $470–570** ⊞ LH

**Frederick James Shields, ARWS**
British (1833–1911)
The Skylark
Signed, watercolour
9¾ x 6¾in (25 x 17cm)
**£1,400–1,700 / $2,000–2,500** ⚒ Bon

**Benjamin Shipman**
British (1806–82)
Llyn Dinas, North Wales
Inscribed, oil on canvas
24 x 36in (61 x 91.5cm)
**£6,800–7,500 / $9,800–11,000** ⊞ Bne

**Gudrun Sibbons**
German (20thC)
Haymaking
Signed, watercolour
15½ x 19¼in (39.5 x 49cm)
**£670–750 / $1,000–1,100** ⚒ Bea(E)

**Nathaniel Sichel**
German (1843–1907)
Portrait of a young woman
Signed, oil on canvas
19¾ x 17½in (50 x 44.5cm)
**£4,500–5,000 / $6,500–7,250** ⚒ DORO

**Walter Richard Sickert, RA**
British (1860–1942)
Vernets, Dieppe
Inscribed, black and blue ink and pencil
23 x 13½in (58.5 x 34.5cm)
**£3,000–3,600 / $4,400–5,000** ⚒ B

◄ **For further information**
see Camden Town Group
(pages 32–33)

► **Adrian Siegel**
American (1898–1978)
Perseus
Signed, oil on board
48 x 31in
(122 x 78.5cm)
**£400–480**
**$580–700** ⚒ TREA

► **Paul Signac**
French (1863–1935)
Paysage près de Hennebout
Signed and titled, pencil and watercolour
on paper
4¼ x 6in (11 x 15cm)
**£3,200–3,600 / $4,600–5,200** ⚒ P

42ᵀᴴ ROYAL HIGHLAND REGIMENT
—1822—

◄ **Richard Simkin**
British (1840–1926)
An officer of the
Black Watch
Signed and dated
1832, watercolour
16¼ x 11in
(41.5 x 28cm)
**£1,000–1,200**
**$1,500–1,750**
⚒ Bon
*Richard Simkin was a
military artist who
lived in Aldershot
and was a prolific
painter of uniforms
and parades.*

► **Henry John Simpkins, ARCA**
Canadian (b1906)
St Janvier Sugar Camp
Signed, oil on masonite
12 x 16in (30.5 x 40.5cm)
**£280–350 / $400–500** ⚒ WAD

**William Simpson, RI**
British (1823–99)
Cotton Transport, India
Signed, dated 1862 and inscribed, watercolour over pencil
heightened with white
10 x 13¾in (25.5 x 34.5cm)
**£1,600–1,900 / $2,300–2,750** 🔨 B

**John Skelton**
Irish (b1923)
Sail Boat on the River
Signed, oil on canvas laid on board
21 x 25in (53.5 x 63.5cm)
**£2,100–2,500 / $3,000–3,600** 🔨 WA

**Christine Slade**
British (20thC)
Sailing on the Orwell
Signed and dated 1989, pastel
12 x 24in (30.5 x 61cm)
**£450–550 / $650–800** 🔨 GAK

**Charles Sims, RA, RWS**
British (1873–1928)
Summer
Signed, watercolour, bodycolour and tempera
15 x 22in (38 x 56cm)
**£12,500–13,750 / $18,000–20,000** ⊞ Bne

**S. D. Skillett**
British (fl1840–65)
The Clipper
*Challenger* off a
coastline, possibly
Madeira
Signed, oil on canvas
26 x 35¾in
(66 x 91cm)
**£7,500–9,000**
**$11,000–13,000**
🔨 Bon

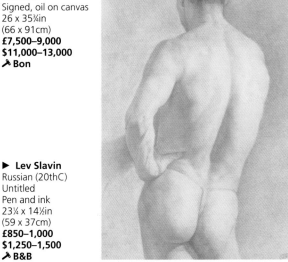

▶ **Lev Slavin**
Russian (20thC)
Untitled
Pen and ink
23¼ x 14½in
(59 x 37cm)
**£850–1,000**
**$1,250–1,500**
🔨 B&B

# Gladys Nelson Smith
# (1888–1980)

An art critic has hailed Gladys Nelson Smith as a fine social Realist. Gladys Smith painted her portraits and figures in landscapes which did not depict the rich and the noble but the lives of ordinary people. Her inspiration was from the likes of the founding fathers of the American Realist movement, Winslow Homer (1836–1910), Thomas Eakins (1844–1916) and John Sloan (1871–1951) who in their painting sought to draw attention to the plight of the huddled masses for whom the reality of the American Dream was very different from what they had been led to believe.

A native of the State of Kansas, Gladys Nelson Smith studied at Corcoran School of Art in Washington and then settled in Washington DC. She had a weekend retreat on a farm in Frederick County, Maryland where she loved to paint. She was also an accomplished painter of still lifes.

► **Gladys Nelson Smith**
American (1888–1980)
Stoop Sitting in Georgetown
Signed, oil on canvas laid on board
17 x 19¼in (43 x 49cm)
**£2,000–2,500 / $3,000–3,600** ⚒ **SLN**

**Louisa Jordan Smith**
American (1873–1928)
Eastern Mountain Landscape
Signed, oil on canvas
18 x 30¼in (45.5 x 77cm)
**£1,200–1,500 / $1,750–2,250** ⚒ **JAA**

► **Marshall D. Smith**
American (20thC)
Feather Palms, Old New Orleans
Signed, oil on board
30 x 24in (76 x 61cm)
**£350–420 / $500–600** ⚒ **TREA**

**Mary T. Smith**
American (b1904))
Untitled
Enamel on wood, c1986
24 x 28in (61 x 71cm)
**£6,000–6,600 / $8,700–9,500** ⊞ **RMG**

┌─────────────────────────────┐
│ ▲ **For further information** │
│ see Outsider Art (pages 144–147) │
└─────────────────────────────┘

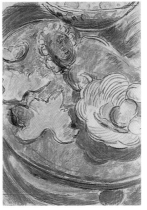

**Sir Matthew Smith**
British (1879–1959)
Still life with figurine
Signed, pastel
29½ x 21¼in (75 x 54cm)
**£3,300–4,000**
**$4,800–5,800** ⚒ **S(O)**

**Reginald Smith**
British (1855–1925)
Wet sands, Fistral Bay, Cornwall
Signed, watercolour
28 x 20½in (71 x 52cm)
**£1,000–1,200**
**$1,500–1,750** ⚒ **G(L)**

**Joop Smits**
Dutch (b1938)
Winter Time, Mourne Mountains, Co Down
Oil on board
11½ x 15½in (29 x 39.5cm)
**£1,300–1,500 / $2,000–2,200 ⊞ WrG**
*Although born in Holland, Joop has lived for many years in Ireland.*
*He graduated from Eindhoven Academy of Art in 1961 and has*
*exhibited in many major European cities including Munich,*
*Amsterdam, Luxembourg and Belfast.*

**Ethel Smul**
American (1897–1978)
Lyrical Chords
Signed, oil on canvas
36 x 28in (91.5 x 71cm)
**£280–340 / $400–500 ↗ TREA**
*Ethel Smul exhibited from the late 1920s to the 1950s at the Salons*
*of America, Society of Independent Artists, National Academy of*
*Design and the Cincinnati Art Museum.*

◀ **Norman Smyth, RUA**
Irish (b1933)
In the Green Lane
Signed, oil on board
12 x 15in (30.5 x 38cm)
**£1,400–1,600**
**$2,000–2,300 ⊞ WrG**

**Lionel Percy Smythe**
British (1839–1913)
Shorthanded, a sketch
Oil on board
9¾ x 15in (25 x 38cm)
**£850–1,000 / $1,250–1,500 ↗ Bon**

## Cincinnati Art Museum

■ 953 Eden Park Drive, Cincinnati, Ohio 45202, www.cincinnatimuseum.com

■ Founded in 1881, the museum is one of the country's oldest visual arts institutions.

■ Eight galleries provide for the display of Cincinnati's permanent collection of over 80,000 works of art.

**Frank Sohn**
American (b1888)
The Pet Lamb
Signed, oil on canvas
29 x 21in (73.5 x 53.5cm)
**£420–500 / $600–720 ↗ TREA**

**Vladimir Sokolov**
Russian (1923–97)
Summer, 1960
Signed and dated verso, oil on board
11½ x 16in (29 x 40.5cm)
**£780–860 / $1,100–1,250 ⊞ B&B**

**Vladimir Sokolov**
Russian (1923–97)
In the Foothills, 1966
Signed and dated verso, oil on board
14¼ x 19in (36 x 48.5cm)
**£780–860 / $1,100–1,250 ⊞ B&B**

**Simeon Solomon**
British (1840–1905)
Sin Gazing upon Eternal Death
Signed, c1890, pencil
13½ x 16¼in (34.5 x 41.5cm)
**£4,800–5,300 / $7,000–7,700 ⊞ PCG**

**Juan Soler**
Spanish (20thC)
Elegant ladies in the City
A pair, signed, oil
11 x 9in (28 x 23cm)
**£2,250–2,500 / $3,300–3,600 ⊞ Dr**

► **Eileen Alice Soper**
British (1905–90)
Foxcubs
Watercolour
15¼ x 22½in (38.5 x 57cm)
**£1,600–1,900 / $2,300–2,750 ⚒ Bon**

**Carl Frederik Sorensen**
Danish (1818–79)
A Yawl and a Cutter leaving a Fjord
Signed and dated 1877, oil on canvas
17¼ x 14½in (44 x 37cm)
**£2,500–3,000 / 3,500–4,500** ⚓ **Bon**

**Camille Souter, RHA**
British (b1929)
Milk Bottle and Old Turnip
Signed and dated 1973, oil on card
19½ x 13½in (49.5 x 34.5cm)
**£12,000–14,000 / $17,500–20,000** ⚓ **JAd**

**Vladimir Sosnovsky**
Russian (1922–90)
In the Countryside
Oil on board
10 x 9in (25.5 x 23cm)
**£750–825 / $1,100–1,200** ⊞ **ARL**

*Vladimir Sosnovsky was born in Novaya Ushitza, Khmelnitzky Region, Ukraine. As a child he showed a great love of drawing and consequently was sent to an art school for children. In 1939 he joined the Odessa Grekov Art College, but at the onset of WWII was asked to serve at the front after completing only two years of his studies. On returning in 1945 he continued to study under the well-known artist L. Mutchnik, entering the Kiev Art Institute in 1948 and graduating in 1954. He then worked as deputy director at the Odessa Western and Oriental Art Museum, and from 1956 taught painting at the Odessa Theatre and Art College until his death in 1990.*

**Augustus John Ruskin Spear, CBE, RA, PLG**
British (1911–90)
Cornish Impressions
Mixed media
15 x 21½in (38 x 54.5cm)
**£3,200–3,500 / $4,600–5,000** ⊞ **P&H**

*Ruskin Spear was born in west London where he won a scholarship to the Hammersmith School of Art at the age of 15. At the Royal College of Art he studied under Michael Rothenstein, Gilbert Spencer and Charles Mahoney. His instantly recognizable Sickert-influenced portraits of public figures won him a large following at the annual Royal Academy Summer Exhibition. He also painted low-life scenes in the bars and streets of Hammersmith where he lived. He has exhibited widely and his work is represented in many public collections including the Tate Gallery and the National Portrait Gallery. This important early work on paper was executed during a trip to Cornwall in the 1930s, and represents a superb example of St Ives School style between the wars.*

▶ **Richard Phene Spiers**
British (1838–1916)
South East View of Gloucester Cathedral
Signed and dated 1870, watercolour
14¼ x 10in (36 x 25.5cm)
**£200–240**
**$300–350** ↗ WW

**Benjamin Walter Spiers**
British (fl1875–93)
Still Life with Basket of Apples
Signed and dated 1887, watercolour
11¾ x 18½in (30 x 47cm)
**£1,250–1,500 / $1,750–2,250** ↗ B

**Jan Jacob Coenraad Spohler**
Dutch (1837–1923)
Near Amsterdam
Signed, oil on panel
8 x 6¼in (20.5 x 16cm)
**£1,300–1,600 / $2,000–2,300** ↗ Bon

**Georges Spiro**
Italian (1909–94)
Surrealist Landscape
Signed and dated 1960, oil on canvas
18½ x 21¾in (47 x 55.5cm)
**£1,200–1,400 / $1,750–2,000** ↗ BUK

▶ **Leonard Russell Squirrel**
British (1893–1979)
Partridge
Signed, dated 1928 and inscribed, pencil drawing
7 x 10in (18 x 25.5cm)
**£250–300 / $360–440** ↗ GAK

**Louis van Staaten**
Dutch (19thC)
Study of mills and barges on a river
Signed, watercolour
15 x 22in (38 x 56cm)
**£700–850 / $1,000–1,250** ⚲ GAK

**Ruth Stage**
British (b1969)
Tuscan Church
Signed, 1995, egg tempera
8 x 5¾in (20.5 x 14.5cm)
**£650–720 / $950–1,000** ⊞ BRG

◀ **George Stainton**
British (fl1860–90)
Shipping off Cowes, Isle of Wight
Signed, oil on canvas
11 x 19in (28 x 48.5cm)
**£2,500–3,000 / $3,600–4,400** ⊞ Ben

**Clarkson Stanfield, RA**
British (1793–1867)
Eruption of Mount Vesuvius
Initialled 'IM', inscribed verso and dated 1839,
watercolour and bodycolour heightened with
gum arabic on blue paper
9¾ x 13¾in (25 x 35cm)
**£4,000–4,800 / $5,800–7,000** ⚲ P

**Henri Stanier**
British (19thC)
Still life: vase of flowers including crocus, camellia and primula
Signed, oil on panel
8 x 9¾in (20.5 x 25cm)
**£700–850 / $1,000–1,250** ⚲ RBB

**Alexander Molyneaux Stannard**
British (c1878–1975)
Moorland Stream
Watercolour
7 x 10in (18 x 25.5cm)
**£160–200 / $230–300** ⚲ G(L)

**Charles Joseph Staniland, RI**
British (1838–1916)
The Young Bookworm
Watercolour
9 x 7in (23 x 18cm)
**£8,000–9,000 / $11,600–13,000** ⊞ HFA

*Charles Joseph Staniland was born at Kingston-upon-Hull and studied at Birmingham School of Art, Heatherley's, South Kensington School and the Royal Academy School. He was a painter of genre and historical subjects, as well as an illustrator. From 1861, he exhibited at the Royal Academy and from 1863 at the British Institute and the New Watercolour Society.*

▶ **Eloise Harriet Stannard**
British (1828–1915)
Still life, basket of grapes
Signed and dated 1894, oil on canvas
8½ x 12in
(21.5 x 30.5cm)
**£3,000–3,500**
**$4,500–5,000**
⚲ WAD

**Henry J. Sylvester Stannard, RBA**
British (1870–1951)
Back from Market
Signed, inscribed verso, watercolour
13½ x 22½in (34.5 x 57cm)
**£3,000–3,300 / $4,400–4,800** ⊞ SGL

*Henry John Sylvester Stannard, son of Henry Stannard, was a landscape painter who lived in the village of Flitwick, Bedford. He studied at South Kensington School and painted both landscapes and rustic subjects. He had many imitators but few equals. Stannard's watercolours of picturesque old cottages enjoy worldwide fame. He made this subject his own speciality.*

**Lilian Stannard**
British (1877–1944)
By the Lily Pond
Signed, watercolour
10 x 14in (25.5 x 35.5cm)
**£4,000–4,500 / $5,800–6,500** ⊞ Ben

*Lilian Stannard was the daughter of landscape and sporting painter Henry Stannard, and her brothers, Henry and Alexander, and sisters, Emily and Ivy, were all artists. Lilian was one of the most successful of the brood. By the age of 30 she was one of the most celebrated garden painters in England.*

**Theresa Sylvester Stannard**
British (1898–1947)
The Haunt of the Primroses
Signed and inscribed, watercolour and bodycolour
10½ x 14in (26.5 x 36cm)
**£1,300–1,500 / $2,000–2,200** ✒ **P(EA)**

**Gideon Townsend Stanton**
American (1885–1964)
Rainy Night on Canal Street, New Orleans
Signed, c1930, oil on canvas
25 x 30in (63.5 x 76cm)
**£10,000–12,000 / $14,500–17,500** ✒ **NOA**

▶ **William Steene**
American (1888–1965)
Railroad Station in Snow
Signed, oil on board
22¼ x 26½in (56.5 x 67.5cm)
**£5,000–6,000 / $7,250–8,750** ✒ **JAA**
*William Steene was born in New York in 1888. He studied at the Art Students' League, the National Academy of Design, the Acadamie Julian, Fontainbleau School of Art, Academy Colarossi and École des Beaux-Arts, all in Paris. He was a member of numerous art associations including the Mural Painters, the Southern States Art League, and the Salmagundi Club. He attained widespread recognition for his work, exhibiting in the National Academy of Design, Philadelphia Academy of Fine Art and the Mississippi Art Association and many others. His works can be found throughout the USA including the New York City Medical Center and the Georgia Military Academy.*

**Anthony Carey Stannus, RUA**
Irish (1862–1910)
Collecting Seaweed, Guernsey
Signed, watercolour drawing
6 x 12in (15 x 30.5cm)
**£800–950 / $1,150–1,400** ✒ **ROSS**

**Arthur J. Stark**
British (1831–1902)
Horses feeding outside stable, with attendants
Signed and dated 1858, oil on canvas
26 x 36in (66 x 91.5cm)
**£6,500–7,500 / $9,500–11,000** ✒ **RBB**

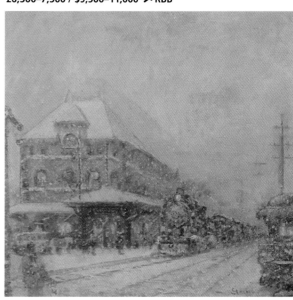

◄ **Eda Sterchi**
American (b1885)
Passage in Tunis
Signed, oil on board
18 x 16in (45.5 x 40.5cm)
**£1,750–2,000**
**$2,600–3,000** ⚒ **TREA**

*Sterchi was born in Olney, a small
town in south central Illinois. She
left for Chicago in 1908 to attend
the Art Institute and travelled to
Paris to study soon after. She met
with early success, exhibiting in
1913 at the American Artists
Club and the International
Artists Union (both in Paris).
She also exhibited at the Salon
d'Automne, American Women's
Club and the Société Nationale
des Beaux Arts. In the USA she
exhibited annually at the Art
Institute of Chicago from 1915
to 1920, and had a one-woman
show there in 1929.*

**Alfred Stevens**
Belgian (1823–1906)
The Beach
Signed, oil on canvas
16 x 12¾in (40.5 x 32.5cm)
**£9,200–11,000**
**$13,500–16,000** ⚒ **S(O)**

**Miller's is a price GUIDE not a price LIST**

**John Stirling**
Scottish (1820–71)
A Lassie and lamb
Signed and inscribed, oil on canvas laid down on panel
21 x 16½in (53.5 x 42cm)
**£3,700–4,500 / $5,500–6,500** ⚒ **Bon**

*John Stirling was born in Aberdeen and probably attended Gray's
School of Art, Aberdeen, or at least associated with J. P. Fraser, who
was head of the school. He showed his work in both Scotland and
England, and made his Academy debut in 1852, showing three works.*

**Will Henry Stevens**
American (1881–1949)
Summer Landscape with Stream and Mountains
Signed, 1925–35, oil on board
16 x 14in (40.5 x 35.5cm)
**£2,500–3,000 / $3,600–4,400** ⚒ **JAA**

◀ **Margaret Stokes**
British (1915–66)
The Bathers
Signed, oil on canvas
15¾ x 13½in
(40 x 34.5cm)
**£1,200–1,400**
**$1,750–2,000**
⚒ JAd

▶ **Arthur Claude Strachan**
British (1865–1938)
A Country Cottage
Watercolour
16¾ x 11¾in
(42.5 x 30cm)
**£8,200–9,000**
**$12,000–13,800**
⊞ BFa

**John Paul Strain**
American (b1955)
On the Buffalo Trail
Signed, gouache
20 x 30in (51 x 76cm)
**£3,700–4,400 / $5,500–6,500** ⚒ CdA

**Philip Eustace Stretton**
British (fl1884–1919)
A Favourite Collie Dog
Signed, oil on canvas
20 x 15½in (51 x 39.5cm)
**£12,000–14,000 / $17,500–20,000** ⚒ S

◀ **Jacob van Stry**
Dutch (1756–1815)
Cattle at Rest
Signed, oil on panel
13 x 19in (33 x 48.5cm)
**£7,500–8,250 / $10,750–12,000** ⊞ SGL

**Henry Stull**
American
(1851–1913)
The stallion Lexington
held by a groom
Signed, oil on canvas
18 x 24in (45.5 x 61cm)
**£14,750–17,750**
**$21,500–25,500**
⚒ S(NY)

▶ **Graham
Sutherland, OM**
British (1903–80)
Cairn
Signed and dated
1944, watercolour,
gouache, pen and
black ink, coloured
chalks and wax crayons
15¾ x 16in
(40 x 40.5cm)
**£40,000–45,000**
**$58,000–65,000** ⚒ S

**Graham Sutherland, OM**
British (1903–80)
Study for a Chained Beast II
Signed, with initials and dated twice, 15.IX.67, ink, chalk,
wash and coloured crayon
25¼ x 19in (64 x 48.5cm)
**£10,500–12,500 / $15,250–18,000** ⚒ P

**Svend Svendsen**
American (1864–1934)
Evening in Winter
Signed, oil on canvas laid on board
23¾ x 19¾in (60.5 x 50cm)
**£600–750 / $870–1,100** ⚒ SLN

◀ **Dorcie Sykes**
British (b1908)
Newlyn moonlight coastal scene
Oil
14 x 19in (35.5 x 48cm)
**£280–350 / $400–500** ⚒ GAK

# St Ives School

The St Ives branch of the Tate Gallery, which exhibits the many artists who have lived and worked in the town, is an important destination for artists and those who appreciate art, it attracts thousands of visitors each year.

St Ives may be synonymous with 20th-century British artists but, before they arrived, the American painter James McNeil Whistler (1834–1903) spent a summer painting there. The St Ives Society of Artists was founded in the early 1900s by potter Bernard Leach but it was the group of artists working there prior to WWII that became known as the St Ives School. The founding fathers were Ben Nicholson and Christopher Wood who visited the town in 1928 and saw the naïve pictures of St Ives Harbour by retired seaman and rag-and-bone man Alfred Wallis. To these art school educated artists the untaught work of Wallis, often on scraps of card, represented a fresh, simple and real approach that they felt they should strive for. 'One finds the influences one is looking for and I certainly found mine', said Nicholson.

When life had returned to normal after WWII, young painters such as Sven Berlin, Peter Lanyon, John Wells and Wilhelmina Barns-Graham exhibited abstract works in the Crypt Gallery near the church. Ben Nicholson, now also painting abstract works, was living in St Ives permanently with his wife, the sculptor Barbara Hepworth. In the 1950s fellow abstract artists Terry Frost, Roger Hilton, Sandra Blow, Trevor Bell, Bob Law and Bryan Wynter, inspired by the local landscapes and seascapes, moved to the town. In this they differed from their American contemporaries whose abstract work was much more influenced by their urban surroundings.

Although mid-20th century British work will never reach the high prices of French and American art of the period, values have steadily increased. Until recently, late Victorian and Edwardian paintings were more expensive but tastes are changing, and St Ives artists in particular are catching up. This is due in part to interior design trends which today are more spare and eclectic and favour post-war British art. At a recent New York sale prices exceeded all expectations. The St Ives masters such as Wood and Heron can fetch over £200,000 ($290,000) and Lanyon £90,000 ($130,000). A Nicholson abstract is regularly worth £250,000 ($362,000) and fashionable drawings range between £7,000 and £15,000 ($10,200 and $21,750). However, other St Ives artists' work can be bought for considerably less. A 1960s Roger Hilton is worth £5,000–10,000 ($7,250–14,500), with Terry Frost's work around the £15,000 ($21,750) mark. Other St Ives artists fetch under £10,000 ($14,500) and some, such as Adrian Ryan, under £5,000 ($7,250). Drawings by most St Ives artists can be picked up for under £1,000 ($1,500). The price of an Alfred Wallis is determined by the size and state of the picture. One which was in good condition recently sold for £30,000 ($44,000), although scrappier ones, which come up more often, are within the £5,000–8,000 ($7,250–11,600) bracket.

◄ **Wilhelmina Barns-Graham**
British (b1912)
Movement in Space No. 1
Signed and dated 1980, gouache on paper
19in (48.5cm) square
**£8,000–8,800**
**$11,600–13,000** ⊞ JLx

► **Sandra Blow, RA**
British (1925)
Ochre Composition
Signed, oil and charcoal on canvas
42 x 36in (106.5 x 91.5cm)
**£2,700–3,250**
**$4,000–4,700** ⚲ P

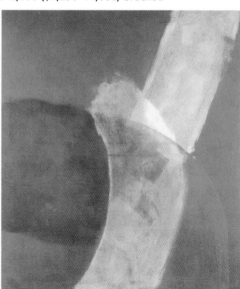

◄ **Terry Frost, RA**
British (b1915)
Challenger II, Blue & Red
Signed, dated 1988 and inscribed, oil on canvas
54¾ x 90in (139 x 228.5cm)
**£7,500–9,000**
**$10,800–13,000** ⚲ P

**Further information**
Artists mentioned in the introduction above may have works appearing elsewhere in this Guide. Consult the index for page numbers.

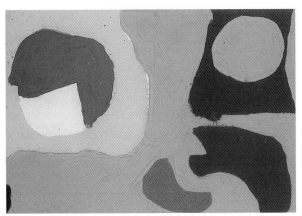

**Patrick Heron**
British (1920–99)
Edinburgh V
Gouache
15 x 23in (38 x 58.5cm)
**£4,800–5,750 / $7,000–8,400** ⚒ P

**Roger Hilton**
British (1911–75)
Red Nude
Initialled and dated 1973, gouache, charcoal and crayon on paper
113/4 x 17in (30 x 43cm)
**£6,000–6,600 / $8,700–9,500** ⊞ JLx

**Ben Nicholson, OM**
British (1894–1982)
Ivory Still Life
Signed, dated 1972 and inscribed, pencil and oil wash on paper
15¾ x 12in (40 x 30.5cm)
**£18,000–21,500 / $26,000–30,000** ⚒ B

**Alfred Wallis**
British (1855–1942)
Big Wave
Paint on board
6½ x 10¼in (16.5 x 26cm)
**£29,250–35,000**
**$42,000–51,000** ⚒ S

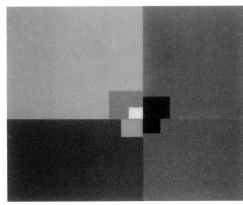

▶ **John Wells**
British (1907–2000)
Composition No. 22
Signed and dated,
oil on board
**£8,000–8,800**
**$11,600–13,000**
⊞ JLx

**Christopher Wood**
British (1901–30)
The Mermaid, 1927
Pen and ink
18 x 24in (45.5 x 61cm)
**£2,600–3,150 / $3,800–4,500** ⚒ P

◄ **Thomas G. Targett**
British (fl1869–88)
A Rainbow Landed
Signed and dated 1881, oil on board
6 x 10in (15 x 25.5cm)
**£2,000–2,200 / $2,900–3,200** ⊞ **CFA**

▶ **Andrea Tavernier**
Italian (1858–1932)
Garden on the Adriatic
Signed, dated and inscribed, oil on panel
11½ x 19¼in (28.5 x 50cm)
**£10,000–12,000 / $14,500–17,500** ⚒ **S(O)**

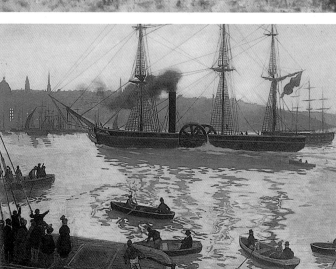

**Aleksandr Tavleev**
Russian (20thC)
Untitled
Pencil drawing
26 x 16¼in (66 x 41.5cm)
**£950–1,150 / $1,400–1,700** ⊞ **B&B**

**Leonard Campbell Taylor, RA**
British (1874–1969)
The First Steam Boat on the Mersey – Sunset, Liverpool Beyond
Signed and inscribed, watercolour and oil on paper
19 x 25½in (48.5 x 65cm)
**£13,000–15,500 / $19,000–22,000** ⚒ **S**

*Leonard Taylor was a versatile painter. His highly finished interiors with figures have a flavour of the Dutch Old Masters, and his still lifes owe much to Chardin. He also painted maritime scenes in Liverpool docks. The picture, Herculaneum Dock, Liverpool 1919, is painted in an almost futuristic style.*

# Boris Tchoubanoff (b1946)

There has always been a cultural affinity between Russia and France and craftsmen and artists in all fields have worked in both countries since the time of Catherine the Great. The Impressionists still influence Russian artists today. Boris Tchoubanoff was born in St Petersburg and went to France to study where he has remained ever since. He and his wife, a descendant of the composer Rimsky Korsakoff, live near Paris. The city inspires his art but it's a romantic, nostalgic image of the city he portrays. His work ignores most of 20th-century art movements – his girls in long white dresses and ribbons painted in a very Impressionistic way could have been painted in late 19th century.

The royal and famous, from the Monaco Royal Family to the conductor Mstislav Rostropovich, all collect his paintings and his work was included in an exhibition at the Hermitage Museum in St Petersburg.

**Boris Tchoubanoff**
Russian (b1946)
Leçon du Piano
Signed, oil on canvas
18¼ x 15in (46.5 x 38cm)
**£3,750–4,000**
**$5,500–5,800** ⊞ **BrS**

**Boris Tchoubanoff**
Russian (b1946)
Parc d'Automne
Oil on canvas
23¾ x 47¼in (60.5 x 120cm)
**£9,500–10,500 / $14,000–15,250** ⊞ **BrS**

**Boris Tchoubanoff**
Russian (b1946)
Les Baigneuses
Oil on canvas
25½ x 32in (65 x 81.5cm)
**£8,250–9,000 / $12,000–13,000** ⊞ **BrS**

**Boris Tchoubanoff**
Russian (b1946)
Les Champs des Coquelicots
Signed, oil on canvas
24 x 19¾in (61 x 50cm)
**£4,750–5,250**
**$7,000–7,500** ⊞ **BrS**

**Joseph Alfred Terry, RBA**
British (1872–1939)
An Italianate Scene
Signed, oil on board
9 x 11in (23 x 28cm)
**£850–950 / $1,250–1,400 ⊞ TBR**

*Joseph Terry was a member of the famous Terry
chocolate family from York. He trained at the York
School of Art and then at the Academie Julian and
Colorossie in Paris, winning a silver medal at the latter.
He moved to Sleights in North Yorkshire and became an
active member of the Staithes Group.*

**Joseph Albert Terry, RBA**
British (1872–1939)
Through the Porta Maria
Signed, watercolour
10½ x 12¼in (26.5 x 31cm)
**£100–120 / $145–175 ⚒ G(L)**

**William Tholen**
Dutch (1860–1931)
Summer Cottage
Signed, oil on canvas
24 x 48in (61 x 122cm)
**£300–330/ $440–480 ⚒ TREA**

**Abbot H. Thayer**
American (1849–1921)
Landscape at Fontainebleau
Signed, oil on canvas
21¾ x 18in (54 x 45.5cm)
**£40,000–50,000**
**$58,000–72,000 ⚒ S**

**► Alistair W. Thompson**
British (b1945)
Sheltering Sheep, Iona
Oil on canvas
20 x 30in (51 x 76cm)
**£1,950–2,350**
**$2,800–3,400 ⊞ CON**

**Edward H. Thompson**
British (1866–1949)
Lake District
Watercolour
12 x 17in (30.5 x 45cm)
**£2,700–3,200 / $4,000–4,600** ⊞ BFa

**Archibald Thorburn**
British (1860–1935)
A Red Deer Stag rolling in a peat hag
Signed and dated 1898, watercolour and bodycolour
14½ x 21in (37 x 53.5cm)
**£8,000–9,500 / $11,500–14,000** ↗ Bon

# William Thornley (fl1858–98)

William Thornley was also known as Georges William Thornley and William A. Thornbery. His work is very similar to Hubert and Charley Thornley, who may have been members of the same family. For a number of reasons artists often use pseudonymns, however Thornley left few clues as to his reasons.

He exhibited works at the Paris Salon and at the Salon of French Artists, also in Paris, receiving an honourable mention in 1881 and a third place medal in 1888. It is believed that Thornley first exhibited Marines at the Royal Academy in 1859 and also at the British Institution from 1861 until it closed in 1867. He continued to exhibit at the Royal Academy until 1898. He also painted a number of landscapes of Holland, Norway. Belgium and Italy but is best remembered for his seascapes.

**William Thornley**
British (fl1858–98)
Hay Barges
Signed, oil on canvas
14 x 12in (35.5 x 30.5cm)
**£4,000–4,500 / $5,800–6,500** ⊞ Ben

**William Thornley**
British (fl1858–98)
Shipping off Whitby Harbour
Signed, oil on canvas
10 x 16in (25.5 x 40.5cm)
**£4,750–5,250 / $7,000–7,500** ⊞ HFA

> **For further information**
> see Marine Art
> (pages 130–133)

► **William Thornley**
British (fl1858–98))
Storm Brewing
Oil on canvas
10 x 16in (25.5 x 40.5cm)
**£4,700–5,200**
**$6,800–7,500** ⊞ HFA

**Joseph Thors**
British (fl1863–1900)
A Norfolk Landscape
Signed, oil on canvas
16 x 24in (40.5 x 61cm)
**£7,850–8,500 / $11,500–12,500** ⊞ HFA

**Joseph Thors**
British (fl1863–1900)
Cottages near Tenbury Wells
Signed, oil on canvas
10 x 14in (25.5 x 35.5cm)
**£2,500–3,000 / $3,600–4,400** ⊞ Ben

◄ **Clara S. Thorward**
American (b1887)
Arizona View
Signed, watercolour on paper
7 x 11in (18 x 28cm)
**£120–140 / $175–200** ⚒ JAA

**Geoffrey Arthur Tibble**
British (1909–52)
Figures in the Drawing Room
Oil on canvas
30 x 25¼in (76 x 64cm)
**£5,500–6,000 / $8,000–8,700** ⊞ MJFA

◄ **Joe Tilson**
British (b1928)
Lufbery and Rickenbaker
Signed, dated and numbered 39/40, silkscreen printed on wove
27¼ x 19¼in (69 x 49cm)
**£800–950 / $1,200–1,400** ⚒ P

**Edward J. Finley Timmons**
American (1882–1960)
Figure in a Rural Landscape
Signed, oil on canvas
16 x 20in (40.5 x 51cm)
**£450–525 / $650–775** ⚒ **JAA**

*Edward J. Finley Timmons was born in Wisconsin and began his studies in the USA before travelling to Spain, England, Holland, France and Italy. At the age of 22 he began exhibiting worldwide and continued to do so until his death.*

**Henry George Todd**
British (1846–98)
Still life study of grapes, apple and nuts on a marble slab
Signed and dated 1895, oil
11 x 9in (28 x 23cm)
**£900–1,200 / $1,300–1,750** ⚒ **GAK**

**Ralph Todd**
British (1856–1932)
Life's Problems (The Unpaid Bill)
Signed, watercolour
10½ x 14½in (26.5 x 37cm)
**£1,500–1,800 / $2,150–2,600** ⚒ **P(Ba)**

**Francis William Topham, RA**
British (1808–77)
The Seaweed Gatherers
Signed and dated 1873, watercolour
23¼ x 32½in (59 x 82.5cm)
**£12,000–14,000 / $17,500–20,000** ⚒ **JAd**

◀ **Julian Otto Trevelyan, RA, LS**
British (1910–88)
Rab
Signed, watercolour
10¼ x 18in (26 x 46cm)
**£4,000–4,800 / $5,800–7,000** ⊞ **NZ**

## Abbreviations

Letters after the artist's name denote that the artist has been awarded the membership of an artistic body. See page 233 for the explanation of abbreviated letters.

**John Trickett**
British (b1956)
Pointer
Signed, oil on canvas
20 x 30in (51 x 76cm)
**£3,500–4,000 / $5,000–5,800 ⊞ WrG**

*John Trickett is regarded as one of the finest dog painters in Great Britain, if not the world. He won the silver medal in the International Animal Painters' competition in France with his painting of a Labrador. Trickett is also collected for his views of the countryside, particularly his images of horses and his Norfolk and Scottish loch scenes. He is a natural colourist with a good eye for composition and feel for atmosphere. His work is held in collections all over the world.*

**W. Wasdell Trickett**
British (b1934)
Study of a hunter 'Maroon Gun' in Stable
Signed and dated 1934, watercolour
13½ x 17½in (34.5 x 44.5cm)
**£200–250 / $300–360 ↗ RBB**

**Geoffrey Tristram**
British (b1954)
In the Potting Shed
Signed, watercolour
13in (33cm) square
**£550–650 / $800–1,000 ↗ Bon**

**Henry Scott Tuke, RA**
British (1858–1929)
Newlyn Fishing Boats
Signed and dated 1903, watercolour
12 x 18in (30.5 x 45.5cm)
**£4,000–4,800 / $5,800–7,000 ↗ B**

▶ **Charles Frederick Tunnicliffe, RA, RE, ARCA**
British (1901–79)
Seclusion of Bucks, Fallow Deer
Signed, watercolour
18 x 23½in (45.5 x 59.5cm)
**£2,500–3,000 / $3,600–4,400 ↗ Bon**

**George Turner**
British (1843–1910)
On the Conway, North Wales
Oil
15 x 25½in (38 x 65cm)
**£2,500–3,000 / $3,600–4,400** ⚒ AH

**Joseph Mallord William Turner, RA**
British (1775–1851)
Falls of the Anio at Tivoli
Watercolour over pencil
11 x 14in (28 x 35.5cm)
**£26,000–30,000 / $38,000–44,000** ⚒ S
In relation to the price, Turner's pictures command – a world record was achieved recently of £2,380,000 – this landscape appears to be a bargain. Its price is due, in part, to the small size of the picture and the quantity of similar art by him currently on the market. It is a pencil drawing as opposed to an oil and the subject matter is not the impressionistic style for which he is known.

**Louis Turpin**
British (20thC)
Up the Garden Path
Oil on canvas
42 x 38in
(106.5 x 96.5cm)
**£5,500–6,500**
**$8,000–9,500** ⊞ LTu

**Arnold Turtle**
American (1892–1954)
Brown County Landscape
Signed, oil on canvas
25 x 30in (63.5 x 76cm)
**£550–700 / $800–1,000** ⚒ TREA

◀ **Walter Frederick Roofe Tyndale**
British (1855–1943)
Figures at Rothenburg, Bavaria
Watercolour
9½ x 5½in (24 x 14cm)
**£1,200–1,400 /**
**$1,750–2,000** ⊞ LH

## Buying at galleries

Even the smartest galleries will have more affordable works by famous names tucked away out of sight. Gallery owners will be only too happy to share their enthusiasm and knowledge so do not be afraid to ask questions.

◀ **Euan Uglow**
British (1932–2000)
Contra-Position, 1993
Pencil on paper
18½ x 17in (47 x 43cm)
**£3,500–4,200**
**$5,000–6,000** 🔨 B

**Fred Uhlman**
British (1901–85)
New York
Signed and dated 1956, oil on canvas
24 x 36in (61 x 91.5cm)
**£6,200–7,000 / $9,000–10,000** 🔨 P

**Franz Richard Unterberger**
Belgian (1838–1902)
Neopolitan Daily Life via Caracciolo
Signed, oil on canvas
31¼ x 51¼in (79.5 x 130cm)
**£78,500–85,000 / $115,000–123,000** ⊞ HFA

**Charles Vacher**
British (1818–83)
Figures by Lake Nemi
Signed and dated 1863, watercolour
18 x 27ins (45.5 x 68.5cm)
**£2,400–2,800 / $3,500–4,000** ⊞ LH

**Robert Vallin**
French (d1915)
A Venetian Backwater
Oil on canvas
21 x 26in (53.5 x 66cm)
**£19,000–21,000 / $27,500–30,000** ⊞ HFA

**John Varley, OWS**
British (1778–1842)
Figures crossing a bridge
Signed, watercolour
5¾ x 8¾in (14.5 x 22cm)
**£800–950 / $1,150–1,400** 🔨 Bon

# Keith Vaughan (1912–77)

Keith Vaughan was a shy retiring man whose school days at Christ's Hospital in Sussex imbued him with a love of Italian Renaissance art. Vaughan who is best known for his modern interpretations of Classical scenes, many of which incorporate male nudes, never went to art school. He worked in an advertising agency, painting in his spare time. Fluent in German he acted as an interpreter in World War II, but when he came into contact with fellow painters Graham Sutherland and John Minton his confidence grew and he was given an exhibition at Lefevre Gallery, London, in 1942.

The 1950s were Vaughan's most prolific and successful period. He painted The Theseus mural of the Festival of Britain and some of his most accomplished and interesting male nudes. He became associated with the young artists of the day such as Lucian Freud and John Craxton. However, Keith Vaughan shunned honours. He taught at a number of art schools but refused the offer of becoming a professor at the Royal College of Art and declined his election as an associate of the Royal Academy.

Vaughan's journals have been published and give a fascinating insight into his intense and obsessive way of working and unfulfilled love life. Recently a cache of his sketchbooks has come to light, which is awakening a new generation to his talents.

**Keith Vaughan**
British (1912–77)
Blue Figure Study
Ink, wash, gouache and acrylic
30½ x 22in (77.5 x 56cm)
**£4,500–5,500 / $6,500–8,000** 🔨 P

**Keith Vaughan**
British (1912–77)
Theseus
Oil on board
16 x 33in (40.5 x 84cm)
**£21,000–25,000 / $30,000–36,000** 🔨 S

▶ **Keith Vaughan**
British (1912–77)
Two Figures
Signed and dated 1951, gouache and crayon
16 x 13in (40.5 x 33cm)
**£4,500–5,000 / $6,500–7,250** 🔨 B

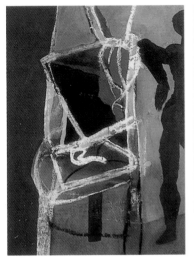

**Keith Vaughan**
British (1912–77)
The Chair
Signed and dated 1950, gouache
14¼ x 10½in (36 x 26.5cm)
**£4,800–5,400 / $7,000–8,000** 🔨 P

**Keith Vaughan**
British (1912–77)
Odysseus seen by the Sirens
Signed and dated 1953, oil on board
12¾ x 10in (32.5 x 25.5cm)
**£4,000–4,500 / $5,800–6,500** 🔨 P

**Keith Vaughan**
British (1912–77)
Boy in the Garden
Signed and dated 1948, gouache and charcoal
11¾ x 15¾in (30 x 40cm)
**£6,300–7,500 / $9,000–11,000** 🔨 P

**Benjamin Vautier**
German (1829–98)
Adding the Bill
Oil on canvas
11¼ x 13¾in (28.5 x 35cm)
**£18,000–19,500 / $26,000–28,500  ⊞ HFA**

**Elihu Vedder**
American (1836–1923)
Head for Picture of Crucifixion
Signed, oil on canvas board
9½ x 9¼in (24 x 23.5cm)
**£2,400–2,800 / $3,500–4,000  ↗ SHN**

**Salomon Leonardus Verveer**
Dutch (1813–76)
Dutch River Scene
Signed and inscribed, watercolour
12 x 16½in (30.5 x 42cm)
**£1,350–1,600 / $2,000–2,300  ↗ P(EA)**

**Johann Christian Vollerdt**
German (1708–69)
An evening landscape with numerous figures gathered
around Roman ruins on a hilltop
Signed, oil on panel
9 x 11¼in (23 x 28.5cm)
**£5,000–6,000 / $7,250–8,750  ↗ P**

▶ **Adrianus Jacobus Vrolyk**
Dutch (1834–62)
Dutch street scene
Signed and dated '58, oil on panel
7½ x 11in (19 x 28cm)
**£1,000–1,200 / $1,450–1,750  ↗ Bon**

**Jonathan Wade**
British (b1960)
March Afternoon at Portpatrick, Galloway
Signed, oil on canvas board
9 x 13½in (23 x 34.5cm)
**£350–400 / $500–580** 🔨 **P(Ba)**

**Thomas Charles Wageman**
British (1787–1863)
A portrait of a mother and daughter
Pencil
14½ x 10½in (37 x 26.5cm)
**£200–230 / $300–330** 🔨 **G(L)**

**Thomas Francis Wainewright**
British (fl1831–83)
Fisherfolk mending the nets by their beached vessels
Signed and dated 1855, oil on canvas
31 x 54in (78.5 x 137cm)
**£2,800–3,200 / $4,000–4,600** 🔨 **P(Ba)**

> **Miller's is a price GUIDE not a price LIST**

**Thomas Francis Wainewright**
British (fl1831–83)
The Gathering Storm
Watercolour
16 x 29in (40.5 x 73.5cm)
**£6,800–7,500 / $10,000–11,000** ⊞ **HFA**

**John Wainwright**
British (fl1860–69)
Still Life: Fruit and stuffed birds
Oil on canvas
24 x 20in (61 x 51cm)
**£5,750–6,250 / $8,400–9,000** ⊞ **Dr**

**Edward Wilkins Waite**
British (1854–1924)
The Road Mender
Signed, oil on canvas
20 x 30in (51 x 76cm)
**£6,000–7,500 / $8,700–11,000** ⊞ **Ben**

**Robert Thorne Waite**
British (1842–1935)
St Mary's Church, Beverley
Inscribed verso, watercolour
14½ x 21in (37 x 53.5cm)
**£2,000–2,500 / $3,000–3,600** ↗ **Bon**

**William Walcot**
British (1874–1943)
The Strand
Signed, gouache over traces of pen and ink and pencil
8¾ x 12in (22 x 30.5cm)
**£3,300–4,000 / $4,800–5,800** ↗ **S(O)**

**Ernest Walbourn**
British (1872–1927)
By the Stream
Signed, oil on canvas
24 x 18in (61 x 45.5cm)
**£6,000–7,000**
**$8,700–10,200** ⊞ **Ben**

▶ **Ethel Walker**
British (b1940)
Water Lilies, Rhudel Pond
Signed, oil on board
29 x 32in (73.5 x 81.5cm)
**£3,500–4,200**
**$5,000–6,000** ⊞ **CON**

**Stephen Walker**
British (20thC)
Study of flowers in a Victorian jug
Signed, oil
17 x 14in (43 x 35.5cm)
**£480–550 / $700–800** ⚒ GAK

**Martha Walter**
American (1875–1976)
Summer Bouquet in a Vase
Signed, oil on canvas
22 x 17¾in (56 x 45cm)
**£3,200–3,800 / $4,600–5,600** ⚒ SHN

▶ **Alfred James Wands**
American (1904–80)
Colorado Mountain Landscape
Signed, oil on canvas
30 x 24½in (76 x 62cm)
**£450–500 / $650–720** ⚒ JAA

*Alfred James Wands was born in Washington, DC and led a wide and varied career as a painter, teacher and lecturer. He was a member of many artists' associations and exhibited throughout his life including the Philadelphia Academy of Fine Art, Chicago Art Institute, the Cleveland Museum of Art, the Paris Salon and others. He also founded and taught at the Wands Art School in Estes Park, Colorado.*

▶ **For further information**
see St Ives School
(pages 190–191)

▶ **Alfred Wallis**
British (1855–1942)
Boats at Sea
Oil, gouache and pencil on board
7 x 9in (18 x 23cm)
**£25,000–30,000**
**$36,250–43,500** ⚒ JLX

**George Stanfield Walters**
British (1838–1924)
In the Thames Estuary
Signed, watercolour heightened with touches of white
9¾ x 17in (25 x 43cm)
**£700–850 / $1,000–1,200** ⚒ Bon

**John Ward**
British (b1917)
A Palace, Rome
Signed and dated,
watercolour and ink
9½ x 12½in (24 x 32cm)
**£250–300**
**$350–450** 🖌 G(L)

▶ **Vernon Ward**
British (b1905)
Pennine Farm in Autumn
Signed, oil on panel
16 x 20in (40.5 x 51cm)
**£4,000–4,500**
**$5,800–6,500** ⊞ Dr

**William Henry Waring**
British (fl1886–1928)
Fording the Stream
Signed, oil on mahogany panel
8 x 16in (20.5 x 40.5cm)
**£3,000–3,300 / $4,500–4,750** ⊞ JC

*William Henry Waring lived and worked in
Birmingham, painting mostly in oils,
specializing in landscapes and rural scenes.
He was a popular and active member of the
Birmingham School and exhibited 51 works
at the Royal Birmingham Society of Artists
between 1886 and 1918.*

▶ **Alfred J. Warne-Browne**
British (d1915)
Portrait of Dan Sullivan,
Lifeboatman
Signed, watercolour
7 x 5½in (18 x 14cm)
**£160–180 / $230–260** 🖌 G(L)

## Venice

Few subjects are more commercially
viable than Venice. Perhaps the first
and undoubtedly the greatest artist to
capitalize on this fact was Canaletto
(1697–1768), who was hugely sought
after for his magnificent Venetian
pictures. Many artists painted in the
style of Canaletto. Since the 18th
century, the popularity of Venetian
views has not waned.

Other artists who have painted Venice
include Antoine Bouvard, Giovanni
Grubacs and Robert McInnes.

▶ **Stephen Frank
Wasley**
British (1848–1934)
Venice
Signed, watercolour
and gouache
10 x 14in
(25.5 x 35.5cm)
**£850–1,000**
**$1,250–1,500** ⊞ TBJ

**J. Watkin**
British (19thC)
A grey thoroughbred in a stable
Signed and dated 1868, oil on canvas
19½ x 23½in (49.5 x 59.5cm)
**£700–800 / $1,000–1,200** ⚒ WW

**Dick Watkins**
Australian (b1937)
Such Sweet Thunder
Signed and inscribed, acrylic
on canvas
59¾ x 84in (152 x 213.5cm)
**£7,500–9,000**
**$10,800–13,000** ⚒ P(Sy)

◄ **Franklin Chenault Watkins**
American (1894–1972)
Abstract Landscape with Figure
Signed and inscribed, oil
on canvas
10 x 13in (25.5 x 33cm)
**£650–780**
**$1,000–1,200** ⚒ JAA

**Harry Watson, RWS, ROI, RWA**
British (1871–1936)
The White Dress
Oil on panel
12 x 11in (30.5 x 30cm)
**£1,500–1,800 / $2,200–2,600** ⚒ Bon

**James Watson**
British (fl1895–1925)
Cottages at Runswick Bay
Signed, oil on canvas
20 x 25½in (51 x 65cm)
**£2,700–3,300 / $4,000–4,800** ⚒ DD

**The National Gallery of Australia**

■ Parkes Place, Parkes, Canberra,
www.nga.gov.au

■ The collections include more than 90,000 works
of Australian art including Aboriginal and Torres
Strait Islander art, Asian art and International art.

**James Fletcher Watson**
British (20thC)
Cottages at Eye, Suffolk
Signed and dated 1954, watercolour
10 x 14in (25.5 x 35.5cm)
**£300–350 / $440–500** ↗ GAK

**John Dawson Watson**
British (1832–92)
Mother and Children in Hayfield
Signed and dated 1878, watercolour
10 x 18in (25.5 x 45.5cm)
**£1,600–1,800 / $2,300–2,600** ⊞ LH

*John Dawson Watson lived in London and Cornwall. He exhibited widely, including several times at the Royal Academy, and was elected RBA in 1892 and RWS in 1870. Examples of his work can be found in the Victoria & Albert Museum, London.*

**Raymond C. Watson**
British (b1935)
Teal at Iken Decoy
Signed, watercolour
14 x 19in (35.5 x 49cm)
**£450–500 / £650–720** ↗ GAK

**Robert F. Watson**
British (1815–85)
Sheep resting along
the Highland Pass
Signed, oil on canvas
8 x 12in
(20.5 x 30.5cm)
**£4,250–4,700**
**$6,000–7,000** ⊞ HFA

**Walter J. Watson**
British (b1879)
Mallard and Ducklings on a Riverbank
Signed, oil on canvas
12½ x 16½in (32 x 42cm)
**£27,000–32,000 / $40,000–46,000** ⊞ BuP

▶ **Herbert Parsons
Weaver**
British (1872–1945)
St Sebaldus Church,
Nuremburg
Signed and dated
1935, watercolour
13½ x 9in
(34.5 x 23cm)
**£480–530**
**$700–750** ⊞ LH

**Herbert Parsons Weaver**
British (1872–1945)
Evening Glow
Signed and dated, watercolour
9½ x 13½in (24 x 34.5cm)
**£160–180 / $230–260** ⚹ G(L)

**Jenny Webb**
British (20thC)
Cyclamen
Pastel
16 x 12in (40.5 x 30.5cm)
**£85–100 / $125–145** ⊞ LS

**Kenneth Webb, ARUA, RWA**
British (b1927)
Beached Boats near Roundstone, Connemara
Signed, oil on canvas
14 x 36in (35.5 x 91.5cm)
**£4,200–5,200 / $6,000–7,500** ⊞ WrG

*Kenneth Webb was born in London and studied at Lydney School of Art, Gloucester College of Art and University College, Swansea.*

**William Edward Webb**
British (1862–1903)
Shipping in Rough Seas
Signed and dated 1883, oil on canvas
11½ x 23½in (29 x 59.5cm)
**£1,000–1,200 / $1,500–1,750** ⚹ Bon

◀ **Nils Wedel**
Swedish (1897–1967)
Jockey
Signed and dated
1921, oil on canvas
14½ x 13¾in
(37 x 35cm)
**£600–675**
**$870–1,250** ⚹ BUK

**William Weekes**
British (fl1864–1904)
An Important Meeting
Signed, oil on panel
8 x 11¼in (20.5 x 28.5cm)
**£3,000–3,300 / $4,400–4,800** ⚹ P(Ba)

# Carel Weight (1908–97)

Carel Weight was born in London and studied at Hammersmith School of Art and Goldsmiths' College School of Art. He exhibited at the Royal Academy from 1931 (he was elected RA in 1965), Leicester Galleries and the Royal Society of British Artists, of which he was a member. Weight served in the army during WWII and in 1945 was appointed an Official War Artist. In 1951 he painted a mural for the Festival of Britain's Country Pavillion, and another for Manchester Cathedral in 1963.

Weight was one of the most popular teachers at the Royal College of Art, where he taught from 1947 and was Professor of Painting from 1957 to 1973. His pupils included David Hockney, Peter Blake and Ron Kitaj, and he counted numerous artists as friends – including Lowry, for whom he arranged election to the Royal Academy.

Carel Weight was made Companion of Honour in 1995 and exhibited at most major venues worldwide. His work is in every important collection of modern British art including HRH Queen Elizabeth, the Tate Gallery, the Fitzwilliam and Ashmoleon Museums, and the Imperial War Museum.

**Carel Weight, RA**
British (1908–97)
Vietnam
Signed, oil on panel
28 x 36in (71 x 91.5cm)
**£4,750–5,225 / $7,000–7,500** ⊞ BrG

◀ **Carel Weight, RA**
British (1908–97)
Hammersmith Nights
Signed, oil on board
6 x 8½in (15 x 21.5cm)
**£6,500–7,500 / $9,500–11,000** ⚒ P

**Julian Alden Weir**
American (1852–1919)
Haystacks
Oil on canvas
18 x 24in (45.5 x 61cm)
**£40,000–50,000 / $58,000–72,000** ⚒ S(NY)
*Julian Alden Weir was born at West Point, NY and studied with his father Robert Walter Weir, a landscape painter of the Hudson River School. Julian Weir was one of the earliest American Impressionist painters.*

**Frank S. Weisbrook**
American (fl1918–35)
Drifting Snow
Signed, watercolour
12 x 16in (30.5 x 40.5cm)
**£200–250 / $300–360** ⚒ TREA

**Miller's is a price GUIDE not a price LIST**

**Frank S. Weisbrook**
American (fl1918–35)
Houses in Savanna
Signed, watercolour on paper
12 x 16in (30.5 x 40.5cm)
**£225–270 / $330–380** ↗ **TREA**

**Thaddeus Welch**
American (1844–1919)
Marin County Pastoral View
Signed, oil on canvas
20 x 36in (51 x 91.5cm)
**£11,000–13,000 / $16,000–18,500** ↗ **SK**

**Eloise Long Wells**
American (b1875)
Circus Scene
Signed, oil on board
10in (25.5cm) square
**£300–350 / $440–500** ↗ **TREA**

**Frank Werther**
Australian (b1922)
Near Point Franklin, 1995
Signed and inscribed, oil on canvas
44 x 60in (112 x 152.5cm)
**£1,250–1,500 / $1,750–2,200** ↗ **P(Sy)**

▶ **Edward Wesson**
British (1910–1983)
A Norfolk mill near Potter Heigham
Signed, watercolour
13 x 20in (33 x 51cm)
**£350–400 / $500–580** ↗ **G(L)**

*Edward Wesson was born in Blackheath, London, in 1910. He drew much of his early inspiration from the tidal waters of the River Thames, in particular, the spritsail-rigged barges that later became such popular subjects for his paintings. He saw active service as a gunner in WWII but still found time to pursue his interest in drawing and painting, exchanging his work for rations or selling the odd piece to friends and colleagues who recognized his potential.*

*On being demobbed from the war he was encouraged to exhibit his work, especially in London, and was soon accepted by most of the prestigious societies. He was elected a member of the Royal Institute in 1952 with important commissions for British Rail and the Post Office Savings Bank helping to enhance his reputation still further.*

**James Whaite**
British (fl from 1867)
Fly fishing on the River Conway
Signed, watercolour
11½ x 16½in (29 x 42cm)
**£1,000–1,100 / $1,500–1,600** ⊞ LH

**Charles Arthur Wheeler**
Australian (1881–1977)
Looking down Ryder Lane from the Hotel
Signed with presentation, inscribed, oil on board
11 x 15in (28 x 38cm)
**£300–350 / $450–500** ⚲ RBB

**Jenny Wheatley, RWS, NEAC**
British (b1968)
Red Cup
Signed, acrylic on canvas
24in (61cm) square
**£1,800–2,000 / $2,600–2,900** ⊞ Bne

**David White, ARBSA**
British (b1939)
Abstract Pots and Landscape
Mixed media
14 x 18in
(35.5 x 45.5cm)
**£450–500**
**$650–720** ⊞ Dr

◀ **Ethelbert White**
British (1891–1972)
Devon Fields
Signed and dated 1922,
oil on canvas
23 x 30in
(58.5 x 76cm)
**£3,600–4,000**
**$5,000–5,800** ⚲ B

## Prices

■ The first consideration when pricing a work is the artist and the subject matter.

■ On a decorative level oils are generally more expensive than watercolours, and watercolours generally more expensive than pencil drawings.

■ An artist's work which is out of character, ie a notable landscape artist producing a portrait, will command less.

■ Work completed during the established peak of an artist's career will cost more.

**John White, RI, ROI**
British (1851–1933)
A Devon village with figures and the Swan inn
Signed, watercolour
11 x 18in (28 x 45.5cm)
**£1,700–2,000 / $2,500–3,000** ⊞ LH

**Steve Whitehead**
British (b1960)
Todd's View
Oil on canvas
21 x 30in (53.5 x 76cm)
**£4,000–4,400 / $5,800–6,500** ⊞ P&H

**Frederick Whiting**
British (1874–1962)
Saddling
Signed, watercolour and pencil
12¾ x 17in (32.5 x 43cm)
**£3,250–3,750 / $4,700–5,200** ⊞ AAJ

*Frederick Whiting was educated at Deal and in Chelsea and studied art at St John's Wood Art School, the Royal Academy School and also in Paris. He was correspondent and artist for* The Graphic *in China from 1900–01, and during the Russo-Japanese War, 1904–05.*

▶ **Worthington Whittredge**
American (1820–1910)
Autumn, Hunter Mountain
Signed and dated 1866, oil on board
11½ x 15in (29 x 38cm)
**£40,000–50,000 / $58,000–72,000** 🔨 S(NY)

*Born on a farm near Springfield, Ohio, Worthington Whittredge began as a house and sign painter in Cincinnati, then worked briefly as a photographer and portraitist in Indiana and West Virginia before turning to landscape painting in 1843. Backed by wealthy Cincinnatians, he went to Europe in 1849, where he studied at the Royal Academy in Dusseldorf. From 1854 to 1859 he worked in Rome and afterwards settled in New York to produce views of New York and New England. Whittredge's European landscapes were not well received, however, and it was not until he started painting typical Hudson River School scenes that he began to have success. In 1865, with Gifford and Kensett he travelled along the eastern Rockies and into New Mexico and made a further two trips to the West but produced only about 40 oil sketches and studio paintings based on Western subjects. Most were painted in his New York City studio from sketches made during his first journey to the West in 1866.*

**Bryan Whitmore**
British (fl1880–97)
Riverscapes with Angler, Eel Traps and Boatmen
A pair, signed, watercolour
9 x 17in (23 x 43cm)
**£550–650 / $800–1,000** 🔨 G(L)

**Frederick John Widgery**
British (1861–1942)
Woodbury Common and the Estuary of the Exe
Signed, watercolour
25½ x 31¾in (65 x 80.5cm)
**£3,750–4,200 / $5,000–6,000**  ⊞ JC

▶ **William Widgery**
British (1822–93)
Holcombe Woods
Signed, watercolour
29 x 18½in (74 x 47cm)
**£580–650**
**$850–950**  ↗ Bea(E)

**Olaf Wieghorst**
American (1899–1988)
Nez Perce
Signed, watercolour
9½ x 8in (24 x 20.5cm)
**£5,400–6,400 / $7,800–8,800**  ↗ CdA

*Olaf Wieghorst was a self-taught artist, whose genre is the American West. He became a full-time painter in 1945. In 1948 he swapped one of his paintings for a year's supply of turkeys. In 1982 a private collector bought Wieghorst's Navajo Madonna for £310,000 ($450,000) – believed to be the highest price paid at the time for the work of a living western painter. Born in Viborg, Denmark, on April 30, 1899, he was a stunt rider for a Danish circus before emigrating to the United States at the age of 19. He also served in the US 5th Calvary at Fort Bliss, Texas, 1919–22.*

**Guy Carleton Wiggins**
American (1883–1962)
A Winter Scene
Signed, oil on canvas
12 x 16in (30.5 x 40.5cm)
**£4,000–4,800 / $5,800–7,000**  ↗ SK

*Wiggins summered in Old Lyme, Connecticut where he became one of a group of painters developing a version of impressionism by fusing French technique with American conventions. Though American art was moving more toward realism, Wiggins was dedicated to maintaining his own style, it was based on French impressionism but influenced by Childe Hassam and other American Impressionists.*

*In Wiggins' later career, he founded the Guy Wiggins Art School and travelled extensively around the USA painting scenes of Montana, Massachusetts and Connecticut.*

**Guy Carleton Wiggins**
American (1883–1962)
The Boat Docks
Signed, oil on canvasboard
8 x 11¾in (20.5 x 30cm)
**£2,200–2,600 / $3,200–3,800** 🔨 **SK**

**R. D. Wilcox**
American (late 19thC)
Sailing in Open Waters
Signed and dated 1896, oil on canvas
18 x 30in (45.5 x 76cm)
**£2,000–2,400 / $3,000–3,500** 🔨 **SHN**

**David Wilkie, RA**
British (1785–1841)
The Love Letter
Signed, oil on canvas
25 x 37in (63.5 x 94cm)
**£10,800–11,800 / $15,500–17,250** 🔨 **JAd**

## Ulster Museum

■ Botanic Gardens, Belfast BT9 5AB, www.ulstermuseum.org

■ With nearly 6,000 square metres of galleries there is a wide variety of art in the collections, including permanent displays of Irish Art.

**Norman Wilkinson**
British (1878–1971)
Las Palmas and the
Peak of Tenerife
Signed, oil on canvas
18 x 24in (45.5 x 61cm)
**£4,000–4,500 / $5,800–6,500** 🔨 **Bon**

◄ **Norman Wilkinson**
British (1878–1971)
Vessels moored on
the Thames
Oil on panel
5 x 8in (12.5 x 20.5cm)
**£550–600**
**$800–870** 🔨 **DN**

**Maurice Canning Wilks, ARHA, RUA**
Irish (1911–84)
Antrim Glen
Signed, watercolour
11 x 15in (28 x 38cm)
**£950–1,200 / $1,400–1,750** 🔨 **WA**

**Graeme Willcox**
British (b1964)
The Red King Considers
Oil on canvas
30 x 34in (76 x 86.5cm)
**£3,200–3,800 / $4,700–5,500** ⊞ CON

**Alexander Williams, RHA**
Irish (1846–1930)
Maam Vallery, Connemara
Signed, watercolour
9½ x 16½in (24 x 42cm)
**£620–750 / $900–1,100** ⚒ WA

**Kyffin Williams, ARA, RBA, PRCamA**
British (b1918)
Cottages, Penmynydd, Angelsey
Oil on canvas
19¾ x 30in (50 x 76cm)
**£5,600–6,200 / $8,000–1,200** ⚒ P

**Alexander Williams, RHA**
Irish (1846–1930)
A Foggy Morning, River Liffey
Signed, watercolour and bodycolour
19¼ x 12¾in (49 x 32.5cm)
**£750–850 / $1,100–1,250** ⚒ B

▶ **Peter Williams**
British (20thC)
In the Paddock, France
Signed, oil on canvas
14 x 18in (36 x 46cm)
**£780–850 / $1,100–1,250** ⚒ S

**Terrick Williams, RA**
British (1860–1936)
The Passing Shower, Concarneau
Signed, oil on canvas
10 x 14in (25.5 x 35.5cm)
**£4,500–5,000 / $6,500–7,250** 🔨 **B**

**Walter Williams**
British (1835–1906)
River Scenes
A pair, oil on canvas
8 x 14in (20.5 x 35.5cm)
**£9,000–10,000 / $13,000–14,500** ⊞ **HFA**

**Warren Williams**
British (1863–1918)
View of Snowdon, North Wales
Signed, watercolour
14 x 20in (35.5 x 51cm)
**£2,600–3,000 / $3,800–4,400** ⊞ **BFa**

**Charles Edward Wilson**
British (1854–1941)
The Visitor
Signed, watercolour
21 x 14in (53 x 36cm)
**£14,000–16,000 / $20,000–23,000** ⊞ **BFa**

◄ **Charles Edward Wilson**
British (1854–1941)
Feeding the Rabbits
Signed and dated 1901, watercolour
6 x 9in (15.5 x 22.5cm)
**£3,500–4,200 / $5,000–6,000** 🔨 **S(O)**

**Frank Avray Wilson**
British (b1914)
Abstract in Red
Signed, oil on canvas
22 x 18in (55.5 x 45.5cm)
**£750–800 / $1,100–1,150** ✦ P

**James Perry Wilson**
American (1889–1976)
Dock Scene
Signed, oil on canvas
20 x 24in (51 x 61cm)
**£480–550 / $700–800** ✦ SLN

**John James Wilson**
British (1818–75)
A Fresh Breeze off the Dutch Coast
Signed with initials, oil on canvas
15 x 26in (38 x 66cm)
**£16,500–20,000 / $24,000–30,000** ⊞ Bne

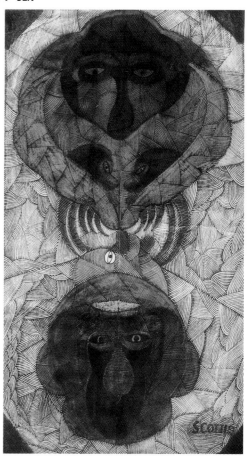

▶ **Scottie Wilson**
Scottish (1889–1972)
Untitled
Signed, ink and
watercolour
18 x 8½in (46 x 21.5cm)
**£1,400–1,600**
**$2,000–2,300** ⊞ BOX

▶ **For further information**
see Outsider Art
(pages 144–147)

◀ **John L. Wimbush**
British (d1914)
A Bolt from the Blue
Signed, oil on canvas
29½ x 39½in
(75 x 100.5cm)
**£6,500–7,500**
**$9,400–10,800** ✦ Bri

**Edward Morison Wimperis**
British (1835–1900)
On the River Bank
Signed and dated 1894, oil on canvas
24 x 36in (61 x 91.5cm)
**£7,000–8,000 / $10,200–11,600** ⊞ **Ben**

**Harry Wingfield**
British (b1910–2002)
Pleased to Meet You
Signed, gouache
11 x 7 in (28 x 18cm)
**£475–550 / $700–800** ⊞ **Dr**
*This is an original illustration for Ladybird Books.*

◀ **Frederick A. Winkfield**
British (1878–1920)
Windsor Castle from the Thames
Watercolour
13 x 20ins (33 x 51cm)
**£7,600–8,400 / $11,000–12,000** ⊞ **HFA**

**William Tatton Winter, RBA**
British (1855–1928)
The Lonely Shepherd
Signed, watercolour
13 x 16½in (33 x 42cm)
**£700–800 / $1,000–1,200** ↗ **Bon**

◀ **Olga Wisinger-Florian**
Austrian (1844–1926)
Bouquet of Lilies of the Valley
Signed, oil on wood
9 x 12¾in (23 x 32.5cm)
**£38,000–45,000 / $55,000–65,000** ↗ **DORO**

**R. Witherspoon**
British (19thC)
Barge Entering Dover Harbour
One of a pair of signed oil on canvas
22 x 11in (56 x 28cm)
**£1,200–1,400 / $1,750–2,000** ⚒ **GAK**

**Alma Wolfson**
Scottish (20thC)
Crail
Signed, oil on canvas
24 x 30in (61 x 76cm)
**£1,950–2,350 / $2,830–3,400** ⊞ **WrG**

▶ **Alfred Wolmark**
British (1877–1961)
Still life of apples
Signed, oil on board
13 x 17¾in (33 x 45cm)
**£1,600–1,800**
**$2,300–3,000** ⚒ **P**

◀ **Alfred Wolmark**
British (1877–1961)
Still life of yellow
flowers in a vase
Signed and dated
1944, oil on board
17¾ x 14¾in
(45.5 x 36.5cm)
**£1,200–1,500**
**$1,750–2,200** ⚒ **P(Ba)**

▶ **Dean Wolstenholme Jnr**
British (1798–1883)
Fly, Winner of Waterloo Cup 1837
Oil on board
8½ x 11in (21.5 x 30cm)
**£4,500–5,000 / $6,500–7,250** ⊞ **AAJ**
*The son of D. Wolstenholme Snr (1757–1837), Dean Wolstenholme*
*was born at Waltham Abbey, Essex. As a young man he studied*
*engraving and made engravings of his father's work. Wolstenholme*
*invented a form of colour printing, later patented by Leighton Brothers.*

◄ **Lewis John Wood**
British (1813–1901)
Figures in a French Town
Signed and dated
1884, watercolour
17½ x 12½in
(44.5 x 32cm)
**£850–950 /**
**$1,250–1,400** ⊞ **LH**
*Lewis John Wood*
*was a landscape and*
*architectural painter*
*and lithographer who*
*lived in London and*
*exhibited from 1836.*
*The majority of his*
*subjects were of*
*northern France and*
*Belgium. He was*
*elected NWS and RI*
*in 1871 and ROI in*
*1883, and his early*
*work was close to*
*that of Thomas Shotter*
*Boys (1803–74).*
*Examples of his work*
*are to be seen in the*
*Victoria & Albert*
*Museum and the*
*British Museum.*

**David Woodlock**
British (1842–1929)
Thoughtful
Signed, watercolour
17¾ x 12½in (45 x 32cm)
**£800–900 / $1,150–1,300** ⚒ **S(O)**

**Miller's is a price GUIDE not a**
**price LIST**

**Kesler E. Woodward**
American (b1951)
August Snow, Denali Park
Signed, oil on canvas
36 x 48in (91.5 x 122cm)
**£3,500–4,000 / $5,000–5,800** ⚒ **CdA**
*Kesler E. Woodward was born in Aiken, South Carolina in 1951.*
*He has been an Alaska resident since 1977, serving as Curator of*
*Visual Arts at the Alaska State Museum and as Artistic Director of*
*the Visual Arts Center of Alaska before moving to Fairbanks in 1981.*
*He recently retired as Professor of Art, Emeritus at the University of*
*Alaska Fairbanks, where he taught for two decades.*

**Stanley Wingate Woodward**
American (1890–1970)
Boat at Sea
Signed, watercolour
14 x 19in (35.5 x 48.5cm)
**£350–400 / $500–580** TREA

**George Wright**
British (1860–1942)
Homewards
Signed, oil on canvas
10 x 16in (25.5 x 40.5cm)
**£5,500–6,500 / $8,000–9,500** P

**George Wright**
British (1860–1942)
Hounds in a Kennel; and Hounds in a Yard
A pair, signed, oil on canvas
13 x 19in (33 x 48.5cm)
**£9,000–10,000 / $13,000–14,500** S(NY)

**George Wright**
British (1860–1942)
A Hunting Scene
Oil on canvas
21 x 35in (53.5 x 89cm)
**£6,200–7,200**
**$9,000–10,300** TMA
*George Wright painted coaching and hunting scenes, a number of which were exhibited at the Royal Academy.*

◀ **Gilbert Scott Wright**
British (1880–1958)
Taking the Fence
Signed, oil on canvas
24 x 36in (61 x 91.5cm)
**£8,500–10,000**
**$12,500–14,500** JAd

◀ **Gilbert Scott Wright**
British (1880–1958)
Asking the Way Home
Oil on canvas
18 x 24in (46 x 61cm)
**£16,500–18,000**
**$24,000–26,000**
⊞ **HFA**

**Richard Henry Wright**
British (1857–1930)
The Grand Canal from the Steps of Santa Maria della Salute, Venice
Signed and dated 1892, watercolour
7 x 10¼in (18 x 26in)
**£1,200–1,400 / $1,750–2,000** ⬈ **Bon**

◀ **W. Wright**
British (20thC)
Fisher folk on the beach at Scarborough South Bay
Signed, oil on canvas
13½ x 17½in (34.5 x 44.5cm)
**£300–350 / $440–500** ⬈ **DD**

# The Wyeth Family

The Wyeth's are America's 'first family' of artists. Newton Cornell Wyeth, known as N.C., illustrated many classic heroic stories. He was killed in a car crash in Chadds Ford, Pennsylvania, and his son Andrew (b1917) has lived thereever since. Opinions about Andrew's reputation are divided. His view of the world is essentially nostalgic; he paints people and landscapes in which there are no cars or signs of modern life. Some critics believe his work gives us insight into the human conditions of nostalgia and loneliness. Leading American critic Sam Hunter feels that his technique is good but that he lacks pictorial ambition and has a banality of imagination. However an original Wyeth or good quality print is always a good buy. Andrew's son Jamie paints scenes from every day life in rural America – houses, animals and gardens.

**Jamie Wyeth**
American (b1946)
Kuerner's Cows
Signed, watercolour on paper
18¾ x 24in (47.5 x 61cm)
**£28,000–32,000 / $41,000–46,500** ⬈ **S(NY)**

**N. C. Wyeth**
American (1882–1945)
Thorgunna, the Waif Woman
Signed, oil on canvas
44¼ x 32¼in (112.5 x 82cm)
**£22,000–25,000 / $32,000–36,000** ⬈ **S(NY)**

**Kate Wylie**
British (1877–1941)
Vase of Flowers
Signed, oil on canvas
27¼ x 22in (69 x 56cm)
**£1,800–2,200 / $2,600–3,200** ⚓ S(O)

**Gordon Hope Wyllie, RSW**
Scottish (b1930)
Morning Argyll
Mixed media
12in (30.5cm) square
**£950–1,100 / $1,400–1,600** ⊞ P&H

*After a successful teaching career, Gordon retired to paint full time in 1990. He is now the Principal Examiner in Art and Design for Scotland and has recently won the Alexander Graham Munro Prize. His delightful landscapes of Scottish Highland scenes are firm favourites with his collectors south of the border.*

**William Lionel Wyllie**
British (1851–1931)
Thames Barges with St Paul's Cathedral and The Tower of London behind
A pair, signed in pencil, etchings
14 x 10in (35.5 x 25.5cm)
**£1,600–2,000 / $2,300–3,000** ⚓ G(L)

◄ **For further information**
see Marine Art (pages 130–133)

**Anthonie Jacobus van Wyngaerde**
Dutch (1808–87)
Dutch Landscape
Oil on panel
11 x 15in (28 x 38cm)
**£1,750–2,000 / $2,500–3,000** ⊞ JDG

# John Yardley (b1933)

John Yardley was born in Beverley, Yorkshire. In 1986 he gave up a career in banking to dedicate himself to painting, beginning mainly by depicting English landscapes before turning to interiors and street scenes in England and abroad. He enjoys huge acclaim with many solo and mixed exhibitions and is now one of the most collected contemporary artists. Elected to membership to the Royal Institute of Watercolours in 1990, John is well known to many 'would be artists' through his teaching books and videos in which he shares the pleasures and frustrations of watercolour painting.

John Yardley, RI
British (b1933)
Awaiting the Tide, Woodbridge
Signed, watercolour
14 x 19½in (35.5 x 50cm)
£1,500–1,650 / $2,200–2,500 ⊞ WrG

◀ John Yardley, RI
British (b1933)
The Flowermarket, Nice
Oil on canvas
24 x 30in (61 x 76cm)
£3,750–4,250 / $5,500–6,250 ⊞ Bne

Anthony Yates
British (20thC)
Bowls Match – Christchurch
Oil
14in (35.5cm) square
£400–450 / $580–650 ⊞ Dr

▶ Eugenio Zampighi
Italian (1859–1944)
Darby and Joan
Signed, oil on canvas
14½ x 20¼in (37 x 51.5cm)
£3,600–4,200 / $5,000–6,000 ⚹ Bon

▶ Fred Yates
British (b1922)
Old Lady of the Sea, Newhaven
Signed, dated 1995 and inscribed, oil on canvas
23¾ x 29½in (60.5 x 75cm)
£1,750–2,000
$2,500–3,000 ⊞ JLx

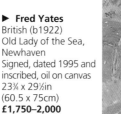

# Bibliography

Archibald, E.H.H., *Dictionary of Sea Painters,* Antique Collectors' Club, 1980.

Arts Council of Great Britain, *British Sporting Painting, 1650–1850,* 1974.

Arts Council of Great Britain, *The Modern Spirit: American Painting 1908–1935,* 1977.

Baigell, Matthew, *A History of American Paintings,* Thames and Hudson, 1971.

Beetles, Chris, Ltd, *The Illustrators, London, 1991, 1992, 1993.*

Bernard, Denvir, *The Impressionists at First Hand,* Thames and Hudson, 1987.

Bindman, David, *Encyclopaedia of British Art,* Thames and Hudson, 1985.

Brook-Hart, Denys, *British 19th Century Marine Painting,* Antique Collectors' Club, 1978.

de Goncourt, Edmond and Jules, *French Eighteenth Century Painters,* Oxford, Phaidon, 1981.

Fielding, Mantle, *Dictionary of American Painters,* Connecticut, Modern Books and Crafts Inc, 1974.

Gaunt, William, *A Concise History of English Painting,* Thames and Hudson, 1973.

Hall, Donald and Corrington Wykes, Pat, *Anecdotes of Modern Art,* Oxford University Press, 1990.

Hall, James, *Dictionary of Subjects and Symbols in Art,* John Murray, 1979.

Heller, Nancy G., *Women Artists, An Illustrated History,* Virago, 1987.

Hemming, Charles, *British Painters of the Coast and Sea,* Victor Gollancz Ltd., 1988.

Hislop, Duncan, *The Art Sales Index 2000/2001,* Art Sales Index Ltd., 2001.

Hook, Philip and Poltimore, Mark, *Popular 19th Century Painting,* Antique Collectors' Club, 1986.

Johnson, J. and Greutzner, A., *Dictionary of British Artists 1880–1940,* Antique Collectors' Club, 1988.

Lucie-Smith, Edward, *The Thames and Hudson Dictionary of Art Terms,* Thames and Hudson, 1988.

Maas, Jeremy, *Victorian Painters,* Barrie and Jenkins, 1988.

McConkey, Kenneth, *A Free Spirit Irish Art 1860–1960,* Antiques Collectors' Club, 1990.

Mallalieu, H.L., *Understanding Watercolours,* Antique Collectors' Club, 1985.

Mallalieu, H.L., *The Dictionary of British Watercolour Artists up to 1920,* Antique Collectors' Club, 1986.

Ottley, H. *Dictionary of Recent and Living Painters and Engravers,* Henry G. Bohn, 1866.

Oxford University Press, *Dictionary of National Biography,* 1975/81/86/90.

Osborne, Harold, *The Oxford Companion to Twentieth Century Art,* Oxford University Press, 1988.

Payne, Andrew Clayton, *Victorian Flower Gardens,* London, Weidenfeld & Nicholson, 1988.

Prendeville, Brendan, *Realism in 20th Century Paintings,* Thames and Hudson, 2000.

Redgrave, Richard and Samuel, *A Century of British Painters,* Oxford, Phaidon, 1981.

Rhodes, Cecil, *Outsider Art, Spontaneous Alternatives,* Thames and Hudson, 2000.

Rothenstein, John, *Modern English Painters,* Macdonald, 1984.

Spalding, Frances, *20th Century Painters and Sculptors,* Antique Collectors' Club, 1990.

Strong, Roy, *The British Portrait 1660–1960,* Antique Collectors' Club, 1990.

Waterhouse, Ellis, *British 18th Century Paintings,* Antiques Collectors' Club, 1981.

Wingfield, Mary Ann, *A Dictionary of Sporting Artists 1650–1900,* Antique Collectors' Club, 1992.

Wood, Christopher, *The Dictionary of Victorian Painters,* Antique Collectors' Club, 1978.

# Directory of Auctioneers

Auctioneers who hold frequent sales should contact us by January 2003 for inclusion in the next edition.

**Berkshire**
Dreweatt Neate, Donnington Priory, Donnington, Newbury RG14 2JE Tel: 01635 553553 fineart@dreweatt-neate.co.uk

**Buckinghamshire**
Bourne End Auction Rooms, Station Approach, Bourne End SL8 5QH Tel: 01628 531500

**Cambridgeshire**
Cheffins, 2 Clifton Road, Cambridge CB2 4BW Tel: 01223 213343 www.cheffins.co.uk

**Cheshire**
Bonhams, New House, 150 Christleton Road, Chester CH3 5TD Tel: 01244 313936

**Cumbria**
Thomson, Roddick & Medcalf, Coleridge House, Shaddongate, Carlisle CA2 5TU Tel: 01228 528939

**Devon**
Bearnes, St Edmund's Court, Okehampton Street, Exeter EX4 1DU Tel: 01392 422800 nsaintey@bearnes.co.uk www.bearnes.co.uk

Michael J Bowman, 6 Haccombe House, Nr Netherton, Newton Abbott TQ12 4SJ Tel: 01626 872890 Mobile: 07789 650202

Taylors, Honiton Galleries, 205 High Street, Honiton EX14 8LF Tel: 01404 42404

**Essex**
G. E. Sworder & Sons, 14 Cambridge Road, Stansted Mountfitchet CM24 8BZ Tel: 01279 817778 www.sworder.co.uk

**Gloucestershire**
Bristol Auction Rooms, St John's Place, Apsley Road, Clifton, Bristol BS8 2ST Tel: 0117 973 7201 www.bristolauctionrooms.co.uk

**Herefordshire**
Brightwells Ltd, Ryelands Road, Leominster HR6 8NZ Tel: 01568 611122 fineart@brightwells.com

**Hertfordshire**
Brown & Merry, Tring Market Auctions, The Market Premises, Brook Street, Tring HP23 5EF Tel: 01442 826446 sales@tringmarketauctions.co.uk www.tringmarketauctions.co.uk

**Kent**
Bonhams, 49 London Road, Sevenoaks TN13 1AR Tel: 01732 740310

The Canterbury Auction Galleries, 40 Station Road West, Canterbury CT2 8AN Tel: 01227 763337

Ibbett Mosely, 125 High Street, Sevenoaks TN13 1UT Tel: 01732 452246/456731

**Leicestershire**
Heathcote Ball & Co, Castle Auction Rooms, 78 St Nicholas Circle, Leicester LE1 5NW Tel: 0116 253 6789 heathcote-ball@clara.co.uk www.heathcote-ball.clara.co.uk

**London**
Bonhams, 10 Salem Road, Bayswater W2 4DL Tel: 020 7229 9090 www.bonhams.com

Bonhams, 101 New Bond Street W1S 1SR Tel: 020 7629 6602 www.bonhams.com

Bonhams, 65–69 Lots Road, Chelsea SW10 0RN Tel: 020 7393 3900 www.bonhams.com

Bonhams, Montpelier Street, Knightsbridge SW7 1HH Tel: 020 7393 3900 www.bonhams.com

Sotheby's, 34–35 New Bond Street W1A 2AA Tel: 020 7293 5000 www.sothebys.com

Sotheby's Olympia, Hammersmith Road W14 8UX Tel: 020 7293 5000

**Merseyside**
Cato Crane & Co, Liverpool Auction Rooms, 6 Stanhope Street, Liverpool L8 5RF Tel: 0151 709 5559 www.cato-crane.co.uk

**Norfolk**
Bonhams, The Market Place, Reepham, Norwich NR10 4JJ Tel: 01603 871443

Keys, Aylsham Salerooms, Off Palmers Lane, Aylsham NR11 6JA Tel: 01263 733195 www.aylshamsalerooms.co.uk

**Northern Ireland**
John Ross & Company, 37 Montgomery Street, Belfast, Co Antrim BT1 4NX Tel: 028 9032 5448

**Nottinghamshire**
Neales, 192–194 Mansfield Road, Nottingham NG1 3HU Tel: 0115 962 4141

**Oxfordshire**
Simmons & Sons, 32 Bell Street, Henley-on-Thames RG9 2BH Tel: 01491 612810 www.simmonsandsons.com

**Republic of Ireland**
James Adam, 26 St Stephens Green, Dublin 2 Tel: 00 3531 676 0261 www.jamesadam.ie

Whyte's Auctioneers, 38 Molesworth Street, Dublin 2 Tel: 00 353 1 676 2888 info@whytes.ie www.whytes.ie

**Scotland**
Bonhams, 65 George Street, Edinburgh EH2 2JL Tel: 0131 225 2266

**Somerset**
Lawrences Fine Art Auctioneers, South Street, Crewkerne TA18 8AB Tel: 01460 73041

**Staffordshire**
Wintertons Ltd, Lichfield Auction Centre, Wood End Lane, Fradley, Lichfield WS13 8NF Tel: 01543 263256

**Suffolk**
Bonhams, 32 Boss Hall Road, Ipswich IP1 5DJ Tel: 01473 740494

**East Sussex**
Gorringes Auction Galleries, Terminus Road, Bexhill-on-Sea TN39 3LR Tel: 01424 212994 bexhill@gorringes.co.uk www.gorringes.co.uk

Gorringes inc Julian Dawson, 15 North Street, Lewes BN7 2PD Tel: 01273 472503 auctions@gorringes.co.uk www.gorringes.co.uk

**West Sussex**
Rupert Toovey & Co Ltd, Star Road, Partridge Green RH13 8RA Tel: 01403 711744 auctions@rupert-toovey.com www.rupert-toovey.com

**Tyne & Wear**
Anderson & Garland (Auctioneers), Marlborough House, Marlborough Crescent, Newcastle-upon-Tyne NE1 4EE Tel: 0191 232 6278

**West Midlands**
Bonhams, The Old House, Station Road, Knowle, Solihull B93 0HT Tel: 01564 776151

**Wiltshire**
Woolley & Wallis, Salisbury Salerooms, 51–61 Castle Street, Salisbury SP1 3SU Tel: 01722 424500

**Yorkshire**
Bonhams, 17a East Parade, Leeds LS1 2BH Tel: 0113 2448011

David Duggleby, The Vine St Salerooms, Scarborough YO11 1XN Tel: 01723 507111 auctions@davidduggleby.freeserve.co.uk www.davidduggleby.com

Andrew Hartley, Victoria Hall Salerooms, Little Lane, Ilkley LS29 8EA Tel: 01943 816363 info@andrewhartleyfinearts.co.uk www.andrewhartleyfinearts.co.uk

Tennants, The Auction Centre, Harmby Road, Leyburn DL8 5SG Tel: 01969 623780

**Austria**
Dorotheum, Palais Dorotheum, A-1010 Wien, Dorotheergasse 17 Tel: 0043 1 515 60 354

**Australia**
Shapiro Auctioneers, formerly Phillips, 162 Queen Street, Woollahra, Sydney NSW 2025 Tel: 00 612 9326 1588

**Canada**
Waddington's Auctions, 111 Bathurst Street, Toronto MSV 2RI Tel: 001 416 504 9100 vb@waddingtonsauctions.com www.waddingtonsauctions.com

**Sweden**
Bukowskis, Arsenalsgatan 4, Stockholm SE111 47 Tel: 08 614 08 00 info@bukowskis.se www.bukowskis.se

**U.S.A.**
The Coeur d'Alene Art Auction, PO Box 310, Hayden ID 83835 Tel: 001 208 772 9009 drumgallery@nidlink.com www.cdaartauction.com

Jackson's Auctioneers & Appraisers, 2229 Lincoln Street, Cedar Falls IA 50613 Tel: 00 1 319 277 2256

Kimball M Sterling, Inc, 125 West Market Street, Johnson City, Tennessee 37601 Tel: 001 423 928 1471 kimsold@tricon.com www.outsiderartauctions.com *Outsider Art auctioneer*

New Orleans Auction Galleries, Inc., 801 Magazine Street, AT 510 Julia, New Orleans, Louisiana 70130 Tel: 00 1 504 566 1849

Phillips New York, 406 East 79th Street, New York NY10021 Tel: 00 1 212 570 4830

Shannon's, 354 Woodmont Road, Milford, Connecticut 06460 Tel: 001 203 877 1711 www.shannons.com

Skinner Inc, The Heritage On The Garden, 63 Park Plaza, Boston MA 02116 Tel: 00 1 617 350 5400

Sloan's, 4920 Wyaconda Road, North Bethesda MD 20852 Tel: 001 301 468 4911 www.sloansauction.com

Sotheby's, 1334 York Avenue, New York NY 10021 Tel: 001 212 606 7000

Treadway Gallery, Inc, 2029 Madison Road, Cincinnati, Ohio 45208 Tel: 001 513 321 6742 www.treadwaygallery.com

# Directory of Galleries

If you wish to be included in next year's directory, or if you have a change of address or telephone number, please contact Miller's advertising department by January 2003. We advise readers to make contact by telephone first before visiting a gallery, therefore avoiding a wasted journey.

**Berkshire**
The Contemporary Fine Art Gallery, 31 High Street, Eton, Windsor SL4 1HL Tel: 01753 854315

The Graham Gallery, Highwoods, Hermits Hill, Burfield Common, Reading RG7 3BG Tel: 0118 983 1070

**Buckinghamshire**
Angela Hone Watercolours Tel: 020 7402 2901/01628 484170

**Cambridgeshire**
artHester, 78 Highsett, Cambridge CB2 1NZ Tel: 01223 522489 arthester@easynet.co.uk

Byard Art, 4 Chapel Street, Duxford CB2 4RJ Tel: 01223 560 400 info@byardart.co.uk www.byardart.co.uk

Cambridge Fine Art, Priesthouse, 33 Church Street, Little Shelford, Nr Cambridge CB2 5HG Tel: 01223 842866

**Cheshire**
Baron Fine Art, 68 Watergate Street, Chester CH1 2LA Tel: 01244 342520

The Bridgegate Gallery, 14 Buraney Court, Pulford, Chester CH4 9ES Tel: 01244 570071 bridgegate.gallery@btinternet.com

**Cleveland**
T B & R Jordan (Fine Paintings), Aslak, Aislaby, Eaglescliffe, Stockton-on-Tees TS16 0QN Tel: 01642 782599

**Cornwall**
The Net Loft Gallery and The Old Customs House Studio, The Harbour, Porthleven TR13 9JD Tel: 01326 564010 www.cornwall-art.co.uk

New Millennium Gallery, Street-an-Pol, St Ives TR26 2DS Tel: 01736 793121 stives@dircon.co.uk www.stives.dircon.co.uk

Shears Fine Art, 58 Chapel Street, Penzance TR18 4AE Tel: 01736350501/361359 dianashears@exchange.uk.com

St Ives Society of Artists, Norway Gallery, Norway Square, St Ives TR26 1NA Tel: 01736 795582 www.stivessocietyofartists.com

**Devon**
J Collins & Son, The Studio, 28 High Street, Bideford EX39 2AN Tel: 01237 473103 biggs@collinsantiques.co.uk www.collinsantiques.co.uk

Gordon Hepworth, Hayne Farm, Sandown Lane, Newton St. Cyres, Exeter EX5 5DE Tel: 01392 851351

New Street Gallery, 38 New Street, The Barbican, Plymouth PL1 2NA Tel: 01752 221450 mail@newstreetgallery.fsnet.co.uk

**Dorset**
Thomas Henry Fine Art, The Old Warehouse, Durngate Street, Dorchester DT1 1JP

Tel: 01305 250388 sealight21@hotmail.com

The Swan Gallery, 51 Cheap Street, Sherborne DT9 3AX Tel: 01935 814465

**Essex**
Brandler Galleries, 1 Coptfold Road, Brentwood CM14 4BM Tel: 01277 222269 john@brandler-galleries.com www.brandler-galleries.com

Simon Hilton, Flemings Hill Farm, Gt. Easton CM6 2ER Tel: 01279 850 107 simonhilton@btopenworld.com

**Gloucestershire**
Alexander Gallery, 122 Whiteladies Road, Bristol BS8 2RP Tel: 0117 973 4692

Benton Fine Art, Regent House, High Street, Moreton-in-Marsh GL56 0AX Tel/Fax: 01608 652153 bentonfineart@excite.com

The John Davies Gallery, Church Street, Stow-on-the-Wold GL54 1BB Tel: 01451 831698 daviesart@aol.com www.the-john-davies-gallery.co.uk

Jonathan Poole, Compton Cassey House, Nr Withington, Cheltenham GL54 4DE Tel: 01242 890224 jonathanpoole@comptoncassey.demon.co.uk

Nina Zborowska, Damsels Mill, Paradise, Painswick GL6 6UD Tel: 01452 812460 enquiries@ninazborowska.com www.ninazborowska.com

**Hampshire**
Maurice Dear, 37 Darlington Gardens, Upper Shirley, Southampton SO15 7QL Tel: 02380 776947

**Kent**
Graham Clarke Ltd, White Cottage, Green Lane, Boughton Monchelsea, Maidstone ME14 4LF Tel: 01622 743938

The Hunt Gallery, 33 Strand Street, Sandwich CT13 9DS Tel: 01304 612792 Tel/Fax: 01227 722287 huntgallery@hotmail.com www.thehuntgallery.com
*Established in 1972, specialising in the work of Michael John Hunt. Topographical and architectural paintings and peaceful, serene interiors.*

Lotus House Studios, 25 Station Road, Lydd, Romney Marsh TN29 9ED Tel: 01797 320585

Redleaf Gallery, 1 Castle Street, Tunbridge Wells TN1 1XJ Tel: 01892 526695

**Leicestershire**
Fine Art of Oakham, 4–5 Crown Walk, Oakham LE15 6AL Tel: 01572 755221 www.fineart-oakham.co.uk

Goldmark Gallery, Orange Street, Uppingham, Rutland LE15 9SQ Tel: 01572 821424

**London**
Arthur Ackermann & Peter Johnson Ltd, 27 Lowndes Street SW1X 9HY Tel: 020 7235 6464 ackermannjohnson@btconnect.com www.artnet.com/ackermann-johnson.html

John Adams Fine Art Ltd, 200 Ebury Street SW1W 8UN Tel: 020 7730 8999

Ainscough Contemporary Art, Drayton Gardens SW10 9QS Tel: 020 7341 9442 art@acag.co.uk www.acag.co.uk

Pascal Allouard Contemporary Art, 6 Saint Mary le Park Court, SW11 4PJ Tel: 020 7223 0850 Pascal.Allouard@Detica.com www.officieldesarts.com/PascalAllouard

Archeus Fine Art, 3 Albemarle Street W1S 4HE Tel: 020 7499 9755 art@archeus.co.uk www.archeus.co.uk

Art First, First Floor Gallery, 9 Cork Street W1X 1PD Tel: 020 7734 0386 artfirst@dircon.co.uk www.artfirst.co.uk

Art Space Gallery, 84 St Peter's Street N1 8JS Tel: 020 7359 7002 mail@artspacegallery.co.uk www.artspacegallery.co.uk

ArtLondon.Com, Suite 958, 28 Old Brompton Road SW7 3SS Tel: 020 7402 2897 info@artlondon.com www.artlondon.com
*Our galleries offer art lovers a rich experience of carefully selected paintings, prints and photographs in a range of genres and styles by international and UK based artists. From landscapes to still life, from traditional to contemporary styles, the works displayed on the site have been chosen for their quality by our professional gallery team. Although we believe in exceptional art, we also believe that art should be obtainable– which is why works are keenly, rather than extravagantly priced. We take pride in our high standards of customer care, and our dedicated team are happy to provide further details about any of the works or artists represented by ArtLondon.Com. We can be contacted by e-mail, fax or phone. ArtLondon.Com. For exceptional, obtainable art.*

Artmonsky Arts, 108a Boundary Road NW8 0RH Tel: 020 7604 3990 gallery@artmonsky.com www.artmonsky.com

Asia Contemporary Art, 49 Lamb's Conduit Street, Bloomsbury WC1N 3NG Tel: 020 7611 5252 mail@asiacontemporaryart.com www.asiacontemporaryart.com

Austin/Desmond Fine Art, Pied Bull Yard, 68/69 Great Russell Street WC1B 3BN Tel: 020 7242 4443 gallery@austindesomond.com www.austindesmond.com

George Babbington, 134 Addison Gardens W14 0DS Tel: 020 7602 5454 george.babbington@btinternet.com www.babbington.net

Kamal Bakhshi Contemporary Japanese Prints, 8 Campden Hill Square W8 7LB Tel: 020 7727 2574 kbahshi@aol.com

Bankside Gallery, 48 Hopton Street SE1 9JH Tel: 020 7928 7521

Barkes & Barkes, 76 Parkway, Camden Town NW1 7AH Tel: 020 7284 1550 www.artrussia.com

Belgrave Gallery, 53 Englands Lane NW3 4YD Tel: 020 7722 5150 sales@belgravegallery.com www.belgravegallery.com

John Bennett Fine Art, 206 Walton Street SW3 2JL Tel: 020 7225 2223

James Birch Gallery, 22 Laystall Street EC1R 4PA Tel: 020 7837 1595

The Blue Gallery, 28/29 Great Sutton Street EC1V 0DS Tel: 020 7490 3833 bluegallery@compuserve.com www.bluegallery.co.uk

Boundary Gallery, 98 Boundary Road NW8 0RH Tel: 020 7624 1126 boundary@agikatz.demon.co.uk

Lena Boyle Fine Art, 40 Drayton Gardens SW10 9SA Tel: 020 7259 2700/020 7373 8247 lena.boyle@btinternet.com www.lenaboyle.com

The Bruton Street Gallery Ltd, 28 Bruton Street W1Y 7DB Tel: 020 7499 9747 art@brutonstreetgallery.com www.brutonstreetgallery.com

Burlington Fine Paintings Ltd, 10 & 12 Burlington Gardens W1X 1LG Tel: 020 7734 9984 pictures@burlington.co.uk www.burlington.co.uk

Caelt Gallery, 182 Westbourne Grove W11 2RH Tel: 020 7229 9309 art@caeltgallery.com www.caeltgallery.com

Cardiff & Rayner, 29 Stokenchurch Street, Fulham SW6 3TS Tel: 020 7736 5916 Cardiff&Rayner@POBox.com

Anna-Mei Chadwick, PO Box 22504 W8 5GZ Tel: 020 7938 3757

Keith Chapman (Modern Sculptors), 91 Raymouth Road SE16 2DA Tel: 020 7232 1885 keithchapman@talk21.com

Jonathan Clark, 18 Park Walk SW10 0AQ Tel: 020 7351 3555 clark@jc-art.com www.jc-art.com

Collins & Hastie Ltd, 5 Park Walk SW10 0AJ Tel: 020 7351 4292 caroline@chelseaart.co.uk www.chelseaart.co.uk

Jonathan Cooper, Park Walk Gallery, 20 Park Walk SW10 0AQ
Tel: 020 7351 0410
mail@jonathancooper.co.uk
www.jonathancooper.co.uk

Cynthia Corbett Gallery, 15 Claremont Lodge, 15 The Downs SW20 8UA
Tel: 020 8947 6782
corbettcc@hotmail.com

Coskun Fine Art, 93 Walton Street SW3 2HP Tel: 020 7581 9056
gulgallery@aol.com
www.coskunfineart.com

Counter Editions Ltd, 5–9 Hatton Wall EC1N 8HX Tel: 020 7692 0000
www.countereditions.com

Alan Cristea Gallery, 31 Cork Street W1S 3NU Tel: 020 7439 1866

Curwen Gallery, 4 Windmill Street, off Charlotte Street W1P IHF
Tel: 020 7636 1459
pryle@curwengallery.com
www.curwengallery.com

Davies & Tooth, 32 Dover Street W1S 4NE Tel: 020 7409 1516
art@davies-tooth.com
www.davies-tooth.com

John Denham Gallery, 50 Mill Lane NW6 1NJ Tel: 020 7794 2635

William Drummond (Convent Garden Gallery Ltd), 8 St. James's Chambers, 2 Ryder Street, St. James's SW1Y 6QA
Tel: 020 7930 9696

Eaton Gallery, 34 Duke Street, St James's SW1Y 6DF Tel: 020 7930 5950

Enitharmon Press, 26B Caversham Road NW5 2DU Tel: 020 7482 5967
books@enitharmon.co.uk
www.enitharmon.co.uk

Fine Art Commissions, 107 Walton Street SW3 2HP Tel: 020 7589 4111
info@fineartcommissions.com
www.fineartcommissions.com

Fleur de Lys Gallery, 227A Westbourne Grove W11 2SE Tel/Fax: 020 7727 8595
fleurdelysgallery@yahoo.com
www.fleur-de-lys.com

Liliane Fredericks, Flat 1, 32 Stanhope Gardens SW7 5QY
Tel: 020 7373 9830
liliane@netcomuk.co.uk

Frost & Reed Ltd, 2–4 King Street, St James's SW1Y 6QP
Tel: 020 7839 4645
www.frostandreed.co.uk

Gallery K, 101–103 Heath Street, Hampstead SW3 6SS
Tel: 020 7794 4949
art@galleryk.co.uk

Gallery Niklas von Bartha, 22 Brechin Place Tel: 020 7370 4754
info@vonbartha.com
www.vonbartha.com

Martyn Gregory Gallery, 34 Bury Street, St James's SW1Y 6AU
Tel: 020 7839 3731

Grosvenor Prints, 28–32 Shelton Street, Covent Garden WC2H 9HP
Tel: 020 7836 1979

Paul Hahn, 5 Lower Grosvenor Place SW1W 0EJ Tel: 020 7592 0224
paulhahn@hahngallery.co.uk

Laurence Hallett (LAPADA)
Tel: 020 7798 8977
Mobile: 077 88 44 29 39
DST104KEY@cwctv.net
*By appointment only*

Hanga Ten, Hurlingham Studios, Ranelagh Gardens SW6 3PA
Tel: 020 7371 9677
japart@hangaten.co.uk

Hanina Gallery, 180 Westbourne Grove W11 2RH Tel: 020 7243 8877
hanina@globalnet.co.uk
www.hanina-gallery.co.uk

Benjamin C. Hargreaves, 90 Kenyon Street, Fulham SW6 6LB
Tel: 020 7385 7757

Hart Gallery, 113 Upper Street, Islington N1 1QN Tel: 020 7704 1131
www.hartgallery.co.uk

Rebecca Hossack Gallery, 35 Windmill Street WIT 2JS Tel: 020 7436 4899
rebecca@r-h-g.co.uk www.r-h-g.co.uk

Kate Howe Fine Art, 32 Sumner Place SW7 3NT Tel: 020 7225 5272
kate.howe@lineone.net

James Hyman Fine Art, 9 North Square NW11 7AB Tel: 020 8455 7882
jameshymanart@aol.com
www.artnet.com/jhyman.html

Images, 248 Verulam Court, Woolmead Avenue NW9 7AZ
Tel: 020 8202 7949
nc.images@btinternet.com
www.images-art.co.uk

Independent Gallery, 3a Compton Avenue N12XD Tel: 020 7704 2297
pop.art@btinternet.com

Gillian Jason Modern & Contemporary Art, 40 Inverness Street NW1 7HB
Tel: 020 7267 4835
art@gillianjason.com
www.gillianjason.com

Mark Jason Fine Art, 71 New Bond Street W1S 1DE Tel: 020 7629 4080
info@jasonfineart.com
www.jasonfineart.com

Kings Road Gallery, 436 King's Road SW10 0LJ Tel: 020 7351 367
tanya@kingsroadgallery.com
www.kingsroadgallery.com

Stephen Lacey Gallery, One Crawford Passage, Ray Street EC1R 3DP
Tel: 020 7837 5507
stephenlaceygallery@lineone.net

Julian Lax, 37–39 Arkwright Road, Hampstead NW3 6BJ
Tel: 020 7794 9933

Frederic Leris, 25 Yoakley Road N16 0BH Tel: 020 8800 4091
fredericleris@virgin.net

Long & Ryle, 4 John Islip Street SW1P 4PX Tel: 020 7834 1434
gallery@long-and-ryle.demon.co.uk
www.long-and-ryle.co.uk

MacLean Fine Art, 10 Neville Street SW7 3AR Tel: 020 7589 4384
info@macleanfineart.com
www.macleanfineart.com

John Martin, 38 Albermarle Street W1S 4JG Tel: 020 7499 1314
info@jmlondon.com
www.jmlondon.com

Menier Gallery, 51 Southwark Street SE1 Tel: 020 7407 5388

Messum's Contemporary Gallery, 8 Cork Street W1X 1PB
Tel: 020 7437 5545
enquiries@messums.com
www.messums.com

Messum's Galleries, Duke Street, St James's SW1 Tel: 020 7839 5180
www.messums.com
*Traditional and Impressionist paintings*

Duncan R Miller Fine Arts, 6 Bury Street, St. James's SW1Y 6AB
Tel: 020 7839 8806
DMFineArts@aol.com
www.duncan-miller.com

New Grafton Gallery, 49 Church Road SW13 9HH Tel: 020 8748 8850

Offer Waterman & Co, 11 Langton Street SW10 0JL Tel: 020 7351 0068
info@waterman.co.uk
www.warterman.co.uk

Panter & Hall, 9 Shepherd Market, Mayfair W1J 7PF Tel: 020 7399 9999
enquiries@panterandhall.co.uk
www.panterandhall.co.uk

Michael Parkin Fine Art Ltd, Studio 4, Sedding Street SW1W 8EE
Tel: 020 7730 9784

Piano Nobile Fine Paintings, 129 Portland Road W11 4LW
Tel: 020 7229 1099
art@pianonobile.freeserve.co.uk
www.piano-nobile.com

The Piccadilly Gallery, 43 Dover Street W1S 4NU Tel: 020 7629 2875
www.piccadillygall.demon.co.uk

Pollock Fine Art, 21 Beak Street, off Regent Street W1
Tel: 020 7434 9947
sjpollock8@aol.com
www.popmodart.com

Portal Gallery, 43 Dover Street, Piccadilly W1S 4NU Tel: 020 7493 0706
portalgallery@btinternet.com
www.portal-gallery.com

The Red Mansion, 9 Park Square West NW1 4LJ Tel: 020 7486 8862
nk@redmansion.co.uk
www.redmansion.co.uk

Ryan Fine Art, 74 Vanbrugh Park SE3 7JQ Tel: 020 8305 0854
darrell@ryanfineart.com

Scolar Fine Art, 35 Bruton Place W1J 6NS Tel: 020 7629 4944
art@scolarfineart.com
www.scolarfineart.com

The Sheridan Russell Gallery, 16 Crawford Street W1H 1BS
Tel: 020 7935 0250

The Sladmore Gallery, 32 Bruton Place, Mayfair W1X 7AA
Tel: 020 7499 0365
sculpture@sladmore.com
www.sladmore.com

John Spink, 9 Richard Burbidge Mansions, 1 Brasenose Drive SW13 8RB Tel: 020 8741 6152

Walton Gallery, 12 Gloucester Road SW7 4RB Tel: 020 7854 2097
matthewsfineart@aol.com
www.waltongallery.com

Whitford Fine Art, 6 Duke Street, St James's SW1Y 6BN
Tel: 020 7930 9332

Will's Art Warehouse, Unit 3 Heathman's Road, Parson's Green, Fulham SW6 4TJ Tel: 020 7371 8787
will@wills-art.demon.co.uk
www.wills-art.com

Wiseman Originals Ltd, 34 West Square SE11 4SP Tel: 020 7587 0747
wisemanoriginals@compuserve.com
www.wisemanoriginals.com

Wolseley Fine Arts, 12 Needham Road W11 2RP Tel: 020 7792 2788
info@wolseleyfinearts.com
www.wolseleyfinearts.com

Christopher Wood Gallery, 20 Georgian House, 10 Bury Street SW1Y 6AA Tel: 020 7839 3963
www.christopherwoodgallery.com

Wyllie Gallery, 44 Elvaston Place SW7 5NP Tel: 020 7584 6024

## Merseyside
Boydell Galleries, Liverpool
Tel: 0151 932 9220
www.boydellgalleries.co.uk

## Oxfordshire
4Impressions, 43 Oakthorpe Road, Oxford OX2 7BD Tel: 01865 516556
jessielee@fourimpressions.com

Wiseman-Noble, 40/41 South Parade, Summertown, Oxford OX2 7JL
Tel: 01865 515123
sarahjane@wisegal.com
www.wisegal.com

Wren Gallery, Bear Court, 34 Lower High Street, Burford, Oxon OX18 4RR
Tel: 01993 823495
enquiries@wrenfineart.com
www.wrenfineart.com

## Republic of Ireland
Apollo Gallery, 51C Dawson Street, Dublin 2 Tel: 00 3531 671 2609
art@apollogallery.ie
www.apollogallery.ie

The Frederick Gallery, 24, South Frederick Street, Dublin 2
Tel: 00 3531 670 7055 fredgal@aol.ie
www.frederickgallery.com

Royal Hibernian Gallery, 15 Ely Place, Dublin 2 Tel: 00 3531 661 2558
rhagallery@eircom.net
www.royalhibernianacademy.com

Hugh Lane Gallery, Charlemont House, Parnell Square North, Dublin 1 Tel: 00 3531 874 1903
info@hughlane.ie www.hughlane.ie

## Scotland
Barclay Lennie Fine Art, PO Box 16772, Glasgow G11 5WF
Tel: 0141 334 8983
barclaylennie@hotmail.com
www.barclaylennie.com

Roger Billcliffe Fine Art, 134 Blythswood Street, Glasgow G2 4EL Tel: 0141 332 4027
roger@rbfa.demon.co.uk
www.billcliffegallery.com

Carlton Gallery, 10 Royal Terrace, Edinburgh HU5 4JY
Tel: 0131 556 1010
mail@carltongallery.co.uk
www.carltongallery.co.uk

Cyril Gerber Fine Art, 148 West Regent Street, Glasgow G2 2RQ
Tel: 0141 221 3095/204 0276
gerber@compassgallery.fsbusiness.co.uk

Glasgow Print Studio, 22 King Street, Glasgow G1 5QP
Tel: 0141 552 0704

Kilmorack Gallery, By Beuly, Invernesshire IV4 7AL
Tel: 01463 783230
art@kilmorackgallery.co.uk
www.kilmorackgallery.co.uk

The Leith Gallery, 65 The Shore, Edinburgh EH7 5DD
Tel: 0131 553 5525 info@the-leith-gallery.co.uk www.the-leith-gallery.co.uk

Mainhill Gallery, Ancrum, Jedburgh TD8 6XA Tel: 01835 830 545
mainhill@lineone.net
www.mainhill.border.co.uk

The Scottish Gallery, 16 Dundas Street, Edinburgh EH3 6HZ
Tel: 0131 558 1200
mail@scottish-gallery.co.uk
www.scottish-gallery.co.uk

**Shropshire**
Wenlock Fine Art, 3 The Square, Much Wenlock TF13 6LX Tel: 01952 728232

**Somerset**
Adam Gallery, 13 John Street, Bath BA1 2JL Tel: 01225 480406
info@adamgallery.com
www.adamgallery.com

Seven Worcester Terrace, London Road, Bath BA1 6PY
Tel: 01225 426791

**Surrey**
Peter Bennett, 88 Ennerdale Road, Kew Gardens TW9 2DL
Tel: 020 8332 9164
bennett_fine_art@compuserve.com

Bourne Gallery Ltd, 31–33 Lesbourne Road, Reigate RH2 7JS
Tel: 01737 241614
bournegallery@aol.com
www.bournegallery.com
*We specialize in fine traditional paintings from the 19th century to the present day. Open Tuesday to Saturday 10am–5pm. Situated 5 minutes from junction 8 on the M25 south of London near Gatwick.*

Henry Boxer, 98 Stuart Court, Richmond Hill, Richmond TW10 6RJ
Tel: 020 8948 1633
www.outsiderart.co.uk

**East Sussex**
Rye Art Gallery, 107 High Street, Rye TN31 7JE Tel: 01797 222433

**West Sussex**
The Antique Print Shop, 11 Middle Row, East Grinstead RH19 3AX
Tel: 01342 410501

The Canon Gallery, New Street, Petworth GU28 0AS
Tel: 01798 344422

Folio Fine Art, High Seat, 1 High Street, Billingshurst RH14 9PJ
Tel: 01403 782697

Peter's Barn Gallery, South Ambersham, Midhurst GU29 0BX Tel: 01798 861388
peters.barn@ic24.net
www.petersbarngallery.co.uk

**Wales**
The Albany Gallery, 74b Albany Road, Cardiff CF2 3RS
Tel: 029 2048 7158
albanygallery@btinternet.com
www.albanygallery.com

**Warwickshire**
The Stour Gallery, 10 High Street, Shipston-on-Stour CV36 4AJ
Tel: 01608 664411
stourgallery@dial.pipex.com

**West Midlands**
Driffold Gallery, 78 Birmingham Road, Sutton Coldfield B72 1QR
Tel: 0121 355 5433

Numberninethegallery, 9 Brindley Place, Birmingham B1 2JA
Tel: 0121 643 9099
www.numberninethegallery.com

**Worcestershire**
Haynes Fine Art of Broadway, Picton House Galleries, 42 High Street, Broadway WR12 7DT
Tel: 01386 852649
email@haynes-fine-art.co.uk
www.haynesfineart.com

John Noott Fine Paintings, High Street, Broadway WR12 7DP
Tel: 01386 854868/852787
john@jnoott.clara.net

**Yorkshire**
Nautical Fine Arts, 21 Meadowcroft Road, The Ridings, Driffield YO25 5NJ Tel: 01377 241074
michael@jwhitehand.fsnet.co.uk
www.nauticalfinearts.com

Sutcliffe Galleries, 5 Royal Parade, Harrogate HG1 2SZ
Tel: 01423 562976

Walker Galleries, 6 Montpelier Gardens, Harrogate HG1 2TF
Tel: 01423 567933
www.walkerfineart.co.uk

**Italy**
Galleria del Leone, 597 Guidecca, 30133, Venice Tel: 0039041 5288001
info@galleriadelleone.com

**Russia**
Alla Bulyanskaya Gallery, Hall 47, Central House of Artists, 10 Krymsky Val, Moscow 117049
Tel: 007 095 737 7392
info@allabulgallery.com
www.allabulgallery.com

**South Africa**
The Everard Read Gallery, 6 Jellicoe Avenue, Rosebank 2196, Johannesburg
Tel: 00 27 11 788 4805
gallery@everard.co.za

**U.S.A.**
Aaron Galleries, 50E Oak, 2nd Floor, Chicago Il 60611
Tel: 001 312 943 0660
aarongal@interacces.com
www.aarongalleries.com

Adams Davidson Galleries, 27–29th Street NW, Suite 504, Washington DC 20008-5545
Tel: 001 202 965 3800
cooper@adgal.com
www.adgal.com

American Primitive Gallery, 594 Broadway, 205 New York NY 10012
Tel: 001 212 966 1530

Roy Boyd Gallery, 739 N. Wells, Chicago IL 60610 Tel: 001 312 642 1606
roy.boyd@worldnet.att.net
www.royboydgallery.com

Jan Cicero Gallery, 835 W. Washington, Chicago IL 60607
Tel: 001 312 733 9551
cicero@concentric.net

Clark Art, 300 Glenwood Avenue, Raleigh, North Carolina 27603
Tel: 001 919 832 8319

Conner Contemporary Art Gallery, 1730 Connecticut Avenue NW, 2nd Floor, Washington DC 20009
Tel: 001 202 588 8750
info@connercontemporary.com
www.connercontemporary.com

Eastwick Art Gallery, 245 W. North Avenue, Chicago IL 60610
Tel: 001 312 440 2322

Kathleen Ewing Gallery, 1609 Connecticut Avenue NW, Washington DC 20009 Tel: 001 202 328 0955
ewinggal@aol.com
www.kathleenewinggallery.com

Paco Filici, 411 West Monroe, Austin, Texas 78704 Tel: 001 512.326.5141
www.pacof.com

Richard Gray Gallery, 875 N. Michigan, Chicago IL 60611
Tel: 001 312 642 8877
info@richardgraygallery.com
www.richardgraygallery.com

Gruen Galleries, 226 W. Superior, Chicago IL 60610
Tel: 001 312 337 6262
lisa@gruengalleries.com
www.gruengalleries.com

Guarisco Gallery Ltd, 2828 Pennsylvania Avenue NW, Washington DC 20007
Tel: 001 202 333 8533
guarisco@mindspring.com
artnet.com/guarisco.html

Anton Haardt Gallery, 2858 Magazine Street, New Orleans LA 705115
Tel: 001 504 891 9080
www.antonart.com

Jane Haslam Gallery, 2025 Hillyer Place NW, Washington DC 20009
Tel: 001 202 232 4644
haslem@artline.com
www.janehaslemgallery.com

Indigo Arts, 151 N. 3rd Street, Philadelphia PA 19106
Tel: 001 215 922 4041
www.indigoarts.com

Kenyon Oppenheimer Inc., 410 N Michigan Ave., Chicago IL 60611
Tel: 001 312 642 5300
joppen@audubonart.com
www.audubonart.com

Klein Art Works, 400 N. Morgan, Chicago IL 60622
Tel: 001 312 243 0400
art@kleinart.com www.kleinart.com

Matt Lamb, 13465 Quail Run Court, Lockport, Illinois 60441
Tel: 001 708 301 8317
www.mattlamb.com

Lindsay Gallery, 986 N.High Street, Columbus, Ohio 423201
Tel: 001 614 291 1973
www.lindsaygallery.homestead.com

Lyons Weir Gallery, 300 W. Superior, Chicago IL 60610
Tel: 001 312 654 0600
www.lyonswiergallery.com

Ricco Maresca Gallery, Third Floor, 529 West 20th Street, New York NY 10011 Tel: 001 212 627 4819
csolomon@riccomaresca.com
www.riccomaresca.com

Marsha Mateyka Gallery, 2012 R Street NW, Washington DC 20009
Tel: 001 202 238 0088
www.marshamateykagallery.com

Thomas McCormick Gallery, 835 W. Washington, Chicago IL 60607
Tel: 001 312 226 6800
gallery@thomasmccormick.com
www.thomasmccormick.com

Richard Norton Gallery, 612 Merchandise Mart Plaza, Chicago IL 60654 Tel: 001 312 644 8855
NortonGallery@aol.com
www.RichardNortonGallery.com

Okuda Gallery, 3112 M Street NW, Washington DC 20007
Tel: 001 202 625 1054
okudaint@bellatlantic.net
www.galleryokuda.com

Parish Gallery, 1054 31st Street NW, Washington DC 20007
Tel: 001 202 944 2310
parishgallery@bigplanet.com
www.parishgallery.com

The Ralls Collection, 1516 31st Street NW, Washington DC 20007
Tel: 001 202 342 1754
maralls@aol.com
www.rallscollection.com

Alla Rogers Gallery, 1054 31st Street NW, Canal Square, Washington DC 20007 Tel: 001 202 333 8595
allarogers@cs.com
www.allarogers.com

Luise Ross Gallery, 568 Broadway, New York 10012 Tel: 001 212 343 2161
www.luiserossgallery.com

Judy A Saslow Gallery, 300 West Superior, Chicago
Tel: 001 312 943 0530
jsaslow@corecomm.net
www.jsaslowgallery.com

St. Luke's Gallery, 1715 Q Street NW, Washington DC 2009
Tel: 001 202 328 2424

Wood Street Gallery, 1239 N. Wood, Chicago IL 6022 Tel: 001 773 227 3306
woodgall@aol.com
www.woodstreetgallery.com

Sonia Zaks Gallery, 311 W Superior, Suite 207, Chicago IL 60610
Tel: 001 312 943 8440

Zenith Gallery, 413 7th Street NW, Washington DC 20004
Tel: 001 202 783 2963
zenithga@rols.com
www.zenithgallery.com

Zolla/Lieberman Gallery, 325 W. Huron, Chicago IL 60610
Tel: 001 312 944 1990
zollaart@aol.com
www.zollaliebermangallery.com

Quester Gallery, 77 Main Street, PO Box 446, Stonington, Connecticut 06378 Tel: 001 860 535 3860

# Directory of Specialists

If you wish to be included in next year's directory, or if you have a change of address or telephone number, please contact Miller's advertising department by January 2003. We advise readers to make contact by telephone first before visiting, therefore avoiding a wasted journey.

## Exhibition & Fair Organisers

**West Sussex**
Hodgson Events, Smithbrook, Lodsworth GU28 9DG
Tel: 01798 861815
hodgsonevents@talk21.com
www.hodgsonevents.com

## Framers

**Cambridgeshire**
The Cottage Gallery, 11/12 High Street, Huntingdon PF18 6TE
Tel: 01480 411521

**Greater Manchester**
Dixon Bate Framing, 94–98 Fairfield Street, Manchester M1 2WR
Tel: 0161 273 6974

**Hampshire**
Academy Arts Centre, Winton Road, Petersfield GU32 3HA
Tel: 01730 261624
nixy@compuserve.com

**Kent**
Simon Beaugié Picture Frames, Manor Farm Workshops, Kingsnorth, Ashford TN26 1NL
Tel: 01233 733353

**London**
Art & Soul, G14 Belgravia Workshops, 157 Marlborough Road N19 4NF Tel: 020 7263 0421

John Campbell Master Frames, 164 Walton Street SW3 2JL
Tel: 020 7584 9268
www.campbellofwaltonstreet. co.uk

Chelsea Frame Works, 106 Finborough Road SW10
Tel: 020 7373 0180

Alec Drew Picture Frames Ltd, 5/7 Cale Street, Chelsea Green SW3 3QT Tel: 020 7352 8716
adrew@hugill.demon.co.uk
www.hugill.demon.co.uk

Framework Picture Framing, 5–9 Creekside SE8 4SA
Tel: 020 8691 5140
enquiries@frameworkgallery.co.uk

Pendragon Fine Art Frames, 1–3 Yorkton Street, Shoreditch E2 8NH Tel: 020 7729 0608

## Gallery Hire

**Lincolnshire**
Yarrow Gallery, Art Department, Oundle School, Glapthorn Road, Oundle, Peterborough PE8 4EN
Tel: 01832 274 034
www.oundleschool.org.uk./school/arts/yarrow/html

**London**
Abbott & Holder, 30 Museum Street WC1A 1LH
Tel: 020 7637 3981
abbott.holder@virgin.net
www.artefact.co.uk/AaH.html

The Air Gallery, 32 Dover Street W1X 3RA Tel: 020 7409 1255
admin@airgallery.co.uk
www.airgallery.co.uk

Alchemy Gallery, 157 Farringdon Road EC1R 3AD
Tel: 020 7278 5666

Art Connoisseur Gallery, 95–97 Crawford Street, London W1H 1AN Tel: 020 7258 3835

Artbank Gallery C, 114 Clerkenwell Road EC1M 5SA
Tel: 020 7608 3333
info@artbank.com
www.artbank.com

Atrium Gallery, Whiteleys, Queensway W2 4YN
Tel: 020 7229 8844

Charlotte Street Gallery, Charlotte Street, Fitzrovia, London W1 2NA
Tel: 020 7255 2828
gallery@28charlottestreet.com
www.28charlottestreet.com

The Coningsby Gallery, 30 Tottenham Street W1 9PN
Tel: 020 7636 7478

Ebury Galleries, 200 Ebury Street SW1
Tel: 020 7730 8999

The Gallery in Cork Street, 28 Cork Street W1S 3NG
Tel: 020 7287 8408
enquiries@galleryincorkst.com
www.gallery27.com

Highgate Gallery, 11 South Grove, Highgate N6 6BS
Tel: 020 8340 3343
admin@hlsi.demon.co.uk

Lauderdale House Arts & Education Centre, Waterlow Park, Highgate Hill N6 5HG
Tel: 020 8348 8716/8341 2032

Mall Galleries, 17 Carlton House Terrace SW1Y 5BD
Tel: 020 7930 6844
jdestonmallgalleries@pipex.uk www.mallgalleries.org.uk`

South London Gallery, 65 Peckham Road SE5 8UH
Tel: 020 7703 9799
mail@southlondonart.com
www.southlondonart.co.uk

Space Studios, 8 Hoxton Street N1 6NG Tel: 020 7613 1925
mail@spacestudios.org.uk
www.spacestudios.org.uk

Westminster Gallery, Central Hall, Storey's Gate SW1 9NH
Tel: 020 7222 8010
events@wch.co.uk
www.wch.co.uk

**Merseyside**
Hanover Galleries, 11–13 Hanover Street, Liverpool L1 3DN
Tel: 0151 709 3073

**Oxfordshire**
Merriscourt Gallery, Sarsden, Chipping Norton OX7 6QX
Tel: 01608 658 989
merriscourtpaintings@btinternet.com www.merriscourt.com

**Republic of Ireland**
Royal Hibernian Academy, Gallagher Gallery, 15 Ely Place, Dublin 2 Tel: 00 353 1 661 2558
rhgallery@eircom.net
www.royalhibernianacademy.com

## Insurance

**Dorset**
Gwennap Stevenson Brown Ltd, Kerris House, 12 Brickfields Business Park, Gillingham SP8 4PX Tel: 01747 821188
paulinegwennap@aol.com

**London**
Aon Ltd, 8 Devonshire Square EC2M 4PL Tel: 01444 414141

AXA Art Insurance
Tel: 020 7626 5001
helen.george@axa-art.co.uk
www.axa-art.co.uk

Blackwall Green (Jewellery and Fine Art), Lambert Fenchurch House, Friary Court, Crutched Friars EC3N 2NP
Tel: 020 7560 3381
cstephens@fgroup.co.uk

Byas Mosley & Co Ltd, International Fine Art Division, William Byas House, 14–18 St Clare Street WC3N 1JX
Tel: 020 7481 0101

Crowley Colosso, Friary Court, Crutched Friars EC3N 2NP
Tel: 020 7560 3000

Needham Jobson & Co, Byron House, 102 Wimbledon Hill Road SW19 7PB Tel: 020 8944 8870

Sedgwick Fine Art, Sedgwick House, The Sedgwick Centre E1 8DX Tel: 020 7377 3456

## Lighting

**Surrey**
Acorn Lighting Products, 27 Marlyns Drive, Guildford GU4 8JU Tel: 01483 564180

## Packers & Shippers

**Cornwall**
3 Lanes Transport, 5 Albany Terrace, St Ives TR26 2BS
Tel: 07970 896256
info@3lanes.com
www.3lanes.com

**London**
Art Move, Unit 3, Grant Road SW11 2NU Tel: 020 7585 1801
artmove@dircon.co.uk

Momart Ltd, 199–205 Richmond Road E8 3NJ Tel: 020 8986 3624
enquiries@momart.co.uk

## Publications

**London**
Art Monthly, 4th Floor, 28 Charing Cross Road WC2B 0DG
Tel: 020 7240 0389
artmonthly@compuserve.com
www.artmonthly.co.uk

The Art Newspaper, 70 South Lambeth Road SW8 1RL
Tel: 020 7735 3331

**West Midlands**
Antiques Magazine, H.P. Publishing, 2 Hampton Court Road, Harborne, Birmingham B17 9AE Tel: 0121 681 8000
Subs 01562 701001
subs@antiquesmagazine.com
www.antiquesmagazine.com

## Restoration

**Hampshire**
Association of British Picture Restorers, P O Box 32, Hayling Island PO11 9WE
Tel/Fax: 0239 2465115
abpr@lineone.net

The Conservation Studio, Chandler's Ford SO53 2FX
Tel/Fax: 023 8026 8167
sales@winstudio.co.uk
www.winstudio.co.uk

**London**
Deborah Bates, 191 St John's Hill SW11 1TH Tel: 020 7223 1629
deborah@deborahbates.com
www.deborahbates.com

**Scotland**
Alder Arts, 4 The Square, Beauly, Invernesshire IV4 7BX
Tel: 01463 782247

# General Cataloguing Terms

The conventional cataloguing system used by the auction houses has been maintained and many of the terms and phrases are explained below.

**Forenames or initials and surname** indicates that in their opinion the work is by the artist named.
A work catalogued with the name(s) of an artist, without any qualification, is in their opinion, a work by the artist.

**'Attributed to...'** In their opinion probably a work by the artist, but less certainly than in the preceding category.

**'Studio of...' 'Workshop of...'** In their opinion a work by an unknown hand in the studio of the artist which may or may not have been executed under the artist's direction.

**'Circle of...'** In their opinion a work by an as yet unidentified but distinct hand, closely associated with the named artist, but not necessarily his pupil.

**Medium** The material used in a painting, i.e. oil, tempera, watercolour, etc.

**'Follower of ... 'Style of...'** In their opinion a work by a painter working in the artist's style, contemporary or nearly contemporary, but not necessarily his pupil.

**'Manner of...'** In their opinion, a work in the artists's style, but of a later date.

**'After...' 'Signed...'/'Dated...'/'Inscribed...'** In their opinion signature/date/inscription are from the hand of the artist.

**'Bears signature, date or inscription...'** In their opinion, signature/date/description have been added by another hand.

# Glossary

We have defined here some of the terms that you will come across in this book. If there are any terms or technicalities you would like explained or you feel should be included in future, please let us know.

**academy:** A group of artists meeting for teaching and/or discussion.

**acrylic:** A synthetic emulsion paint.

**bodycolour:** Opaque pigment made by mixing watercolour with white pigment. Same as gouache.

**cartoon:** A full size early design for a painting.

**collage:** A work of art in which pieces of paper, photographs and other materials are pasted to the surface of the picture.

**Conté:** A brand name for synthetic black, red or brown chalk.

**counterproof:** A mirror-image reproduction, achieved by wetting a drawing or engraving, laying a damp sheet of clean paper on it and then running both through a press.

**drawing:** Representation with line.

**dry-point:** The process of making a print by engraving directly on to a copper plate with a steel or diamond point.

**edition:** The run of a print published at any one time.

**engraving:** The process of cutting a design into a hard surface (metal or wood) so that the lines will retain the ink. Engravings can be roughly divided into three types: Relief, Intaglio and Surface. Each has its own special method of printing.

**etching:** A technique of print making developed in the 16th century, in which a metal plate is covered with an acid-resistant substance and the design scratched on it with a needle revealing the metal beneath. The plate is then immersed in acid, which bites into the lines, which will hold the ink.

**genre:** Art showing scenes from daily life.

**gouache:** Opaque watercolour paint.

**grisaille:** Painting in grey or greyish monochrome.

**impression:** An individual copy of a print or engraving.

**lithograph:** A print made by drawing with a wax crayon on a porous prepared stone which is then soaked in water. A grease-based ink is applied to the stone which adheres only to the design. Dampened paper is applied to the stone and is rubbed over with a special press to produce the print.

**linocut:** A design cut in relief on linoleum mounted on a wooden block.

**measurements:** Dimensions are given height before width.

**mixed media:** Art combining different types of material.

**montage:** The sticking of layers over each other, often done with photographs using an unusual background.

**oil:** Pigment bound with oil.

**pastel:** A dry pigment bound with gum into stick-form and used for drawing.

**patina:** Refers to the mellowing with age, which occurs to all works of art.

**plate:** The piece of metal etched or engraved with the design used to produce prints.

**print:** An image which exists in multiple copies, taken from an engraved plate, woodblock, etc.

**proof:** A print of an engraving usually made before lettering engraver worked on it adding title, dedication, etc.

**provenance:** The record of previous owners and locations of a work of art.

**recto:** The front of a picture.

**remarque proofs:** Proofs with some kind of mark in the margin to denote superiority to ordinary proofs.

**silkscreen:** A print-making process using a finely meshed screen, often silk, and stencils to apply the image.

**state:** A term applied to prints–to the different stages at which the artist has corrected or changed a plate–and the prints produced from these various 'states', which are numbered first state, second state, etc.

**still life:** A composition of inanimate objects.

**tempera:** A medium for pigment mostly made up of egg yolk and water, commonly used before the invention of oils.

**verso:** The back of a picture.

**wash:** A thin transparent tint applied over the surfaces of a work.

**watercolour:** Transparent, water soluble paint, usually applied on paper.

**woodcut:** Print made from a design cut into a block of wood.

# Index to Advertisers

# Index to Abbreviations

| | | | | |
|---|---|---|---|---|
| **A** | Associate | | **OSA** | Ontario Society of Artists |
| **AAA** | Allied Artists' Association | | **OWS** | Old Watercolour Society, London |
| **b.** | born | | **P** | President |
| **BWS** | British Watercolour Society | | **PS** | Pastel Society |
| **CBE** | Commander of the British Empire | | **RA** | Royal Academy |
| **CH** | Companion of Honour | | **RBA** | Royal Society of British Artists |
| **cm** | centimetre | | **RBC** | Royal British Colonial Society of Artists |
| **d.** | died | | **RBSA** | Royal Birmingham Society of Artists |
| **DBE** | Dame Commander of the British Empire | | **RCA** | Royal College of Art |
| **DCM** | Distinguished Conduct Medal | | **RCA** | Royal Canadian Academy of Arts |
| **F** | Fellow | | **RDS** | Royal Dublin Society |
| **fl.** | Flourished | | **RE** | Royal Society of Etchers and Engravers |
| **H** | Honorary Member | | **RGI** | Royal Glasgow Institute |
| **ICA** | Institute of Contemporary Arts | | **RHA** | Royal Hibernian Academy, Dublin |
| **in** | Inch | | **RI** | Royal Institute of Painters in Watercolours |
| **IS** | International Society of Sculptors, Painter and Gravers | | **RIA** | Royal Irish Academy |
| | | | **ROI** | Royal Institute of Oil Painters |
| **Jnr** | Junior | | **RP** | Royal Institute of Portrait Painters |
| **LG** | London Group | | **RSA** | Royal Scottish Academy |
| **MM** | Military Medal | | **RSMA** | Royal Society of Marine Artists |
| **NCA** | National College of Art, Dublin | | **RSW** | Royal Scottish Watercolour Academy |
| **NEAC** | New English Art Club | | **RUA** | Royal Ulster Academy of Arts |
| **NG** | National Gallery | | **RWA** | Royal West of England Academy, Bristol |
| **NPG** | National Portrait Gallery | | **RWS** | Royal Society of Painters in Watercolours |
| **NGI** | National Gallery of Ireland | | **Snr** | Senior |
| **NSA** | New Society of Artists | | **SWA** | Society of Women Artists |
| **NWS** | New Watercolour Society | | **VP** | Vice President |
| **OBE** | Order of the British Empire | | **WCSI** | Watercolour Society of Ireland |
| **OM** | Order of Merit | | **WIAC** | Women's International Art Club |

# Key to Illustrations

Each illustration and descriptive caption is accompanied by a letter code. By referring to the following list of auctioneers (denoted by *) and galleries (•) the source of any item may be immediately determined. Inclusion in this edition in no way constitutes or implies a contract or binding offer on the part of any of our contributors to supply or sell the goods illustrated, or similar articles, at the prices stated. Advertisers in this year's directory are denoted by †.

If you require a valuation for an item, it is advisable to check whether the gallery or specialist will carry out this service and if there is a charge. Please mention Miller's when making an enquiry. Having found a specialist who will carry out your valuation it is best to send a photograph and description of the item to the specialist together with a stamped addressed envelope for the reply. A valuation by telephone is not possible.

Most galleries are only too happy to help you with your enquiry; however, they are very busy people and consideration of the above points would be welcomed.

**AAJ** • Ackermann, Arthur & Peter Johnson Ltd, 27 Lowndes Street, London SW1X 9HY Tel: 020 7235 6464 ackermannjohnson@btconnect.com www.artnet.com/ackermann-johnson.html

**ACG** • Cristea Gallery, Alan, 31 Cork Street, London W1S 3NU Tel: 020 7439 1866

**AG** * Anderson & Garland (Auctioneers), Marlborough House, Marlborough Crescent, Newcastle-upon-Tyne, Tyne & Wear NE1 4EE Tel: 0191 232 6278

**AH** *† Hartley, Andrew, Victoria Hall Salerooms, Little Lane, Ilkley, Yorkshire LS29 8EA Tel: 01943 816363 info@andrewhartleyfinearts.co.uk www.andrewhartleyfinearts.co.uk

**ARL** • ArtLondon.Com, Suite 958, 28 Old Brompton Road, London SW7 3SS Tel: 020 7402 2897 Mobile: 07785 707427 info@artlondon.com www.artlondon.com

**B(Ba)** * Bonhams, 10 Salem Road, Bayswater, London W2 4DL Tel: 020 7313 2700 www.phillips-auctions.com

**B(C)** * Bonhams, 65–69 Lots Road, Chelsea, London SW10 0RN Tel: 020 7393 3900 www.bonhams.com

**B(EA)** * Bonhams, 32 Boss Hall Road, Ipswich, Suffolk IP1 5DJ Tel: 01473 740494

**B(Ed)** * Bonhams, 65 George Street, Edinburgh, Scotland EH2 2JL Tel: 0131 225 2266

**B(L)** * Bonhams, 17a East Parade, Leeds, Yorkshire LS1 2BH Tel: 0113 2448011

**B(Nor)** * Bonhams, The Market Place, Reepham, Norwich, Norfolk NR10 4JJ Tel: 01603 871443

**B(NW)** * Bonhams, New House, 150 Christleton Road, Chester, Cheshire CH3 5TD Tel: 01244 313936

**B(S)** * Bonhams, 49 London Road, Sevenoaks, Kent TN13 1AR Tel: 01732 740310

**B(WM)** * Bonhams, The Old House, Station Road, Knowle, Solihull, West Midlands B93 0HT Tel: 01564 776151

**B&B** • Barkes & Barkes, 76 Parkway, Camden Town, London NW1 7AH Tel: 020 7284 1550 www.artrussia.com

**B** * Bonhams, 101 New Bond Street, London W1S 1SR Tel: 020 7629 6602

**Bea(E)** * Bearnes, St Edmund's Court, Okehampton Street, Exeter, Devon EX4 1DU Tel: 01392 422800 nsaintey@bearnes.co.uk www.bearnes.co.uk

**Ben** •† Benton Fine Art, Regent House, High Street, Moreton-in-Marsh, Gloucestershire GL56 0AX Tel/Fax: 01608 652153 bentonfineart@excite.com

**BFa** • Baron Fine Art, 68 Watergate Street, Chester, Cheshire CH1 2LA Tel: 01244 342520

**BG** • Boydell Galleries, Liverpool, Merseyside Tel: 0151 932 9220 www.boydellgalleries.co.uk

**Bne** • Bourne Gallery Ltd, 31–33 Lesbourne Road, Reigate, Surrey RH2 7JS Tel: 01737 241614 bournegallery@aol.com www.bournegallery.com

**Bon** * Bonhams, Montpelier Street, Knightsbridge, London SW7 1HH Tel: 020 7393 3900 www.bonhams.com

**Bon(C)** * See B(C)

**BOX** • Boxer, Henry, 98 Stuart Court, Richmond Hill, Richmond, Surrey TW10 6RJ Tel: 020 8948 1633 www.outsiderart.co.uk

**BRG** •† Brandler Galleries, 1 Coptfold Road, Brentwood, Essex CM14 4BM Tel: 01277 222269 john@brandler-galleries.com www.brandler-galleries.com

**Bri** * Bristol Auction Rooms, St John's Place, Apsley Road, Clifton, Bristol, Gloucestershire BS8 2ST Tel: 0117 973 7201 www.bristolauctionrooms.co.uk

**BrS** • The Bruton Street Gallery Ltd, 28 Bruton Street, London W1Y 7DB Tel: 020 7499 9747 art@brutonstreetgallery.com www.brutonstreetgallery.com

**BUK** * Bukowskis, Arsenalsgatan 4, Stockholm, Sweden-SE111 47 Tel: 08 614 08 00 info@bukowskis.se www.bukowskis.se

**BuP** •† Burlington Fine Paintings Ltd, 10 & 12 Burlington Gardens, London W1X 1LG Tel: 020 7734 9984 pictures@burlington.co.uk www.burlington.co.uk

**CAG** * The Canterbury Auction Galleries, 40 Station Road West, Canterbury, Kent CT2 8AN Tel: 01227 763337

**CdA** * The Coeur d'Alene Art Auction, PO Box 310, Hayden, U.S.A. ID 83835 Tel: 001 208 772 9009 drumgallery@nidlink.com www.cdaartauction.com

**CEL** • Counter Editions Ltd, 5–9 Hatton Wall, London EC1N 8HX Tel: 020 7692 0000 www.countereditions.com

**CFA** • Cambridge Fine Art, Priesthouse, 33 Church Street, Little Shelford, Nr Cambridge, Cambridgeshire CB2 5HG Tel: 01223 842866

**CG** • The Canon Gallery, New Street, Petworth, West Sussex GU28 0AS Tel: 01798 344422

**CGC** * Cheffins, 2 Clifton Road, Cambridge, Cambridgeshire CB2 4BW Tel: 01223 213343 www.cheffins.co.uk

**CON** • The Contemporary Fine Art Gallery, 31 High Street, Eton, Windsor, Berkshire SL4 1HL Tel: 01753 854315

**CW** • Christopher Wood Gallery, 20 Georgian House, 10 Bury Street, London, SW1Y 6AA Tel: 020 7839 3963 www.christopherwoodgallery.com

**DD** * David Duggleby, The Vine St Salerooms, Scarborough, Yorkshire YO11 1XN Tel: 01723 507111 auctions@davidduggleby.freeserve.co.uk www.davidduggleby.com

**DN** * Dreweatt Neate, Donnington Priory, Donnington, Newbury, Berkshire RG14 2JE Tel: 01635 553553 fineart@dreweatt-neate.co.uk

**DORO** * Dorotheum, Palais Dorotheum, A-1010 Wien, Dorotheergasse. 17, 1010 Austria Tel: 0043 1 515 60 354

**Dr** •† Driffold Gallery, 78 Birmingham Road, Sutton Coldfield, West Midlands B72 1QR Tel: 0121 355 5433

**FdeL** •† Fleur de Lys Gallery, 227A Westbourne Grove, London W11 2SE Tel/Fax: 020 7727 8595 fleurdelysgallery@yahoo.com www.fleur-de-lys.com

**G(L)** * Gorringes inc Julian Dawson, 15 North Street, Lewes, East Sussex BN7 2PD Tel: 01273 472503 auctions@gorringes.co.uk www.gorringes.co.uk

**GAK** * Keys, Aylsham Salerooms, Off Palmers Lane, Aylsham, Norfolk NR11 6JA Tel: 01263 733195 www.aylshamsalerooms.co.uk

**HFA** •† Haynes Fine Art of Broadway, Picton House Galleries, 42 High Street, Broadway, Worcestershire WR12 7DT Tel: 01386 852649 email@haynes-fine-art.co.uk www.haynesfineart.com

**HG** • Hart Gallery, 113 Upper Street, Islington, London N1 1QN Tel: 020 7704 1131

**JAA** * Jackson's Auctioneers & Appraisers, 2229 Lincoln Street, Cedar Falls IA 50613, U.S.A. Tel: 00 1 319 277 2256

**JAd** * James Adam, 26 St Stephens Green, Dublin 2, Ireland Tel: 01 6760261 www.jamesadam.ie

**JBG** • James Birch Gallery, 22 Laystall Street, London EC1R 4PA Tel: 020 7837 1595

**JC** • J Collins & Son, The Studio, 28 High Street, Bideford, Devon EX39 2AN Tel: 01237 473103 biggs@collinsantiques.co.uk www.collinsantiques.co.uk

**JDG** • John Denham Gallery, 50 Mill Lane, London NW6 1NJ Tel: 020 7794 2635

**JLx** • Julian Lax, 37–39 Arkwright Road, Hampstead, London NW3 6BJ Tel: 020 7794 9933

**JN** •† John Noott Fine Paintings, High Street, Broadway, Worcestershire WR12 7DP Tel: 01386 854868/852787 john@jnoott.clara.net

**JSp** • John Spink, 9 Richard Burbidge Mansions, 1 Brasenose Drive, London SW13 8RB Tel: 020 8741 6152

**KMS** * Kimball M Sterling, Inc, 125 West Market Street, Johnson City, Tennessee 37601, U.S.A. Tel: 001 423 928 1471 kimsold@tricon.com www.outsiderartauctions.com

**L** * Lawrences Fine Art Auctioneers, South Street, Crewkerne, Somerset TA18 8AB Tel: 01460 73041

**LGA** • The Leith Gallery, 65 The Shore, Edinburgh, Scotland EH7 5DD Tel: 0131 553 5525 info@the-leith-gallery.co.uk www.the-leith-gallery.co.uk

**LH** •† Laurence Hallett (LAPADA), London Tel: 020 7798 8977 Mobile: 077 88 44 29 39 DST104KEY@cwctv.net

**LS** • Lotus House Studios, 25 Station Road, Lydd, Romney Marsh, Kent TN29 9ED Tel: 01797 320585

**LTu** • Louis Turpin, 19 Udimore Road, Rye, East Sussex TN31 7DS Tel: 01797 222307 www.louisturpin.co.uk

**MJFA** • Mark Jason Fine Art, 71 New Bond Street, London W1S 1DE Tel: 020 7629 4080 info@jasonfineart.com www.jasonfineart.com

**MLM** • Matt Lamb, 13465 Quail Run Court, Lockport, Illinois 60441, U.S.A. Tel: 001 708 301 8317 www.mattlamb.com

**MP** • Michael Parkin Fine Art Ltd, Studio 4, Sedding Street, London SW1W 8EE Tel: 0207 7730 9784

**MSM** • Messum's Galleries, Duke Street, St James's, London SW1 Tel: 020 7839 5180 www.messums.com

**N** * Neales, 192–194 Mansfield Road, Nottingham, Nottinghamshire NG1 3HU Tel: 0115 962 4141

**NGG** • New Grafton Gallery, 49 Church Road, London SW13 9HH Tel: 020 8748 8850

**NOA** * New Orleans Auction Galleries, Inc., 801 Magazine Street, AT 510 Julia, New Orleans, Louisiana 70130, U.S.A. Tel: 00 1 504 566 1849

**NZ** •† Nina Zborowska, Damsels Mill, Paradise, Painswick, Gloucestershire GL6 6UD Tel: 01452 812460 enquiries@ninazborowska.com www.ninazborowska.com

| | | |
|---|---|---|
| **P** | * | See B |
| **P(Ba)** | * | See B(Ba) |
| **P(EA)** | * | See B(EA) |
| **P(Ed)** | * | See B(Ed) |
| **P(L)** | * | See B(L) |
| **P(Nor)** | * | See B(Nor) |
| **P(NW)** | * | See B(NW) |
| **P(NY)** | * | Phillips New York, 406 East 79th Street, New York NY10021, U.S.A. Tel: 00 1 212 570 4830 |
| **P(S)** | * | See B(S) |
| **P(Sy)/ SHSY** | * | Shapiro Auctioneers, formerly Phillips, 162 Queen Street, Woollahra, Sydney NSW 2025, Australia Tel: 00 612 9326 1588 |
| **P(WM)** | * | See B(WM) |
| **P&H** | • | Panter & Hall, 9 Shepherd Market, Mayfair, London W1J 7PF Tel: 020 7399 9999 enquiries@panterandhall.co.uk www.panterandhall.co.uk |
| **PCG** | • | The Piccadilly Gallery, 43 Dover Street, London W1S 4NU Tel: 020 7629 2875 www.piccadillygall.demon.co.uk |
| **PLH** | • | Paul Hahn, 5 Lower Grosvenor Place, London SW1W 0EJ Tel: 020 7592 0224 paulhahn@hahngallery.co.uk |
| **PN** | • | Piano Nobile Fine Paintings, 129 Portland Road, London 020 7229 1099 |
| **PWG** | • | Park Walk Gallery, 20 Park Walk, Chelsea, London SW10 0AQ Tel: 020 7351 0410 www.jonathancooper.co.uk |
| **RBB** | * | Brightwells Ltd, Ryelands Road, Leominster, Herefordshire HR6 8NZ Tel: 01568 611122 fineart@brightwells.com |
| **RMG** | • | Ricco Maresca Gallery, Third Floor, 29 West 20th Street, New York NY 10011, U.S.A. Tel: 001 212 627 4819 csolomon@riccomaresca.com www.riccomaresca.com |
| **ROSS** | * | John Ross & Company, 37 Montgomery Street, Belfast, Co Antrim BT1 4NX Tel: 028 9032 5448 |
| **RTo** | * | Rupert Toovey & Co Ltd, Star Road, Partridge Green, West Sussex RH13 8RA Tel: 01403 711744 auctions@rupert-toovey.com www.rupert-toovey.com |
| **S** | * | Sotheby's, 34–35 New Bond Street, London W1A 2AA Tel: 020 7293 5000 www.sothebys.com |
| **S(NY)** | * | Sotheby's, 1334 York Avenue, New York NY 10021, U.S.A. Tel: 001 212 606 7000 |
| **S(O)** | * | Sotheby's Olympia, Hammersmith Road, London W14 8UX Tel: 020 7293 5000 |
| **SGL** | • | The Swan Gallery, 51 Cheap Street, Sherborne, Dorset DT9 3AX Tel: 01935 814465 |
| **SHN** | • | Shannon's, 354 Woodmont Road, Milford, Connecticut 06460, U.S.A. Tel: 001 203 877 1711 www.shannons.com |
| **SK** | * | Skinner Inc, The Heritage On The Garden, 63 Park Plaza, Boston, MA 02116, U.S.A. Tel: 00 1 617 350 5400 |
| **SLN** | * | Sloan's, 4920 Wyaconda Road, North Bethesda, MD 20852, U.S.A. Tel: 001 301 468 4911 www.sloansauction.com |
| **StI** | • | St Ives Society of Artists, Norway Gallery, Norway Square, St Ives, Cornwall TR26 1NA Tel: 01736 795582 www.stivessocietyofartists.com |
| **SWO** | * | G. E. Sworder & Sons, 14 Cambridge Road, Stansted Mountfitchet, Essex CM24 8BZ Tel: 01279 817778 www.sworder.co.uk |
| **TAY** | * | Taylors, Honiton Galleries, 205 High Street, Honiton, Devon EX14 8LF Tel: 01404 42404 |
| **TBJ** | • | T B & R Jordan (Fine Paintings), Aslak, Aislaby, Eaglescliffe, Stockton-on-Tees, Cleveland TS16 0QN Tel: 01642 782599 |
| **TEN** | * | Tennants, The Auction Centre, Harmby Road, Leyburn, Yorkshire DL8 5SG Tel: 01969 623780 |
| **TMA** | *† | Brown & Merry, Tring Market Auctions, The Market Premises, Brook Street, Tring, Hertfordshire HP23 5EF Tel: 01442 826446 sales@tringmarketauctions.co.uk www.tringmarketauctions.co.uk |
| **TREA** | * | Treadway Gallery, Inc, 2029 Madison Road, Cincinnati, Ohio 45208, U.S.A. Tel: 001 513 321 6742 www.treadwaygallery.com |
| **TRL** | * | Thomson, Roddick & Medcalf, Coleridge House, Shaddongate, Carlisle, Cumbria CA2 5TU Tel: 01228 528939 |
| **WA** | *† | Whyte's Auctioneers, 38 Molesworth Street, Dublin 2, Republic of Ireland Tel: 00 353 1 676 2888 info@whytes.ie www.whytes.ie |
| **WAD** | * | Waddington's Auctions, 111 Bathurst Street, Toronto, MSV 2RI, Canada Tel: 001 416 504 9100 vb@waddingtonsauctions.com www.waddingtonsauctions.com |
| **WG** | • | Walker Galleries, 6 Montpelier Gardens, Harrogate, Yorkshire HG1 2TF Tel: 01423 567933 www.walkerfineart.co.uk |
| **WHI** | • | Whitford Fine Art, 6 Duke Street, St James's, London SW1Y 6BN Tel: 020 7930 9332 |
| **WL** | * | Wintertons Ltd, Lichfield Auction Centre, Wood End Lane, Fradley, Lichfield, Staffordshire WS13 8NF Tel: 01543 263256 |
| **WO** | •† | Wiseman Originals Ltd, 34 West Square, London SE11 4SP Tel: 020 7587 0747 wisemanoriginals@compuserve.com www.wisemanoriginals.com |
| **WrG** | •† | Wren Gallery, Bear Court, 34 Lower High Street, Burford, Oxon, Oxfordshire OX18 4RR Tel: 01993 823495 enquiries@wrenfineart.com www.wrenfineart.com |
| **WW** | * | Woolley & Wallis, Salisbury Salerooms, 51–61 Castle Street, Salisbury, Wiltshire SP1 3SU Tel: 01722 424500 |
| **WyG** | • | Wyllie Gallery, 44 Elvaston Place, London SW7 5NP Tel: 020 7584 6024 |

# Index